Praise for *Doing Life*

A striking and powerful narrative.
—*San Francisco Chronicle*

Tough . . . courageous . . . a stunning mixture of legalese and Brooklyn street jargon. Bello captures the pain and triumph of Jerry Rosenberg.
—*Roanoke Times & World-News*

A book about a different kind of hero. A real underdog who had to fight the system for every inch. A guy who never quit—a book that never lets go.
—Clark Howard, author of *Zebra* and *Six Against the Rock*

Fast-paced and compulsively readable. Bello has a remarkable gift for transforming Rosenberg's life into a series of emotionally charged scenes.
—Ralph Gardner, *The American Lawyer*

A fascinating and compelling book.
—Judge Jerry Pacht, *Los Angeles Times Book Review*

Doing Life is a truly inspiring story of a uniquely remarkable man who, but for a cruel twist of fate, might well have been one of the country's foremost criminal lawyers.
—William M. Kunstler

In the pervasive atmosphere of violence and fear, Jerry knew that his life depended on fighting back at every turn, that his sanity depended on every available weapon: words and fists, law books and courts.
—Dan Pochoda, Special Counsel, NYC Board of Correction

Rosenberg's tale is fascinating, as are the questions raised about the relationship between criminal and legal thinking.
—*Phoenix Republic*

DOING LIFE

THE EXTRAORDINARY SAGA OF AMERICA'S GREATEST JAILHOUSE LAWYER

STEVE BELLO

Published by Graymalkin Media, LLC

www.graymalkin.com

This edition published in 2022

Book design by Timothy Shaner

ISBN: 978-1-63168-145-5

Printed in the United States of America

1 3 5 7 9 10 8 6 4 2

FOR JANE

and

FOR JENNIFER AND SOPHIE

To become a lawyer, they oughtta

make you do some time in jail.

—JERRY ROSENBERG

INTRODUCTION

BY RON KUBY

Jerome Samuel Rosenberg spent forty-six years in a New York State prison. He had the dubious distinction of being the state's longest-serving inmate, but more important, he was the greatest "jailhouse lawyer" who ever lived. He died in prison on June 1, 2009 at seventy-two years old.

Many of those who knew him, or knew of him, do not mourn his passing. He was convicted of a 1962 murder of two police detectives in a botched robbery in New York City. And he wasn't just a good kid who fell into the wrong company. At the time of the murders, he was on parole after serving a four-year bid at Comstock State Prison for an armed robbery. Not the nice Jewish boy suburban moms of the 1960s dreamed their daughters would marry. He was sentenced to death.

But "Jerry the Jew"—the prison nickname that he wore with pride—was not going quietly. He never did. This was before the days of prison libraries, and decades before prisoners had much access to counsel, so his family obtained law books for him. Jerry studied. He took a law correspondence course from the Blackstone School of Law in Chicago, an accredited law school that was part of a much older American tradition of legal study. Of course, he was never admitted to the bar. A double murder conviction won't get you past the Character and Fitness Committee.

His legal education, though, was more than sufficient for his own purposes. He spotted a loophole in New York's death penalty law, and his sentence was commuted by then-Governor Nelson Rockefeller. Spared the death penalty, Jerry was doing life.

He began reviewing cases for his fellow prisoners, finding errors made by attorneys who were incompetent, diffident, or both. He began writing writs for others behind bars, sometimes securing their freedom, sometimes reducing their sentences. He became the only jailhouse lawyer in history to be permitted to formally represent another prisoner in open court—demonstrating his skill in 1974 before US District Judge Whitman Knapp, who came to the bench fresh from leading a two-year investigation into police corruption in New York City.

Jerry played a pivotal and controversial role in the Attica rebellion. A die-hard capitalist (after all, he was an armed robber), he was widely respected by the inmates in D-Yard. When the prisoners were given a court order promising amnesty to end the uprising, it was Jerry who ripped up the document, correctly noting that it was not worth the paper it was printed on. It was a fateful decision. Jerry was ready to die, but he was not ready to be fooled. The very Governor Rockefeller who spared Jerry the death penalty called in the State Troopers, who murdered prisoners and hostages alike.

For close to four decades, Jerry was the only "lawyer" many prisoners had. He helped many hundreds of people navigate their way through the legal maze that imprisoned them. After the legal battles of the 1970s began to secure rudimentary law libraries for prisoners, Jerry became a jailhouse law professor. He called upon prisoners to use their minds, to use words instead of bullets. He was an inspiration to those who had given up all hope.

But for all of his skill, he could never free himself. He argued an appeal before the very judge who had originally sentenced him to death. The judge commented "When I send them away, they never come back. . . . Not only did [Rosenberg] come back, . . . he came back as a lawyer." Jerry's original conviction, though, was reaffirmed time and time again. Eligible for parole in 1982, Rosenberg was turned down every two years until his death.

On the back cover of the first edition of *Doing Life*, my late mentor, the great William M. Kunstler, said, "But for a cruel twist of fate, [Jerry] might well have been one of the country's foremost criminal lawyers." The "cruel twist of fate," of course, was Jerry's role in the murder of two policemen. He brought his "fate" upon himself. Yet he paid for that crime with close to half a century of devotion to his fellow prisoners, and to the law. People will disagree as to whether the scales balance, or on which side they tip. But no one can deny that Jerry the Jew made a remarkable contribution to the life of the law. *L'chaim*, Jerry.

RON KUBY *is a criminal defense and civil rights lawyer in New York.*

PART ONE

If you live in an abnormal situation,

you gotta behave abnormally.

Otherwise you go nuts!

1

There were three of them facing the bench that morning in 1978—the plaintiff, his attorney, and a lawyer for the State of New York. It was a federal courtroom in Manhattan's Foley Square, and the rise and fall of their voices was all but extinguished by the thick royal-blue-and-gold carpeting underfoot.

"Mr. Rosenberg," the judge said, turning to the plaintiff's attorney. "How do you respond to the state's latest assertion that your client deliberately bypassed this issue in his appeal four and a half years ago?"

"He was denied effective assistance of counsel at the time, Your Honor," Rosenberg told him quickly. "Needless to say, that was long before I entered the case."

He is a small, effervescent man of forty-one, this lawyer, wearing a slightly outmoded herringbone sports coat and flannel slacks and a pair of aviator-style tinted glasses. And yet despite the trappings of respectability, there is a lingering aura of street life about him—in his gestures and intonation and occasionally in his choice of words.

"And what about this procedural objection the state raises as governed by the rule in *Johnston v. Marsh*?" the judge asks him.

"Totally irrelevant, Your Honor," the lawyer says. "It is our position that the State of New York has lost jurisdiction over Mr. Wylie, that his release to federal authorities in November of 1972 constituted a waiver, and that Mr. Wylie's further imprisonment is manifestly illegal."

This was the heart of the issue. For although Ruben Wylie had already completed a four-year federal sentence for interstate transport of untaxed cigarettes and was then serving his third year of a seven-year state sentence for hijacking the truck, Rosenberg had recently become convinced that the validity of the state conviction could be attacked through the back door.

"This is a highly complex issue, Your Honor," Assistant Attorney General Wallace Heilman sputtered. "This notion of a waiver goes far beyond the substance of the petition, and I respectfully request a continuance until the twenty-third of this month."

"Motion denied," the judge told him with a disdainful rap of the gavel. He had allowed Heilman three adjournments already. But more than that, he loathed this particular combination of arrogance and laziness in a lawyer—an attitude, he found, that had begun to characterize virtually the entire state attorney general's office.

"Your Honor," Rosenberg said, groping instinctively for some way to harness the judge's impatience, "I submit that these delays are unconscionable, and I would point out for Your Honor's consideration that Mr. Wylie is clearly eligible for bail under Title 28, United States Code, Section 2243, pending a final disposition of this proceeding."

There was a long pause. As a rule, no one would even bother to make such a motion when the prisoner in question is doing seven years.

"Title 28, did you say?" The judge scratched his head and glanced quickly over at his law clerk, who was nodding vigorously.

"Objection, Your Honor!" Heilman shouted, springing to his feet. "As Your Honor knows, before Your Honor could even *consider* an application for bail," he said, "we would have to prepare a probation report and other necessary documentation—"

"The only documentation necessary is my signature," the judge told him sharply, and he began fishing in annoyance through the papers at the back of Wylie's case file.

"Mr. Wylie," he said, staring disgustedly right at Heilman, "does your mother still reside at Two Fourteen East One Hundred Forty-fifth Street in the Bronx?"

"Yes, sir!" Wylie told him, scarcely able to believe which way the conversation seemed to be headed.

"Your Honor," Heilman babbled, "I can assure you that the People are not prepared to argue these grounds on such short notice."

"That's the People's problem, Mr. Heilman," the judge snapped, reaching for his gavel. "And if you want to avoid it next time, try and remember not to string me along."

He turned back to the plaintiff. "I am setting bail at five thousand dollars bond, Mr. Wylie," he said, staring gruffly at him over the top of his glasses. "And if you fail to show up for that hearing on the twenty-third, I will personally send a vanload of marshals over to your mother's house with bazookas. Is that clear?"

He banged his gavel, hopped down off the bench, and headed for his chambers, Wylie staring after him in mute astonishment as a pair of marshals shouldered their way to the front of the courtroom.

"Nice goin', Jerry," one of the marshals said, quickly approaching Wylie's attorney. He unsnapped a pair of handcuffs from the back of his belt, tightened them firmly around the attorney's wrists, and began riffling carefully through the contents of his briefcase.

"Gimme a break, Chief," the lawyer told him. "You know that stuff's all protected by attorney-client privilege."

"You got a pastrami sandwich in there, it ain't protected," the marshal reminded him, poking around some more till he was finally satisfied. He closed the snap of the briefcase and motioned the lawyer toward the corridor, where a high-security elevator would whisk them down to the third-floor catwalk that connects the courthouse to the Metropolitan Correctional Center next door.

"Don't hit no lieutenants in there, Jerry," Wylie told him, profoundly grateful but totally unable to put the feeling into words. He reached out and clasped his attorney's manacled hands in both his own. "You take good care of yourself in there, Jerry," he whispered. "Y'hear?"

For Jerry Rosenberg, flat-out victories like the Wylie case are always tinged with a note of desperate irony.* For he has spent the past sixteen years of his life in prison. And ever since the day in 1966 when he sprung himself out of the Sing Sing Death House with a brilliantly argued petition to Governor Rockefeller, he has struggled ceaselessly—but so far unsuccessfully—to obtain his own release.

In the meantime, however, he has built a reputation for himself as the most accomplished and successful jailhouse lawyer in the country. And within the closed world of prison society, his accomplishments have made him into an authentic jailhouse legend. In 1967 he became the first man in New York State prison history to earn a bona fide law degree from behind bars. And in the years since then he has used that knowledge on behalf of hundreds of his fellow prisoners, springing dozens of them from lengthy jail terms and shortening the sentences of many others.

In 1974 he became the first prisoner ever to be permitted to represent a client in a jury trial. Since then he has won cases against policemen and prosecutors and high-ranking public officials—and the United States Supreme Court has recognized him as the attorney

* At a final hearing six weeks later, Ruben Wylie was allowed to take a plea to eight years in lieu of a new trial. And since he had already earned three years' good-time credit, he promptly walked out of the courtroom a free man.

of record in several major cases in recent years, including a precedent-shattering appeal in 1977 on behalf of Carmine Galante, allegedly the most powerful organized crime figure ever to do time in the federal prison system.

And yet, despite Jerry's unparalleled accomplishments—and the fact that he technically becomes eligible for parole in April of 1982—no one who knows anything about the New York State criminal-justice system believes that his parole is any kind of foregone conclusion.

The reason for their pessimism has to do with the highly provocative nature of the crime Jerry was convicted of: a double police homicide that monopolized the front pages of the city's tabloid press for weeks on end during the summer of 1962. As far as the parole board is concerned, Jerry is simply a cop killer—one of three men who became the subject of a nationwide manhunt and who finally surrendered in a blaze of publicity in the city room of the New York *Daily News*. It doesn't matter that no physical evidence was ever discovered linking him to the scene of the crime, or that the gun he allegedly possessed was only fired at the ceiling, or that he could have copped out to simple armed robbery if he'd been willing to implicate his old friend and co-defendant Anthony Portelli, or that many of the witnesses against him had been systematically tortured by the police. It doesn't matter that Jerry never killed *anyone* on that Friday afternoon in May. All that matters is that he was convicted and sentenced to the electric chair in connection with that crime, and that the substantial doubts about his involvement have been brushed aside consistently by state and federal courts at every level. Unfortunately for Jerry, he also has the national climate of hysteria over violent crime to contend with now, as well as the enormous political muscle of the Patrolmen's Benevolent Association, an organization that firmly believes in the deterrent power of long sentences, particularly where a cop killing is concerned.

Parole, then, has never struck him as a particularly good bet, but he continues to attack the circumstances of his conviction and imprisonment through the courts, as he has for the past sixteen years. He's come pretty close on a number of occasions, most notably in June of 1971, when the United States Court of Appeals for the Second Circuit came within an inch of setting him free. Jerry had argued in a beautifully crafted appeal that he had been victimized by an avalanche of slanderous pretrial publicity, that he had been denied the right to cross-examine certain of the witnesses against him, and that the testimony of the key prosecution witnesses had been extracted by means of threats and violent physical abuse. A three-judge panel considered these claims and finally split 2 to 1 against him. But the dissenting judge ruled in Jerry's favor on all three issues. And if only one of his two colleagues had seen fit to concur, Jerry would have walked through the gates of Attica State Prison a free man.

Because of his unique accomplishments and congenital abrasiveness—and the threat he always poses to institutional routine—Jerry has been a frequent target of official harassment for most of his prison career. And as a result, he's also been a sitting duck for stool pigeons hoping to barter their sentences in return for information—often imaginary information—against an inmate whom they know the administration is out to get.

When I first came to know him in January of 1978, Jerry had just been transferred out of the reasonably comfortable eleventh-floor dorms at the Metropolitan Correctional Center and placed in administrative segregation on the ninth floor, where, except for visits and court appearances, he was spending the entire day locked up in a vicious-looking six-by-ten-foot metal cage furnished with a light bulb, a grizzly little cot, and an open toilet.

The transfer had come swiftly in the wake of a series of accusations by an old friend and former client named Kenny Wedra. Jerry had been hearing for months that Wedra was "wrong," that he had in fact been transferred to the MCC solely in order to spy and squeal. But Jerry had disbelieved the rumors.

"I'm very slow to *mark* a guy," he says. "Especially when he happens to be a friend."

Wedra himself is now confined in the stool-pigeon wing on the third floor. And whenever he's escorted to other parts of the prison—the infirmary, the Attorneys' Conference Room, or the tiny open-air exercise yard on the roof—the hallways are always cleared well in advance, and he is required to wear a heavy brown canvas hood over his head. For his own protection.

"A rat is the lowest thing in the world," Jerry told me one bone-chilling afternoon several weeks after his transfer to the ninth floor. "And this was a guy I trusted, a guy I'd been locking with for close to a year." He lit up a cigarette from one of the three packs he usually carries, filled his lungs to capacity, and exhaled a dense plume of smoke. "Believe me when I tell you, I'd rather die first. I would definitely have myself killed or kill myself before I would become an informer. That's the way we live in jail, the bright guys, the good guys."

He rolled the cigarette thoughtfully between three fingers for a moment. "It's not just a matter of principle, either," he finally said. "It's a way of life. Because if you go for their scumbag deals and you submit to their crummy fuckin' harassment and intimidation, these places can turn you into a zombie overnight. I've seen it happen to guys even after fifteen or twenty years of standing up to it every day. But not me. I'll never bend to these people. I mean that sincerely. Even four years ago when they offered me my freedom if I'd agree to perjure myself by ratting on some county-court judge. 'No fuckin' good,' I told them, and I've never regretted it for a minute. If I wanted to get out the *wrong way*, I had plenty of better chances sixteen years ago.

"Anyhow, it was common belief in the joint that this mutt Kenny Wedra had his own brother pinched on the street for cocaine. That's how low he is. I'll give you another example. Last month he told me he needed some money for Christmas presents for his kids. Okay, I got lotsa friends on the street. 'I'll have the money for you Thursday morning,' I told him. Sure enough, Wednesday night the goon squad rolls into my cell and tears me down. Long-handled mirrors, the whole bit. Not only did they find the currency, they got my pepper, a couple of those little bottles of cognac you get on airplanes, and some special food I had stashed away under the lip of the sink. It makes me nauseous just thinking about it."

He removed his tinted glasses to reveal a pair of deeply sunken eyes and a jagged scar across his forehead that he received in the aftermath of the Attica rebellion in September of 1971.

"Hell, I can handle solitary confinement," he said. "That ain't nothin'. It's the goddamn *pepper* that drives you crazy when they snatch it away."

One of the nice things about the MCC, as compared with the state prisons where Jerry has done most of his sixteen years, is the opportunity to get to the phone. Upstate he was allowed one phone call a week, *collect*. But at the MCC there's a pay phone on almost every floor, and except during lock-ins and counts, inmates with dimes are permitted to make as many calls as they wish. Of course, Jerry's transfer to the ninth floor has complicated things a bit, but he still manages to log an hour or two a day on the phone, some of it legal business, some of it purely social.

"I'm gettin' addicted to contact in this joint," he told me. "I don't know what the hell I'm gonna do when they send me back upstate."

He had been waiting for almost a year for his nine-million-dollar lawsuit against former State Special Prosecutor Maurice Nadjari to come to trial—a Byzantine affair that occasionally flashed to life for a pretrial hearing and then lapsed back into dormancy, as criminal cases crowded in ahead of it on the court's scrambled calendar. But in the meantime he'd been able to convince Federal District Judge Charles D. Stewart that, since it was a federal case, he was entitled to residence at the MCC during the entire pretrial period—close to his family and the phone and his buddies on the street.

And he was also blissfully close to his current girl friend, a twenty-eight-year-old former stewardess and mother of two named Arlene Castelli, whom Jerry met in the eighth-floor visiting room soon after his arrival. He had eventually managed to get her credentialed as his legal assistant, and they were now in the habit of seeing each other three or four times a week in the privacy of the Attorneys' Conference Room—an arrangement that had the old-line puritanical members of the staff buzzing with indignation and innuendo and that had given Jerry some of the deepest moments of both joy and anguish that he had known in his entire life.

"Sometimes I don't think I can stand it no more," he says. "Just knowing she's out there and beautiful and full of love for me and I'm stuck up here in this fuckin' place. Listen to me when I tell you, I never knew what *hard time* was before I met this woman. I'd let them beat me every day if that's what would get me to the phone."

And yet despite the fact that the phone has become a near-obsession for Jerry, he still keeps all his phone numbers on little scraps of paper that are constantly sifting out of his pockets fore and aft. For long-distance calls he prefers the push-button pay phone on the eleventh floor, where, since he knows the access code, he's able to call anywhere in the country for a dime. He also calls his seventy-two-year-old mother, Rose, several times a day. During the week she's less than half a mile away from the MCC, still working in the family business, a prosperous advertising specialties firm that Jerry's father and two older brothers built from scratch.

His high-volume telephone habits have also put him back in touch with a lot of old friends, at least one of them by sheer coincidence. He was waiting on line one day, rapping with a friend from the sixth floor, when the guy on the phone ahead of them turned around and asked them if they wanted to play a number. He had just phoned in a bet to the bar and grill in his old neighborhood, the guy said, and he still had one of his buddies on the line.

"Sure," Jerry told him, "I wanna bet my prison number. Tell him to put down five dollars on eight thirty-one for Jerry the Jew."

The guy repeated the instructions into the phone and then handed Jerry the receiver in surprise. "There's somebody having a beer over there says he knows you," the guy told him.

It turned out to be Johnnie-Boy Rizzo, a dear friend of his from Sing Sing whom Jerry had represented in a landmark case almost six and a half years earlier and with whom he had fallen completely out of touch. They chatted happily for a few minutes, teasing each other and breaking each other's chops in the time-honored Italian fashion.

"So listen, Johnnie," Jerry finally asked him. "When are we gonna get together?"

There was an awkward silence on the other end of the line, and Jerry was well aware that many former prisoners are absolutely phobic about the idea of setting foot back inside a prison.

"Well, I don't know, Jerry," Rizzo finally croaked. "Maybe next week sometime. I got a lot of things need my personal attention over here."

"How about next week, Tuesday, in the evening," Jerry nudged. "We'll just sit around, shoot the breeze. You ever been in the MCC?"

"Nah," Rizzo said.

"It's nothin' to get uptight about, believe me. I mean, you ain't on parole or nothin', am I right?"

"Nah, nothin' like that," Rizzo told him glumly. "Okay, Jerry, I'll see you Tuesday around six thirty, seven o'clock. Awright?"

"You know where it is, huh?"

"Yeah, I know where it is," Rizzo assured him.

Even so, Jerry called him virtually every day until that Tuesday rolled around, always with a funny anecdote or some hair-raising tale of official corruption or ineptitude. But he always made sure to run down the arrangements for the visit at the end of every call. Where and when and where to park, what to say to the lobby officer on the way up, and also to please bring him a roll of dimes for the phones. It's not that Jerry felt any cosmic urgency about this particular visit. It's just that reminding people to do the things they promised has become a way of life.

I met John Rizzo for an hour beforehand on that Tuesday evening in February of 1978—curious mostly about Jerry's starring role in the Rizzo case, in which he had become the first inmate ever to represent a client in a jury trial.

"He pulls very big with Italians, I guess that's obvious," Rizzo told me. "He's a nervy fuckin' ballsy little guy, a helluva guy to do time with. If he was six feet tall he woulda been dangerous." He paused for a thoughtful swallow of Sambuca. "You know, when I got hurt that time up at Sing Sing, Jerry practically took the whole joint out on strike. That's the only reason they ever treated me medically. It's the strangest thing in the world, but the officials upstate really respect him. They hate him, but they respect him. I saw him get on the phone one time and call up the clerk of the prison. It had something to do with how they were calculating a guy's release date. Well, Jerry ran down this long, complicated legal argument, and then he says, 'Now we can do one of two things. Either you send the man home like you know you oughta, or else we hash the whole thing out in a court of law.' And sonofabitch if they didn't cut the guy loose the next day. I mean, it's gotten to the point now where the *threat* of his getting involved in a guy's case is enough to make sure they do the right thing. A fabulous guy to have on your side."

We took a cab to the MCC around six forty-five, with Rizzo sweating buckets and clearly dreading this first contact with the world of prison since his release from Sing Sing in 1973. In the lobby downstairs he practically jumped out of his skin as a kid on his way out from a visit accidentally kicked over a freestanding metal ashtray and sent it toppling to the floor with a tremendous crash.

"I'm not usually like this," Rizzo told me, steadying his nerves with a cigarette. "It's just the smell of the place that's setting me off. Whether they're two hundred years old like Sing Sing or brand new like this one . . ." His voice trailed off distractedly, and we watched for a moment as one of the guards hassled a pair of women on their way up to the seventh floor, dumping the contents of their pocketbooks onto a wooden tray. "Look at how fuckin' brutal and callous these people are," Rizzo muttered. "And this is what Jerry's gotta put up with all his fuckin' life."

Our number was finally called, and Rizzo danced around in a nervous little circle as a hack swept his body with a buzzing, hand-held metal detector. And then we were in the elevator, our left wrists still glistening from the ultraviolet stamp that would distinguish us from any potential escape artists on our way back out through the lobby.

Moments later we stepped out into one of the regular social visiting rooms at the MCC—one to each floor, each of them no bigger than four hundred square feet, with eight rows of fiberglass stacking chairs that can be moved around to form little semiprivate clusters. In the evenings and on the weekends, the noise level in the rooms is often shattering, and children especially seem to suffer from the oppressive and totally sterile milieu.

The heavy armored door at the front finally *clunked* open, and a bored-looking hack escorted Jerry through this final checkpoint, subjecting him to a surprisingly thorough body frisk.

"Hey, I'm doing a life bid here, leave me alone," Jerry growled at the guy, his eyes twinkling at his old friend Rizzo halfway across the room.

And then within a matter of seconds Rizzo's apprehension and paranoia melted away. He met Jerry halfway to the gate and hugged him tight, squeezed his chin and his cheeks, thumped him on the back, and finally picked him up bodily and swung him around, all of this accompanied by a chorus of insults and epithets and imprecations, both of them grinning from ear to ear.

It was childish and stupid and totally hilarious, and they spent the next hour and a half running through a vast repertoire of jailhouse anecdotes and stories and real-life pranks, laughing hysterically and topping each other every time.

"Remember that night we broke into the meat locker right before Thanksgiving?" Rizzo asked him. "And we pinched those six hundred frozen chickens . . . terrible-looking birds, all screwed up and frosty-looking like they'd been in there for twenty years?"

"Remember the time we buried all the spoons?" Jerry shouted back. "Or the time you chopped off the dead branch with a buzz saw and crashed it through the warden's window?"

And so it went, tears of glee streaming down their faces.

"It was worth it, y'know?" Rizzo told him. "All those crazy things we done. When we could get over on 'em like that, we had a month made. We could do a month laughing. I think them stunts we pulled was the only thing that kept me sane."

And then the conversation came to an awkward halt.

"Everything is scheming in here," Jerry finally told him. "You remember. Scheming for the smallest things in life that you can get on the streets like nothing. It's like your whole fuckin' life gets spent just waiting for the next shakedown." He looked up at Rizzo and sensed that his old friend was growing uncomfortable again.

"It's the hacks I really forgot about," Rizzo told him. "The viciousness of these people, even in little ways. They're all borderline cases. They're too scared to steal and be criminals, and yet they don't have the heart or the guts to go out and do something legal. 'Cause this ain't no fuckin' *work* what they're doin' . . ."

Just then an alarm bell began ringing distantly several floors below.

"Good," Rizzo chuckled. "Maybe a hack got hit."

Jerry smiled and stretched expansively, pointing to a short, curly-headed correctional officer on the other side of the room. "See that nitwit over there?" he asked Rizzo. "Name's Delguercio; a new guy. A couple of weeks ago he didn't know me from Adam. Anyhow he busts in on me and Arlene one time in the Attorneys' Conference Room and starts yelling he caught me feeling up my lawyer. 'No,' I says. 'I wasn't feeling her up, I was kissing her. And besides she ain't my lawyer.' Already I got the guy confused. 'Well,' he says, 'you're not allowed to kiss her, either.' 'Of course I am,' I tell him. 'I don't see no sign where it says no attorney-kissing permitted.' 'Well, there should be,' he says. 'Maybe so,' I tell him. 'But what there should be and what there is, is two different things.' By this time he's all fucked up and he can't remember what he thought he had me on. 'Forget about it, sonny,' I told him. 'You just made a pretty foolish move there, but I give you my word I won't tell the lieutenant nothin' about it.' I swear to God, Johnnie, he turned on his heel and walked out of there and I haven't heard one peep out of him ever since."

Rizzo chuckled appreciatively and got slowly to his feet. "Hell, it's only eight fifteen," Jerry told him. "Stay till eight thirty; you'll get an elevator right away."

But Rizzo had had more than enough, and he gave Jerry a final brokenhearted hug and promised to come in and see him again whenever he got the chance.

"It's a fuckin' miracle," Rizzo told me several minutes later as we pushed through the revolving door into the deep-frozen February night. "You have any idea what kinda shape the average guy is in after fifteen or twenty years in one of these places? You know what the mental anguish can do to a guy? You know how many times they've trashed his cell, destroyed his legal papers, thrown him in the hole?"

He stepped off the curb and tried in vain to hail a speeding cab.

"You notice that scar he's got all up and down his forehead? A trooper did that to him up at Attica, cracked his head wide open with a rifle butt. It's more than a scar, actually. It's nerve damage. Take a look at his right eye sometime when he's got his glasses off. You'll see the pupil in there is all closed up tight, no bigger than a pinhead. And then he gets these terrible attacks, cluster headaches, they're called. Excruciating. I seen him one time just about ready to put his head through the wall. They finally pulled in an outside specialist who told him he needed an operation, neurosurgery. Told him they could reduce the pain a little, but there was a fifty-fifty chance that half his face would end up paralyzed. Of course, Jerry told 'em *no* right away, but at first I didn't understand. 'You gotta be a tough guy in jail,' he shouted at me, real exasperated. 'I'm five foot five and a half and ninety-eight pounds dripping wet,' he screamed. 'How am I gonna survive in this jungle with half my face on the blink?' "

Rizzo gave up on the idea of a cab and headed quickly in the direction of Centre Street, tucking his head down against the wind.

"Just remember one more thing about Jerry," he told me. "All the jackpots he's been in, all the beatings and shakedowns and time in the hole . . . that's all been 'cause of helpin' other people. I visited him in the infirmary once after a really bad beating, right after he'd put his name on another man's legal papers for the first time. And I'll never forget what he told me. 'A lot of people got the wrong impression about what a tough guy is,' he said. 'They think he's good with his fists . . . or he just boldly walks into a joint and beats the shit out of some guy to form a reputation. Uh-uh. I call those guys pieces of garbage. I'll tell you what a tough guy is,' he said. 'The tough guy is the guy who can deal with the backlash of something he believes in . . . who refuses to submit to the dehumanization and the degradation and the horrendous brutality that these assholes are always dishing out.'

"You deal with strong principles in jail," Rizzo told me. "And nobody deals with 'em stronger than Jerry."

That February evening in 1978 came relatively early in my acquaintance with Jerry Rosenberg. I had been hearing about him and his accomplishments for several years before that, however, having written a television documentary on prison life in 1975 and having begun to hear bits and pieces of the legend that surrounds him in the course of that research. To me, the very idea of a practicing jailhouse attorney was fascinating. But at that point I had no direct way to pin down any of the rumors.

Three years later I had the opportunity to meet him in person. What I thought I was interested in was background material for another film project. But a week later, having spent close to four hours a day with him in an intense, multifocused, and often uproarious nonstop conversation, I had begun to consider the idea of telling Jerry's story in a book.

Above all, I sensed in those first meetings that I would have his complete attention. Clearly he had reached the point in his life where he wanted his story told. And as we came to trust each other in the months ahead, I was astonished again and again by his willingness to open his life to me in a truthful way, even when the glimpse it provided into his nature was unflattering or potentially threatening to his position and privileges in the institution.

Since those early days in 1978, I have spent many hundreds of hours with him in prison visiting rooms, conference areas, and courtrooms throughout the state. And I have lugged home tens of thousands of pages of trial transcripts, court records, legal briefs, newspaper coverage, and hundreds of hours of tape-recorded interviews and notes. It was an organic process, each new source or long-forgotten court appearance unlocking scores of other leads, until finally a coherent picture gradually began to emerge.

In between were long stretches of uncertainty as a chaotic jumble of data and contradictory personal impressions quickly began to accumulate. It is part of Jerry's nature, I would discover, to be in a state of constant change. And it is part of the nature of imprisonment, I would also learn, that nothing disappears faster than the artifacts of personal history. In their place one finds the prisoner's *jacket*, or reputation—an exotic brew of fact, opinion, myth, and bravado that tends to resist verification by its very nature, especially in Jerry's case, where the texture is now so richly embroidered that even *he* sometimes loses track of the early specifics. Eventually, however, because so many of his exploits—both legal and extralegal—proved to be traceable through court records and other public documents, I was finally able to pin down a factual, step-by-step chronology—the chronological bones around which this book then quickly began to grow.

Along the way I was reminded over and over again just how fragile Jerry's privileged lifestyle behind bars really is. There would be frequent unexplained interruptions in his ability to make phone calls and receive visits. And, of course, our working relationship was further complicated by the enormous gulf between *his* world and the free-world culture in terms of which I was constantly attempting to measure his behavior and achievements. Always I was asking and rephrasing and redefining a basic set of unanswerable questions, a set of doubts and hopes and paradoxes that hovers around Jerry like some strange halo and that continues to baffle even those who have known him for many years. How, for example, could an environment as oppressive as the Sing Sing Death House have failed to extinguish the last drop of ambition in anyone, let alone a semiliterate hood from Bath Beach? What possible destiny might have awaited him if he had remained on the streets? ("At the rate he was going?" says his old friend Richie Moretti. *"Forget about it!"*) And what, for that matter, does it say about the relationship between criminal and legal thinking that Jerry should have been so passionately attracted to—and adept at—both?

In the end, however, I found myself looking less for answers than for the man himself—a quest, I continually rediscover, that raises still further questions every step of the way, not only about Jerry but about the brutal system in which he finally and paradoxically has discovered fertile ground for his talents. Above all, I find myself wondering what would have happened if the system hadn't chosen to fight him quite so hard. And what plans they have for him now that he has ostensibly fulfilled their own widely disparaged goal of rehabilitation.

My previous contact with the world of prison was just enough for me to appreciate the significance of the opportunity that Jerry's story represented, not only for its epic and human qualities, but as an opportunity to explore the hidden world of prison life.

As I found myself drawn deeper and deeper into this unfamiliar world, I gradually came to rely on the wisdom and perspective of a large number of people, some of them Jerry's friends and former clients on both sides of the criminal fence, some of them scrupulously neutral observers with a special expertise in some branch of law or criminology. To all of them—a group both too numerous and for the most part too reclusive to mention—I would like to express my enormous appreciation.

2

During Jerry's stay at the MCC, I usually visited him around three o'clock in the afternoon. The Attorneys' Conference Room wasn't very crowded at that hour, and we were generally able to get a private cubicle all to ourselves. But it didn't always work out that way. And once when we were stuck at the long table in the anteroom waiting for a cubicle to open up, I made the mistake of pulling out a map of Brooklyn, hoping to get him talking about his old neighborhood.

As soon as he saw it, he quickly jammed it back inside my jacket pocket. "Maps is a big pinch in here," he rasped. "They'll think we got an escape going, I swear to God."

But a few minutes later, when the hack seemed to be tied up for a moment at the gate, he asked to see the map again. He unfolded it reverently and stared at it with a sense of total incomprehension.

"I ain't seen one of these things in so long," he whispered, twisting it around and around. But he just couldn't get his bearings, and he finally pushed it away in embarrassment. Nevertheless, it must have jogged his memory because, for the first time in the many hundreds of hours we'd spent together, he began to talk about his childhood.

"I grew up old," he told me. "Like when I was twelve, I was hanging around with guys in their twenties. I never stood with kids my own age. Come to think of it, I never *was* a kid."

He tilted his chair back against the windowsill, a nostalgic grin playing at the corners of his mouth.

"I remember getting throwed out of Hebrew School when I was seven," he said. "That's 'cause I never listened to the rabbi. Public school was even worse. My father used to walk me over every morning just to make sure I got there. I'd say good-bye, walk in the front door and right out the back. Spend the whole day at Coney Island. But the guys we really hated were the monitors, the kids in the stairways with the armbands. They were stool pigeons. We used to throw them down the stairs, take their armbands off, and break them."

He paused for breath, took a huge, furtive bite out of the Hostess Twinkie he'd brought into the room with him, and then slipped the open package back into his jacket pocket.

"The first time I ever saw the inside of a police station I was nine years old," he said, sweeping the incriminating Twinkie crumbs off the top of the table. "Still just a baby. I pinched my brother's watch, sold it to the janitor for five dollars, and went to Coney Island. Then I got lost and the cops picked me up and hauled me into the precinct. I went on all the rides that day, though. One of the best days of my entire life." He laughed at the memory, then fell silent for a moment, his eyes far away. "I guess I just happened to choose a life which ain't the best fuckin' life . . ."

He fumbled for a cigarette and lit it with a throwaway lighter embossed with the name and address of his parents' advertising specialties firm.

"I got no explanations or excuses," he said. "I'm me, and that's just the way it happened."

I asked him to tell me a little bit more about Coney Island.

"I practically lived there," he said. "By the time I was twelve, me and my buddy Joey DiNisio were shaking down the concessionaires on the boardwalk for five dollars a week protection money. We had a little shack under the boardwalk we called the Bop House. It had a record player in there and a lot of kids hanging around. Anytime a cop used to come down on the beach with his horse, a couple of minutes later all you'd see is his horse all alone and the cop's hat floating in the fucking water. We beat him up, threw him down, and that was the end of it."

Of course, this is the same Jerry who readily admits he never won a fistfight in his life. "The first time I ever got in tight with the Italian kids was in fourth grade," he said. "Three of them jumped me in the boys' room, beat the shit out of me. But I never gave up. I was still punching away when the gym teacher came in to break it up. The Italian kids jumped through the window and disappeared, but I wouldn't rat on 'em. Three weeks' detention, they gave me, but I still wouldn't squeal. That's when they started showing me some respect."

The first official entry on his juvenile record shows a hearing in family court for possession of three cases of cherry bombs.

"I wasn't into fireworks," Jerry explains. "They weren't for me; they were for sale. We'd just ripped off a guy who brought them over from Jersey in the trunk of his car. The cops knew the whole story but couldn't prove it, so they pinched us for possession instead."

Curiously enough, the case was never disposed of. And neither were several other early juvenile infractions—all of them smoothed over through connections on the street.

Meanwhile, back at home Jerry was taking a solid drubbing from his older brothers, Marty and Nathan, both of whom were "sprouting wings," as his mother liked to say. With Marty the fights were tooth and nail, and with Nathan they were verbal. But either way Jerry inevitably wound up with the short end of the stick.

"I don't think Jerry ever walked out of that house with a good feeling in his gut," his friend Richie Moretti recalled many years later. "He couldn't stand up to them intellectually, and he couldn't stand up to them physically. He'd finally hit the door in a rage, his shoulders hunched and his head cocked, a huge Borsalino hat practically swallowing up his neck."

For Jerry's father, Lou, his son's delinquency was the only major blot on an otherwise exemplary if modestly proportioned life. He was by turns intimidated, awed, disgusted, and estranged from his son. And yet he was always there when Jerry needed him in a pinch. For Lou was a firm believer in the axiom that age is often the only cure for life's most serious problems. There had been a streak of wildness in him, too, as a boy—a streak he had burned out as an amateur club fighter in the thirties. He had toyed briefly with the idea of turning professional but had opted instead to take over his father's millinery shop in the then-Jewish neighborhood of South Harlem. He had parlayed a modest success there into a shoestring coin-machine business, leasing pinballs and jukeboxes and placing them in bars and restaurants wherever he could talk his way in. There's no question that Lou occasionally rubbed elbows with some of Brooklyn's most illustrious racketeers as he made his rounds, and no question, either, that some of them had become close personal friends. But by 1948 he had successfully made the transition into the white-collar world of advertising specialties—matchbooks, calendars, giveaways, and premiums—a business that had grown and deepened in pace with the postwar boom. By the mid-fifties he had broadened the business to include sales-incentive plans and complex merchandising programs. And while it provided the five of them with a more than comfortable living, there were many times when he missed the action and excitement of the streets and the high-voltage characters who had been his friends. Perhaps Jerry was more in touch with this side of his father's nature than were Marty and Nathan. Perhaps Lou unconsciously *endorsed* his son's wild behavior, flashing him covert signs of approval in between the stiff lectures and indignant harangues.

In any case, his strategy in the face of Jerry's delinquency, though well intentioned, was ultimately disastrous. Time after time he would buy his son's way out of scrapes, trudging down to the precinct house in the middle of the night to make bail or grease the palm of the desk sergeant, who by this time had become something of an old family friend. There would be a fierce argument in the car on the way home, a hysterical confrontation with his mother in the doorway, and a brief flurry of phone calls in an attempt to line him up a job, none of which ever lasted for more than a week.

For his mother, Rose, Jerry's behavior was an absolute nightmare. Her own father had been a pioneer labor organizer with the International Bakery Workers' Union—a dynamic, cultured, scholarly man who also knew how to handle the rough and tumble of the streets.

Lou was safe and steady as a rock, but he paled before the memory of her father's reach and grasp. Understandably, then, she had very lofty ambitions for her sons. Nathan, calm and patient and very thorough, would make a wonderful doctor, she thought. Marty was argumentative and aggressive and sharp as a tack and seemed destined in her mind's eye for a career in law or politics. But for Jerry a professional life of any kind was clearly out of the question.

Perhaps his most solid accomplishment during this period was his role as lead singer in a short-lived rock-'n'-roll band called The Blue Notes. They had only one gig during their brief career, a cocktail lounge on Bath Avenue known as The Nineteenth Hole. They packed the place with friends and relatives on opening night, but business fell off precipitously thereafter.

"The incredible thing about Jerry," Richie Moretti recalls, "is that he actually went out and did these things. Always in motion, always scheming for action, and to hell with the consequences. But what a personality this kid had. He was so damn much fun to be with. 'Leave it to me,' he'd say. 'Let me handle this.' He was absolutely fearless. And the amazing thing is he often came out smelling like a rose."

His father blames Jerry's fate on the neighborhood, his mother blames it on "too much love." Sifting through the ashes of his early childhood, one finds other anomalies as well. His size, for one thing, and a history of chronic illness throughout his infancy. Curiously, in his only surviving baby picture, he's wearing a dress and pincurls, and tears of grief are streaming down a precious little face that can only be described as pretty.

"Everybody thought he was a girl," his mother recalls. "All the women in the supermarket would come over and admire him just like a little princess. Oh, I wanted a girl all right," she freely admits, "especially after Marty and Nathan. But once he was here, I didn't mind. I had to get used to what I got."

When Jerry was ten years old, the family moved into a house of their own on Fifteenth Avenue in the Bath Beach section of Brooklyn, one of the legendary fiefdoms in the history of organized crime. Their neighbor down the street was none other than Joseph Profaci, the King-fish of the Brooklyn mob and one of the most celebrated gangsters of his generation. Several of his ranking henchmen lived on the side streets nearby, and the entire neighborhood was suffused with the aroma of illicit wealth.

Any kid who grew up in Bath Beach during the forties and fifties as Jerry did had no choice but to come to terms with the mob presence in one way or another. The Jewish kids, for the most part, withdrew into a private world that centered around home, school, and temple—a carefully controlled environment where values like hard work, scholarship, thrift, and compassion could sometimes be instilled, a world where Jerry happened to be an absolute flop. For him the numbers joints and candy stores and the small-time hoods who ran them had far more to offer. Acceptance, for one thing. For Jerry was small for his age and physically underdeveloped—and he had also managed to get himself suspended from school regularly starting in fourth grade. Perhaps he was clinically hyperactive, perhaps he had some simple learning disability that could easily be identified and *therapized* out of existence today. But whatever the reason, his teachers all quickly came to the conclusion that he was no damn good. He couldn't read, he couldn't understand basic arithmetic, and his constant troublemaking in the classroom brought things to an absolute standstill several times a day. Small wonder, then, that no one at school made a very serious effort to curb his truancy. And given the run of the streets for most of the day, it's not surprising, either, that his closest friends were the junior-grade mobsters who hung out in the candy stores all up and down Bath Avenue. By the age of thirteen he was working part time behind the counter of a local numbers joint, dealing stolen cameras out of the back room and impressing his superiors with his insatiable appetite for action. In fact, his behavior there was so remarkable—and so out of ethnic character—that they soon christened him with the nickname he would bear proudly for the rest of his life.

And yet no one had ever doubted his intelligence, at least not since the spring of 1952, when his despairing parents had taken him for an evaluation by a clinical psychologist in nearby Bensonhurst. Dr. Seymour Glaser administered a battery of tests, including the Stanford-Binet IQ Test and the Minnesota Multi-Phasic Inventory, and pronounced him bright as a whip. But not bright enough to avoid building up a juvenile record almost as long as his arm.

His mother remembers warning him during this period that "the day will come when nobody will be here to take care of you, when they'll just take you away and there'll be no one left to bail you out."

And yet the arrests continued to pile up: receiving stolen property in 1954, burglary in 1955, assault and robbery a year and a half later. But one way or another the charges were always dropped. And for every entry on the official record, there were scores of other encounters with the cops, many of which ended in savage beatings down by the waterfront.

"I hate everything that wears a badge," he was fond of saying even then. "Including the postman."

3

By the time he was twelve years old, Jerry's parents had begun to spend at least part of every summer in the Catskills, mostly in order to get him away from the pernicious influence of the Bath Beach neighborhood. At first it was just a week or two at a rooming house in Monticello. But by the middle fifties the family business was prospering nicely, and they were able to afford a cottage for the entire season. And it was at Durschlag's cottages in Monticello during the summer of 1954 that seventeen-year-old Jerry first met the woman he'd be pursuing for the rest of his free-world life.

Well, *woman* is hardly the right word. For Rose-Ann Cozza was exactly three months younger than Jerry, on her own that summer for the first time in her life and working for peanuts in the hotel kitchen. The summer was also providing her with her first glimpse of middle-class living. And the Rosenbergs in particular must have struck her as a family that had just about everything her own family lacked. She was the second oldest of five children, her twice-divorced mother constantly struggling just to keep things together and moving them frequently—from New York to Florida eleven years before, and endlessly from apartment to apartment and town to town ever since. She had spent most of her early adolescence caring for her three younger brothers and sisters, one of whom was seriously ill. And now that she was away from home, she was fiercely determined to start living her life *exactly* as she wished. Jerry intrigued her the minute she laid eyes on him—his wildness and worldly assurance so different from the lazy southern boys who'd begun to hit on her the year before. Jerry at least was a *mensch*, a man with a vision, however bizarre. And as she got to know him better, his dream of the big time and his crazy spending habits must have tasted to her like caviar and champagne.

Their relationship was cemented when Jerry gallantly faced down her boss, a strapping former clubhouse boxer named Harry Waldheim, who had been holding up her wages, claiming that Rose-Ann's working papers had not yet arrived from Florida. Jerry sauntered into Waldheim's kitchen one morning and, using his best Brooklyn snarl, managed to scare the guy out of his wits, invoking the names of several well-known mobsters and threatening to send up a sedan full of torpedoes to straighten the situation out. Rose-Ann's wages flowed steadily from that day forth.

Jerry had certainly never met anyone like her—serious and pretty and extremely bright, the kind of girl he would never in a million years have encountered under the Coney Island boardwalk. And best of all, she actually *liked* him. They quickly became inseparable, hanging out around the swimming pool by day and the deserted dining room in the evenings. They were both great talkers, always picking up new little expressions and turns of phrase. And they would often sit up half the night telling stories and analyzing life ad infinitum, trying to top each other like a pair of vaudeville comics.

"I saw quite a bit of Jerry back in Brooklyn that summer," says his old friend Moretti, "and every other word out of his mouth was Rose-Ann, Rose-Ann, Rose-Ann. He absolutely worshipped her. And when I finally met her, I could right away understand why. She was a beautiful kid, very sensual and very sensitive, with wonderful rounded cheeks and a light in her eye like none of us had ever seen. She was obviously fascinated by Jerry as a person, and I'm sure she got him thinking about himself and his life in a lot of new ways. She had that deep, introspective, adolescent turn of mind. She questioned everything. And somehow she also relaxed him, allowed him to drop his tough-guy act whenever he was around her for very long. She quickly became the only alternative to the violence and delinquency that was threatening to overwhelm him, a haven of calm and quiet and peace of mind."

At first the more she saw of Jerry, the more intrigued Rose-Ann became. Here was a person her own age who seemed to operate on the basis of pure instinct—fiercely intelligent, uproariously funny, and yet deeply disturbed. There seemed to be absolutely no structure to his life. He would come and go on a whim, drive to Niagara Falls on a dare. His world never seemed to have any consequences. But the pressures at work on him were clearly enormous.

"His nails were bitten down so deep, I believe his fingers must have been in constant pain," Moretti recalls. "And when the pop-top soda cans came out a couple of years later, he was in real trouble. The only way he could get them open was to tear off the cover of a matchbook and slide it under the ring. He was really suffering a lot and doing everything he could to hide it. Sometimes I'd see him pacing around nervously when he didn't know anyone was watching, wearing a hole in the sidewalk back and forth. 'Don't worry about it,' he'd be muttering to himself. 'Everything's gonna work out just fine.'"

What he was worried about only became clear to Rose-Ann in bits and pieces. He showed up one weekend all bruised and puffy from a run-in with the cops in Brooklyn. Another time a pair of state troopers stopped them on the highway just outside of town and practically dismantled his car bare-handed, looking in vain for a cache of drugs. Rose-Ann knew for a fact that Jerry's only vice was nicotine, and she resented the frisk far more than he did.

"Fortunes of war," he told her with a shrug, struggling to wedge the front seat back into the car. "I see those mutts again, I'm gonna throw a hot stove at them."

Another time she was over at the cabin when there was a knock at the door and a trio of detectives from the city barged through the door. "I'll be right with you, fellas, let me get my jacket," Jerry chirped, his nonchalance only ninety-eight percent convincing. "Which precinct?"

No sooner was he out the door than Jerry's mother, Rose, fished the number of their current bailbondsman out of her handbag, urging Lou to call even though it was the middle of the night.

"Let him stew," Lou told her wearily.

But Rose wouldn't hear of it. "I don't want him to spend the night in jail," she shrieked.

And, as usual, Jerry didn't have to. He was released on his own recognizance and was back in the Catskills by noontime the next day.

"At this point in Jerry's career, his parents had excellent contacts," an old friend remembers, "and they were able to smooth over almost anything short of aggravated assault. The problem, of course, was that Jerry never got to experience the full consequences of his own behavior, and I sometimes wonder if he ever really had a good enough reason to put all that craziness behind him."

"He used to run through people like the Yellow Pages," says Rose-Ann, "eagerly pouncing on anyone in a jam, organizing his time and energies around their plight, often with no possible benefit for himself except the distraction and sense of purpose it sometimes provided."

As the summer wore on, she began to see this pattern as a possible attempt to avoid the chaos and confusion and perhaps even the self-destructiveness that lay at the heart of his own behavior.

"Hey, look at you," she screamed at him one night when he came in all cut and bleeding from an encounter with a loan shark. "These other people don't need help, you do!"

But his main problem, of course, was not his penchant for helping others but his seemingly manic determination to stay in hot water himself.

"The trouble with Brooklyn," Richie Moretti explains, "is that you had ten thousand little guys running around with big ideas. And none of them really wanted to steal. They just wanted to be accepted by Solly D. or Joe 'Fish' or some other *made* guy over there at the bar. They just wanted to impress him. But to do that they had to hang out and spend money and act tough. And every once in a while they actually had to go out there and knock over a joint. Do you have any idea how hard it is to rob and steal? It's gotta be one of the toughest things in life to do really well. And the really vicious part is that once you're in that life, you can't really drop out of it. Because then you're a punk or a scumbag, and maybe all of a sudden they start worrying you're going to squeal. We all knew what happened to stool pigeons. Take my word for it, the pressures on those kids were simply enormous."

Two months later Rose-Ann was pregnant and comfortably installed in Marty's old room in the house on Fifteenth Avenue. For Rose and Lou it was just another routine shock. They knew all too well that Jerry would be totally unable to handle the responsibilities of a family, but at least the relationship with Rose-Ann promised to inject a measure of stability into his life, and the prospect of a grandchild toddling around the house was an attractive one.

No doubt Jerry was head over heels in love with the girl, delighted with the ripple of surprise and attention that her presence with him inevitably created. And yet the rhythms of his life hadn't changed a bit. He was still sleeping late, working the back room at the numbers joint most afternoons, and hanging around the mob-controlled gambling clubs at night.

Sometimes days would go by and Rose-Ann would never see him at all. And then on the third night he'd show up hungry and horny at three o'clock in the morning.

"Let's go get some Chinese food, Rosie," he'd coax her, picking out a dress for her from the little closet.

Sometimes she'd go and sometimes she wouldn't, but either way he'd usually manage to wake up his parents in the room next door.

"What d'you bother coming back here for?" Lou would yell after him from the top of the stairs. "Running around all night with your bum friends . . . who needs this aggravation?"

"You want your father to have a heart attack over you?" Rose would chime in through the open doorway. "For God's sake, Jerry, show a little consideration!"

And then he and Rose-Ann would be out on the streets again, and all the doubts and confusions they both were feeling would fall away and the world would once again seem to be smiling beneficently.

"It's real easy to be in love with Jerry at three o'clock in the morning," Rose-Ann remembers. "In twenty minutes we'd be in Manhattan. He knew all the best restaurants in Chinatown—which ones were open late, which ones had the finest lobster Cantonese. We'd sit in a booth in the back for hours, smooching and dreaming about another kind of life."

Jerry was also genuinely excited about the baby. And when Rose-Ann's gradually rounding tummy could no longer be concealed, he began to take her out more often in the early evenings as well.

"He was the proudest young pregnant papa in Brooklyn," Richie Moretti remembers. "I guess it proved he could do something, like it was the first legitimate accomplishment of his entire life."

Unfortunately, this accomplishment only inspired Jerry to more exalted levels of larcenous ambition. He showed up one night with a gorgeous mink jacket, flashing it under his brothers' noses before draping it excitedly around Rose-Ann's shoulders. He took her out for dinner to a fancy mob spot in Sheepshead Bay and then to the movies on Cropsey Avenue, closer to home. On their way out they were surrounded by plainclothesmen from the Twenty-first Precinct, who stripped the coat off Rose-Ann's shoulders and threw Jerry into the back of an unmarked police car at the curb. He spent the night in the station house lockup. But before Lou came down to bail him out the next morning, he and Jerry's mother had decided to put an end to their son's experiment in adult living. They made a flurry of long-distance calls, finally located Rose-Ann's mother in Galveston, and quickly placed the girl on a Texas-bound Greyhound, promising to send the rest of her belongings by Railway Express.

"We just thought the responsibilities of a family were driving him right off the deep end," his mother remembers. "Jerry was absolutely furious, screaming at us through the bars of the holding tank. But the mink coat was the last straw. 'If you get a regular job and stick with it for a couple of months, maybe we'll reconsider,' Lou told him. 'But you'll never be able to support a wife and child with a crowbar and a pair of dice.' "

Two weeks later Jerry was on a bus to Texas himself, drawn to Rose-Ann's side by a curious and insistent magnetism, and perhaps also by a part of himself that yearned for the decent and legitimate life that by now had just about slipped through his fingers.

Rose-Ann's mother had recently remarried for the third time, and Jerry made a surprisingly solid impression on her and her new husband, an enormous, gentle Dutchman known simply as The Rock. They were amazingly warm and generous toward Jerry at first, buying him a secondhand car and solemnly encouraging him when he said he wanted to set up a small jewelry business there in town. What appealed to him about the jewelry trade, he said, was the hundred and fifty percent markup. He carried through on this lofty ambition to the extent of buying some semiprecious stones from a wholesaler at the Jewelry Exchange in Houston and selling them at construction sites and shopping centers out of the trunk of his car. But he held back the only valuable piece that he'd acquired—a slim, diamond-encrusted engagement ring with which he proposed to Rose-Ann when she was seven and a half months pregnant.

"I know he wanted to legitimize the child," she says. "But I know he was also convinced that we really *could* make the marriage work. He never gave up on himself or on us as a couple, no matter how impossible things looked or how hard we'd fought the night before. And that was something I truly loved about him, something very fine and very precious."

They were married June 6, 1955, before a justice of the peace in the small town of Rosenberg, Texas. Jerry had spotted the place on a map the week before and had ruled out every other suggestion that Rose-Ann and his future in-laws had made. It wasn't a joke, either. It just seemed to him like the best way to sanctify the event, to make it special. They went in two cars: Rose-Ann enormously pregnant and alone with Jerry in the front seat of the '48 Ford her parents had bought him, her sister and two brothers following behind with the grown-ups in The Rock's brand new El Camino.

And then, just as suddenly, Jerry was headed back to New York. For the umpteenth time Rose-Ann listened to the ritual promises of "a place of our own," nodding automatically for the benefit of her parents, who were still largely under the spell of Jerry's charm and stylish good nature. He promised to send for her as soon as the baby was able to travel. And meanwhile he'd have his hands full with all the arrangements.

"I'll take care of everything," he told her. "My brother's even got a civil service job all lined up and waiting for me," he said. "You wait and see."

The baby was born three weeks later in the charity ward of St. Luke's Hospital in Galveston, news of the event reaching Jerry and his parents in the form of a telegram from Rose-Ann's mother the next day. Jerry, of course, wasn't very far along with the "arrangements," but the telegram struck an unexpectedly responsive chord in Rose and Lou. Suddenly here was the daughter they'd always dreamed of having. Suddenly their son and his marriage and his crazy lifestyle didn't seem quite so crazy. So what if Jerry was still in his wild phase? He'd settle down in a couple of years. And in the meantime they'd have the sublime pleasure of a baby girl toddling around the house. Rose was on the phone to the hospital within twenty minutes. Everything had been straightened out, she told Rose-Ann. And they all insisted that she and the baby come live in the house in Brooklyn, at least until Jerry was able to find a job commensurate with his talents. There would be a ticket waiting for her at Delta Airlines as soon as she felt capable of traveling, and they'd have all kinds of baby supplies and equipment set up for her in the room upstairs.

And then Jerry got on the line, so sweet and concerned and proud and excited. Of course she'd come back to Brooklyn, Rose-Ann told him. She couldn't wait to see him and hug him and show him the baby. And for the next ten days, while Rose-Ann was still in the hospital, they all truly believed that things had finally started to go right.

The name Rose-Ann had in mind for the baby was Deborah, but she quickly deferred to Rose, who, for reasons known only to herself, had her heart set on Ronnie. It was to be the first of hundreds of decisions about the child's welfare and upbringing that would be decided by Rose and Lou, both of whom fell madly in love with the little girl at first sight. And there's no question that Jerry's stock in the family rose precipitously as soon as Rose-Ann stepped through the terminal gates at LaGuardia Airport, Ronnie smiling and blinking curiously in her arms. She was a gorgeous child, born with a full head of delicate cornsilk hair, her little features perfectly formed and highly responsive. All five Rosenbergs were waiting for them there in the crowded lobby, the baby cooing and chirping at them despite the noise and confusion.

"Never in the history of the human race has a child received so much undivided attention from so many delirious adults," one old family friend remembers.

Suddenly life in the little house on Fifteenth Avenue revolved around diaper changes and naps and feeding schedules, with endless debates as to the proper strategy for dealing with Ronnie's occasional temper tantrums and chronic wakefulness in the middle of the night.

Rose and Lou actually seemed to *youthen*, both of them feeling more positive and vigorous than they had in years. And for a few months, at least, things actually seemed to be working out rather well.

"At first it was a very educational thing for me being in that household," Rose-Ann remembers. "They're all very bright people, and they exposed me to a lot of mind-opening ideas that I would never have encountered on my own. I loved every minute of those conversations. I soaked it up like a sponge."

Jerry was on the premises more than usual during this early stretch, but his contributions to the intellectual life of the household were almost nil.

"If he was around for more than ten minutes, he'd get zapped," says Rose-Ann, "led into a verbal trap by Marty or Nathan, who'd then squelch him hideously when they were sure he lacked the means to battle his way out."

She came to recognize a pattern in which Rose and Lou were constantly bailing Jerry out of these situations, coming to his rescue in his scrapes with his brothers as well as with the police.

But just as remarkable, she thought, was the unconditional loyalty they showed him, never once writing him off as hopeless or, despite the evidence that was accumulating almost daily, as *bad*.

"Can you help my son?" Richie Moretti remembers Lou beseeching him one time after bailing Jerry out of a felonious assault on Coney Island. "Please talk to him, Richie. Make him understand he can't keep going on like this."

In fact, Richie Moretti was rapidly getting sucked under himself and would later do seven and a half years for bank robbery, four of them in Attica with Jerry. What Lou failed to understand was that all the heat Jerry was drawing to himself was actually a mark of distinction on the candy-store circuit: If you were pulling jobs, or were claiming to, and you *weren't* getting any heat, then you were probably a rat. It was that simple. But Jerry never talked, never supplied the cops with even a scrap of incidental information, inexorably building up his reputation as a real stand-up guy, a guy who'd never talk no matter what they did to him. And as a result, he had begun to come to the attention of some of the real heavyweights in the neighborhood—sober, cautious men who were impressed by his initiative and his nerve but who were understandably troubled by his reckless stunts. There was talk of awarding him a numbers franchise in nearby Crown Heights, and Jerry would occasionally approach them with a scheme of his own. But always the decision was to wait and see. "He's too crazy yet," they'd finally decide. "He's still just a cowboy. Let him learn some common sense."

Perhaps in his heart he knew they were right. Perhaps he was growing genuinely alarmed by the escalating risks all around. Perhaps, as Richie Moretti likes to say, he was simply *pazzo*. Whatever the explanation, on March 3, 1956, he stumbled into the armed forces recruiting station in Brooklyn's Borough Hall and enlisted in the United States Army.

"I don't know *why* the fuck I did it, to be honest with you," Jerry cackled many years later. "Maybe it was the cheap cigarettes . . ."

Whatever his motives, one can imagine the sense of relief Rose and Lou must have felt upon hearing the news. God willing, their son had finally started to channel his aggressiveness into something worthwhile. To Rose-Ann, on the other hand, his decision seemed patently ridiculous.

"I knew he'd never last more than a couple of months," she says. "I saw it more as a cry for help, a need he had for limits and external controls, a need that nobody in his life had ever really been able to supply."

In any case, they all went down to Grand Central Station to see him off, Ronnie now close to a year old and screaming hideously at the sight of Jerry in a crew cut and an olive-drab uniform. He was away for exactly ninety days, returning home one sultry morning in June with a dishonorable discharge in his pocket.

From that point on his life began to oscillate even more wildly than it had before, shimmying out of control with monotonous regularity. He did his first significant stretch of jail time that spring—three months in the Brooklyn House of Detention, charged with the murder of a well-known Bay Ridge gangster named Cesare Marciano. "A meatball case if there ever was one," Jerry remembers with a chuckle. "A ludicrous fabrication." And yet the story was juicy enough that it eventually made the pages of newspapers and detective magazines throughout the country.

Marciano, the police alleged, had masterminded a break-in at Our Lady of Sorrows Roman Catholic Church in Crown Heights, during which the parish jewels had been cleaned out of a safe in the rectory. Joseph Profaci, a deeply religious man, had ordered Marciano to return the jewels. And when he refused, the police maintained, Profaci had turned to Jerry and a well-known triggerman named Louis Brienza and ordered Marciano executed forthwith. The evidence against Jerry consisted exclusively of the testimony of a cocktail waitress named Judy Campodello, who claimed to have been a passenger in the car Marciano was driving at the time he was shot. The only problem was that she had waited eleven months to come forward with her story. And even though her word was sufficient to have Rosenberg and Brienza indicted and held without bail, the case was thrown out of court for lack of substance at a pretrial hearing three months later.

But what a story to have running around in the candy stores and hangouts of Bath Beach. Profaci himself, the story went, had singled Jerry out for this most urgent of assignments. To his parents and Rose-Ann, Jerry's explanation was that the cops had cooked the whole thing up simply to cause him a little grief. But as far as the rest of the world was concerned, he was finally becoming a man of solid notoriety and criminal distinction—a welcome face at last in Brooklyn's most disreputable circles. "At that time, right after the Marciano case," he says, "I could go anywhere I wanted in New York and never have to pay for nothin'. Gambling joints, taverns, restaurants, you name it—the red carpet was always there."

Maybe so. But it was abruptly yanked away on the night of October 12, 1957, when Jerry and his buddy Frankie Morano were caught red-handed in the middle of a holdup at a check-cashing store on Queens Boulevard. Here at last was an infraction so serious that his parents were totally unable to have it squelched, and Jerry and his buddy both eventually pleaded guilty to robbery in the third degree.

"They got me right that time," Jerry says. "But the four years they gave me was way out of line."

He did half of it at the Elmira Reformatory, then turned eighteen and was transferred to Comstock State Prison, a medium-security institution 250 miles upstate. He enrolled in the high school equivalency course there and finally passed the exams a year and a half later—mainly, he says, in order to qualify for good-time credits.

For the most part it was easy time, and Jerry liked to brag afterward that he'd done those four years standing on his head. He had heard enough jailhouse horror stories and spent enough time in precinct lockups so that very little surprised him when he actually got there. In his own mind he was a full-time professional hood, a regular knockaround guy for whom jail time was nothing more than an irritating occupational hazard. And in many ways prison actually served to shore up his identity, confirming that he *was* a pro, making him tougher and more reliable and, he hoped, more valuable once he was back on the streets.

Rose-Ann stuck it out for the first two of those years in Brooklyn, paying lip service at least to the idea of waiting for her man to be set free. Ronnie was still very much the center of attention in the house, and news of her tiniest achievements was faithfully relayed to Jerry by Rose and Lou on their weekly visits. Rose-Ann would visit less frequently; for her the bars and frisks and snarling guards were always a shattering experience. And when she finally did get into the visiting room, her tears and gloominess would often drive him wild.

Once, yielding to his incessant demands, she brought Ronnie up with her. On the surface, at least, the visit was a smashing success—the child painfully shy and unresponsive at first, then gradually loosening up as Jerry dazzled her with a bunch of simple coin tricks she'd always been too young for in the past. And then he taught her a gambling game and allowed her to clean him out of dimes and nickels—hugging and kissing her every time she guessed right, Rose-Ann watching in amazement as the lines of tension and anger and pain slowly melted from his face.

The break finally came in the fall of 1959, precipitated not by anything that had happened in Brooklyn but by Rose-Ann's desire to help out with her mother's recovery from surgery back in Houston. And from fifteen hundred miles away her life with the Rosenbergs was suddenly thrown into sharper focus.

"I came to see that I'd been living off my daughter in a way," she says. "Living off Rose and Lou's infatuation with her, at least. I knew I still had feelings for Jerry; I think I always will. But I also knew damn well that they weren't rehabilitating him up there at Comstock. And that even when he did get out, our life together could never be more than it was before he went away."

She and Ronnie moved in with Rose-Ann's younger sister, Linda, who had her own child now and was working nights as a cocktail waitress at a motel near the Houston airport. Rose-Ann herself soon found a job as a checker at Weingarten's Supermarket in Texas City. And on November 4, 1960, she filed for an out-of-state divorce.

4

In the fall of 1961 Jerry emerged from his four years at Comstock on the dead run and quickly managed to pick up most of the threads of his old life without breaking stride.

There was one big, gaping hole in his life, however, that was left by Rose-Ann. Parole regulations forbade him to leave the state, but he was on the phone with her almost every week. And always, his message was the same. She had taken all the magic out of his life, he would tell her. He missed her like crazy—all the wonderful things they had shared together and laughed about, all the hugs and tears and arguments and nutty stunts. He was sure they could make things work if they tried again. He was working steadily now in the family business, he claimed, with a roster of steady customers and a batch of accounts to service just like his older brothers—the same barely plausible story he'd told to his parole officer. And if she'd only drop the divorce action and come to New York for a week or two, she'd be able to see for herself.

Rose-Ann was sorely tempted by his invitation and half-convinced by the miracle of rehabilitation he so vividly described. But she had a job of her own to look out for and no vacation time for the next six months. "Wait till you're off parole, Jerry," she told him. "When all that craziness is finally behind you, maybe then we can think about trying again."

Six weeks later he jumped parole and flew to Texas City for the weekend, hoping to win her over with a high-pressure, in-person appeal—his heart breaking at the sight of his six-year-old daughter practicing some wobbly gymnastics in a leotard on the front lawn. He did tumbling tricks with her until his muscles shrieked with pain, then took her to a little amusement park nearby and plied her with slush cones and chocolate turtles. He even went to an open house at school and met her teacher, carrying off the role of weekend father with surprising aplomb. But he was determined not to involve her in the struggle that was going on between him and Rose-Ann. And when she asked him why her mommy was acting so upset, he simply said that when people don't get to see each other very often, their feelings can be very confusing and very strong.

Most confusing of all for Rose-Ann was the strong inner temptation she felt to knuckle under and return with him to New York. God knows, she hated those endless shifts behind the cash register. But she had also tasted the sweet nectar of self-respect down here in Texas, and she clung to that feeling with a fierce tenacity that Jerry, in his vulnerability and neediness, was prone to misinterpret as contempt. They fought for five hours straight on Saturday evening and picked up right where they left off the next morning—Jerry walking over from the Bloomfield Avenue Travelodge where he was staying, a dozen eggs and a quart of orange juice tucked under his arm. But the vibes quickly grew so intense and full of venom that Rose-Ann found herself counting the hours till his seven P.M. departure.

It was by far the roughest afternoon Rose-Ann and Jerry had ever spent together, Ronnie banished from the house but hanging around under the windows, trying to make some sense of the noisy dispute playing itself out inside. But in the end, despite all his blustering and extravagant promises, Jerry couldn't budge her.

He finally left, on schedule and empty-handed, Rose-Ann and Ronnie driving him to the airport in the same beat-up '48 Ford in which they had jounced and shimmied to their marriage ceremony in Rosenberg, Texas, almost seven years before. All three of them were teetering close to the brink by this point—brokenhearted and emotionally drained. But Jerry quickly blitzed through the airport gift shop and salvaged the farewell moment with a bunch of funny little going-away presents: some play money and a tiny little stuffed koala for Ronnie, a ten-gallon hat and an ounce of Fabergé for Rose-Ann.

Five days later, at six o'clock on a Friday afternoon, a friend of Rose-Ann's from around the corner called up to say that they were talking about a man on TV who sounded an awful lot like her former husband. And even before she switched on the set, Rose-Ann began to re-experience the numbing sense of dread that had permanently disfigured her life in Brooklyn.

That Friday in New York City had been hot and unseasonably muggy for the eighteenth of May. And Detectives Luke Fallon and John Finnegan were both pretty well wrung out as they neared the end of their decoy shift—posing as the driver and passenger respectively of a battered Checker cab—cruising the crime-ridden side streets off New Utrecht Avenue in Boro Park. Fallon was fifty-six, a twenty-five-year veteran of the force, a man who was nearing the end of a solid but unspectacular career as a cop. "He was a decent, hail-fellow-well-met type of guy," a lawyer friend recalls. "A real hotshot at the beginning. And then he got passed over for a couple of promotions, he got some years on him, and I guess he became more interested in his grandchildren than just about anything else."

His partner Finnegan was twenty-nine and the father of two young children—Big John, they called him—handsome and incorruptible and deeply committed to his work. Finnegan had been a cop for six years, had recently received a citation for outstanding performance, and was, no doubt, the ideal partner for a man like Fallon.

They stopped briefly on their way back to the precinct at a grungy wholesale tobacco warehouse on Forty-eighth Street, Finnegan to pick up a box of candy for his wife's birthday, Fallon for a box of cough drops. The proprietors, David and Robert Goldberg, were only too glad to oblige. Stores on both sides of the street had been held-up recently, and the Goldbergs still hadn't gotten around to installing the sophisticated burglar alarm system that the premises clearly warranted. For they usually maintained an inventory of cigarettes and candy worth well over a quarter-million dollars, and on Fridays like this one they often had several thousand dollars in cash as well. In any case, the two detectives were more than welcome to the candy. Any kind of police presence in the store was cheap insurance, the Goldbergs reasoned. And Finnegan and Fallon, even in plainclothes, were well known to the neighborhood, both of them having served a stint as foot patrolmen on this very beat. They chatted with the Goldbergs for a few moments, then turned to go, Fallon's cough aggravated by the thick haze of tobacco smoke from the runners filling orders in the back, each of them puffing away on his own favorite brand.

Across the street two men watched them leave, looking down on the store from the elevated-subway station less than a hundred yards away. One of them was chubby and heavy-featured, with longish wavy blond hair, wearing a beige topcoat, a wide-brimmed hat, and a pair of Foster-Grant sunglasses. His partner was thinner and shorter but similarly dressed—a man Jerry's friends invariably refer to as *the thin bandit*.

Perhaps the two men didn't recognize Finnegan and Fallon; perhaps they assumed that the coast was now clear. In any case, they barged into the store a few minutes later, guns drawn, each of them holding a handkerchief over the lower half of his face. "You know what's happening," the thin bandit rasped. "Listen up and you won't get hurt." He quickly herded the runners into a room-size humidor at the back of the store, while his chubby partner ransacked the little office for cash, practically dismantling it single-handedly, strewing files and office supplies all over the floor.

A few blocks away Detectives Finnegan and Fallon were making the first of a series of decisions that would turn this routine stickup into a municipal tragedy. They decided to return to the store, whether to pick up an additional item they had forgotten or because they had spotted the two suspicious characters emerging from the subway station, neither of them would live to explain.

The fat bandit, meanwhile, was raging out of control, the handkerchief over his face long since abandoned, unconvinced by David Goldberg's explanation that one of the runners had just left for the bank with the day's receipts. "What about the payroll?" he roared, toppling over the table under which Goldberg was attempting to hide.

In the back of the store, the thin bandit had already bolted the door to the humidor. But he heard his partner's shouts, quickly grasped the nature of the problem, and returned to the humidor for Robert Goldberg, slamming him up against the back wall and screaming at him to reveal the location of the rest of the cash. In the confusion his gun went off with a deafening roar and a blanket of plaster dust rained down on them from above, the bullet having lodged itself deep in the ancient ceiling.

Finnegan and Fallon, meanwhile, had just pulled up for the second time outside the store, and the sound of the gunshot galvanized them into immediate response. They had been trained never to break in on a robbery in progress except when innocent lives were in danger. But the sound of the gunfire must have convinced them that they had no alternative. Fallon went in first, smashing open the door with his foot, squinting into the half-light of the store, his weapon drawn, as the heavy bandit lumbered in confusion to the doorway of the little office. What happened next can never be known with absolute certainty. But there is a persistent rumor in the case that Fallon's service revolver jammed as he attempted to fire at the menacing figure in front of him. Certainly there was no time for him to establish his identity as a cop, and from the bandit's point of view, he may well have appeared as a murderous intruder. All that can be known for sure is that Fallon eventually managed to fire a single shot that slammed harmlessly into the plywood counter, and that the fat man in the same period of time squeezed off three quick rounds of his own, one of which ripped into Fallon's chest and sent him spinning to his death in the doorway.

Finnegan came next and managed to fire all six rounds from his own weapon without laying a scratch on his partner's assailant, who finally shot twice more and fatally wounded the younger cop, bullets slamming into his chest and neck and toppling him backward onto the sidewalk. The fat man stared at the carnage in numb disbelief, then dropped his weapon and lurched out the door, shouting, "I'm a cop! I'm a cop!"

In the back of the store, the thin bandit was bouncing around like a rat in a maze, searching in vain for an exit to the alleyway behind the building. His handkerchief, too, had gotten lost in the confusion, and he grabbed an ink-stained towel from the tax-stamping machine along the far wall, covering his face with it as he dashed past David Goldberg and out into the street. He hung onto the towel—and the hat and sunglasses—until after he skittered around the corner onto New Utrecht Avenue, at which point he tossed them into a trash can and quickly melted into the crowd.

Nevertheless, David Goldberg has always maintained that he caught a glimpse of the man—a glimpse he has variously described as lasting for "a fleeting instant" or "a short time" or "a few seconds," depending on who was conducting the cross-examination. In any event, among the half-dozen "possible" mug shots he picked out at the Butler Street Precinct House that evening was a set belonging to Jerome Samuel Rosenberg. Whether the "picture show" that the cops laid out for him was a fair one or whether it was stacked against a group of known criminals whose *modus operandum* the police thought they recognized was to become the subject of bitter litigation over a period of many years.

Guilty or not, Jerry was undoubtedly aware of the crime by early that evening—if only from the hysterical headlines that screamed the news from every street corner. For a cop killing was still a rarity in 1962, and the last *double* cop killing was far beyond the memory of anyone still active on the force. Hundreds of grim-faced policemen had gathered outside the Boro Park Tobacco Company that afternoon, milling around behind their own barricades, the rage and fury in the air so thick you could cut it with a knife. And hundreds more would volunteer their own time in the days ahead, joining an investigation that was already being described as the largest single police operation in the city's history.

The man in charge was an ambitious fifty-four-year-old Irishman named Raymond V. Martin, the chief of detectives for Brooklyn South, a man who had known and liked Luke Fallon and John Finnegan and whose public statements about the case were consistently charged with self-righteousness, high emotion, and an unconcealed lust for revenge. The case was front-page news for a full week, all seven New York dailies milking the story for every ounce of morbid detail. A small army of hustling reporters camped outside the Butler Street Precinct House in Boro Park, where Martin had set up his command post.

His chief investigating officer in the case was Captain Albert A. Seedman, a beetle-browed, cigar-chomping cop in his early forties, whose thoroughness, penchant for hard work, and near-legendary criminal intuition would eventually lead to his appointment as chief of detectives for the entire city. It was Seedman who arrived at the tobacco store first, having responded to a "10-30" distress bulletin that had been issued as a result of an anonymous phone tip from the Laundromat across the street. "Stunned as I was," he told a reporter, "standing there over the bodies of my two detectives, I still had a pretty good idea of who had done this to them. In fact, I had photos of the suspects right in my jacket pocket."

A curious statement, since no suspects had yet been identified or announced. But it was Jerry's fate to have a photograph of himself nestled snugly in the grasp of the one man on the force who was in a position to do him the greatest damage. The other photograph was of a thirty-four-year-old minor-league mobster named Anthony Delvecchio, who was eventually charged with driving a getaway car that the two bandits were never able to catch up with.

To explain why he had these two photographs in his pocket, Seedman told the reporter a rambling story about a similar holdup at a tobacco wholesaler on Ocean Parkway several weeks before. That robbery still had not been cleared, Seedman admitted, but he'd told his detectives to keep an ear out for anyone who might have been involved. "And sure enough, they picked up the names of Delvecchio and Rosenberg." He'd also discovered that Delvecchio's brother, Red, operated a candy store supplied by a wholesaler very much like the Boro Park Tobacco Company, and he deduced that "Delvecchio may have gotten the idea of robbing such places from talking to his brother." And it was on this highly nebulous basis that Jerry's name originally became linked to the case. "I kept a spare set of photos of the suspects with me to query detectives, other suspects, or just people in the neighborhood,"

Seedman explained. "You never know when something useful could turn up."

Seedman and Martin together made a devastating one-two punch, Seedman flogging the investigation along with furious intensity, Martin calling on a lifetime of press contacts to publicize the case as no single murder case had ever been publicized before. Indeed, the investigation and the press coverage fed each other in the most astonishing way—several newspapers putting up a total of $11,500 in reward money for information leading to the arrest of the perpetrators. As the investigation wore on, Martin would hold press briefings several times a day, and he was often described as "anguished" or "shaken" or "struggling to control his emotions." His explanations and analyses of the crime were invariably taken at face value. And he also managed to keep the press from speculating about the performance and competence of Finnegan and Fallon—and about the appropriateness of their response to the situation they had faced out there on the sidewalk.

"This crime is a slap at everybody, citizens *and* cops," Martin told reporters at a briefing on May 21. And he went on to dream up a scenario for the shoot-out that has never been corroborated by anyone there at the scene. "Those two thugs knew who they were shooting at," Martin proclaimed. "They double-crossed the dead detectives. They tricked my men into relaxing their guard and then shot them down in cold blood." He went on to explain that the heavyset bandit had raised his gun to the ceiling and yelled out: "Don't shoot, I quit," as soon as he caught sight of Fallon in the doorway. And then, according to Martin, as Fallon approached to disarm him, the man lowered his gun and pumped him full of lead. The net effect of this fabrication and almost every other statement Martin made over the next ten days was not only to inflame public opinion but to create a climate of near-hysteria within the police force itself.

As a result, Seedman had far more manpower on the case than he knew what to do with. And his initial problem on the day of the shootings was to keep the hordes of cops out of the store until the fingerprint teams and photographers and ballistics experts had finished their work. But nothing in the way of hard physical evidence was ever turned up on the premises: no fingerprints on the murder weapon, no fragments of clothing or traceable personal possessions of any kind.

The first substantial break in the case came at about five P.M. that Friday when one of the patrolmen combing the neighborhood stumbled across a black fedora that had been abandoned in a nearby trash can—a hat that the Goldbergs were "quite sure" had once graced the head of the thin bandit. Seedman handed it to one of his favorite detectives, a big hambone Irishman named Marty Flanagan. "Here's the hat, Marty," Seedman growled. "Now go out there and find a head to put it on."

Another early break was the discovery of a pair of sunglasses in a clump of bushes several blocks away—sunglasses that the Goldbergs identified as also having been worn by the thin bandit. What was especially hopeful about the find were the initials *G.E.E.* scratched into the frame. "Now we're getting somewhere," Martin told reporters. "This is the best lead we've got so far." Seedman assigned Detective Eddie Lambert to trace down the ownership of the sunglasses, a task that was vastly simplified when Lambert noticed the same three letters scratched into the wall of a phone booth at the candy store owned by Delvecchio's brother, John.

Forty-eight hours later Lambert was able to satisfy himself that the letters *G.E.E.* were not initials at all but were part of a nickname for Louis "The Geezer" Ferrara, a sixteen-year-old part-time employee at the candy store, whose physical stature roughly coincided with the description of the thin bandit. Lambert was elated. He promptly tracked down Ferrara at home and hauled him into Seedman's command post at the Sixty-sixth Precinct. But he scrupulously avoided questioning the boy or tipping his hand in any way, positive that Seedman would consider him a prime suspect in the case and would want to do all the questioning himself.

"Hello, Louie," said Seedman when he strolled into the room about twenty minutes later. "When did you lend Jerry Rosenberg your sunglasses?" Lambert was astonished by the question. For not only had Seedman just handed the kid an alibi; he had also provided him with the "correct" answer, the answer that would quickly whisk him out of the police station and out from under the cloud of suspicion that might well have changed the course of the entire investigation.

That same afternoon a rabbi and a small boy walked into the Boro Park police station and told the desk sergeant that they'd caught a glimpse of the fleeing killers. They were promptly set to work with one of the department's sketch artists. And Martin in his next press briefing told reporters that the rabbi's description was "probably the best we've been able to get so far." Previous descriptions provided by the Goldbergs and the other eyewitnesses in the store were much too vague, he said. "Those people were all too shocked to remember much of anything," Martin admitted. And yet it was the Goldbergs' "possible" identification of Jerry's mug shots that had provided the only corroboration for Seedman's initial hunch in the case, a hunch that was rapidly becoming a self-fulfilling prophecy.

At one point, when asked to comment on the investigation, Martin termed it "intensive, routine police work." But another, more illicit phase of the investigation was going on concurrently in precinct houses all around the city—mostly at night, and largely obscured from press attention by the Martin PR blitz. For whether Martin knew about it or not, the investigation actually amounted to the most extensive campaign of torture and official brutality that the New York underworld had ever seen. A total of 148 known criminals were dragged in for questioning, some of whom later described interrogation techniques so vicious that the American Civil Liberties Union promptly called for the immediate dismissal of every officer involved. "I was stripped naked and beaten with wooden sticks and a rubber hose," one of the suspects testified later. "This lasted for more than two hours. Then they tied a wire around my testicles and ground out lighted cigarettes on my back and neck." Other casualties included several broken bones and black eyes, a dislocated shoulder, and numerous instances of cuts and abrasions so extensive as to require short-term hospitalization.

By this point a third name was on the tip of the interrogators' tongues, in addition to Jerry's and Delvecchio's. For an old woman had surfaced on Sunday morning and had told a patrolman in a frightened whisper that she had seen a man she knew only as "Baldy" running down the street away from the tobacco store shortly after the shootings. Seedman quickly checked the extensive nickname file in the district office and came up with the name of Anthony Portelli, a thirty-three-year-old former gas station attendant who had been arrested nearly forty times in the last five years. Unfortunately for Portelli, he happened to be the only "Baldy" listed in the file.

Seedman was convinced that he now had all three of the names he needed. All he required to issue the arrest warrants was some kind of corroboration. And so the focus of the interrogations now shifted away from "what can you tell us about the shootings" to "what can you tell us about Portelli, Rosenberg, and Delvecchio?" This, of course, is the kind of question where physical brutality often yields the most gratifying results, because implicit in the question is the answer that the interrogator would like to hear. But even so, the steady parade of underworld figures remained mute and unhelpful for the next thirty-six hours. Finally, one of them cracked—a small-time Coney Island bookie named Richie Melville, who had only the most tenuous links to the mob. Melville was a long shot, but he was known to be friendly with an acquaintance of Portelli's named Babe Acarino, and he was also dumb enough to answer the door in person.*

Melville's first stop at the precinct house was a small room down the hall from the command post, where Acarino himself was sprawled on a chair in the corner, his arm in a makeshift sling, his face bruised and puffy, a bloody three-foot length of rubber hose in the hands of the detective who was conducting the interrogation.

Even so, Melville held out for close to eight hours. He was to testify later that he was beaten and kicked without mercy from the moment the door closed behind him, and the scars from the clusters of cigarette burns on his back were still visible months later. But the story he eventually told led indirectly to the arrest of Anthony Portelli in a motel room in Chicago, and it also convinced Chief Martin that he now had enough to issue an emergency bulletin for Jerry's arrest.

Clearly, Melville's story contained at least some elements of truth. Portelli, he claimed, had spent most of Saturday night and Sunday at his apartment and had then asked Melville to drive him to a motel in Union City, New Jersey, where he planned to spend the night and then catch a flight to Chicago from nearby Newark Airport at nine A.M. the next morning. So much for verifiable detail. But Melville went on to recount a series of conversations in which he alleged that Portelli not only confessed to the two murders but also implicated Jerry as the thin bandit in the back of the store. "I panicked, Richie," he quoted Portelli as having told him in the apartment that Saturday evening. "Believe me, those shots are still ringing in my ears. But honest to God, noth-

* In a bizarre sidelight to the investigation, crime throughout the city had dropped to a tiny fraction of its normal level, since no crook in his right mind relished any kind of contact with the police in their present mood.

ing like this would've happened except that idiot Jerry had to go and shoot off his gun. That's what scared off Delvecchio, who was spozed to be waiting for us out front with his brother's car."

A vivid conversation. But certainly nothing Melville couldn't have dreamed up simply by using the names his interrogators told him they were interested in and then plugging those names into the newspaper accounts of the crime that had blanketed the city for the past seventy-two hours. In any event, his statement was sufficient to halt the beatings and to have him arraigned before Magistrate Benjamin Schor as an accessory after the fact—a charge that was quietly dropped six months later in return for his testimony at the trial.

5

It was nearly eight thirty on Monday morning before the crucial details of Melville's story had finally been extracted, and Seedman quickly dispatched Detectives Edward Shea and Herman Frigand to Newark Airport in an attempt to apprehend Portelli before he boarded the plane. They missed him by less than ten minutes but immediately phoned ahead and arranged to have the flight met by detectives in Chicago, who were instructed to tail the suspect and then wait for further instructions once Shea and Frigand had arrived on a later flight. Unsuspecting and unarmed, Portelli rented a car and led them straight to the Lido Motel in nearby Franklin Park, where Shea and Frigand arrested him shortly after noon that same day.

"You got visitors, Baldy," Frigand growled as he clicked a spare key into the motel-room door. "Don't even breathe."

Martin would say later that Portelli "blubbered like a baby" when he was first taken into custody. "But those were crocodile tears," Martin went on to explain. "He was just trying to get sympathy. If he had had a gun with him, he would have used it again. I know the type."

Portelli was promptly hustled back to O'Hare for the return flight, and the *Daily News* described his arrival at Idlewild [later Kennedy] Airport with bouquets of purple prose:

> Portelli, a sentimental thug who has a tattooed heart encircling the word MOTHER on his right, or gun arm, was shaking his head from side to side and biting his lips. "He looks scared to death," said one spectator.
>
> With a grim lane of 50 detectives, patrolmen and airport police alongside, he was the first passenger off when the plane halted near the American Airlines hangar. Virtually all airport business was suspended as hundreds of patrons and employees watched a police wedge lead Portelli through the terminal building and out to a waiting police car.

The *Journal-American* coverage described his arrival at the precinct house and quoted extensively from Martin's next briefing:

> Several hundred persons shouted "Pig," "Rat," and "Murderer" as Portelli literally was carried up the steps of the station house. He didn't see the flag that flew at half-mast atop the building in honor of the slain detectives.
>
> Insp. Martin said Portelli was "crying and praying" while being questioned. "He's sullen and remorseful, but he hasn't said anything," the inspector added. "I think his remorse is just an act." Although police said Portelli had made damaging admissions about his role in the shoot-out, the suspect repeatedly shouted, "I didn't do it, I didn't do it!" as he was dragged up the steps.
>
> Portelli's mother, Mrs. Jennie Russo, 63, appeared downstairs at the station house during her son's quizzing. A tiny, gray-haired woman in a blue house dress, she wore a three-quarter length violet coat and black flat shoes with no socks. She fought a mixture of tears and rage as she sputtered:

"He's not a bad fellow. He's not as bad as they made him out." At one point she broke down completely, wringing her hands and shrieking: "I want to see him. I want to see my son."

Asked if he would allow this, Insp. Martin said: "Why should I? She's been looking at him long enough."

Martin also used the occasion of Portelli's arrival to announce publicly the names of the other two suspects for the first time. "Rosenberg and Delvecchio are members of the top hoodlum element in Brooklyn," he told reporters. "We know that they're armed, we know that they're desperate, and we know that they've vowed never to be taken alive. The commissioner has instructed all 32,000 members of the force to respond accordingly." Martin then went on to recite a long list of other "facts" about the suspects, all of which turned out to be completely false. "We have positive identifications of all three of them in ten other Brooklyn holdups," he said. "They've been pulling these jobs together for years." Martin also falsely claimed that Jerry's fingerprints had been found on a .38-caliber automatic abandoned in a clump of bushes just off New Utrecht Avenue. And as for Portelli, Martin stated flat out: "He's the triggerman, all right. He's the fellow that killed the two cops. We have the gun and the bullets to match."

In fact, as Martin was well aware, no fingerprints whatsoever had been found on either gun, and the only "evidence" linking Jerry and Portelli to the crime still amounted to nothing more than the vague eyewitness identifications and the frantic testimony that had been squeezed out of Richie Melville by means of terror and physical abuse. Nevertheless, the cumulative effect of Martin's falsehoods would live on in the press coverage for weeks to come, whipping up a climate of municipal hysteria that would ultimately infect the conduct of the trial itself.

In an interview years later Seedman would sheepishly attempt to justify the department's performance in the case. "Our detectives were not operating in a vacuum," he said. "The revulsion they felt over the murder of their colleagues was shared by the entire city. Everyone was hopping mad. I even got a letter from a *Daily News* reporter that said, 'I want you to know that the working press applauds your handling of this rotten sonofabitch [Portelli]. The entire nation is with you.' It was the feeling that the public was secretly behind us," Seedman added, "that gave our detectives license to take the measures necessary to find the killers." What Seedman neglected to point out was that the public reaction to the crime—and to the three suspects—was largely determined by the lies and distortions that had been spoon-fed to the press by his boss, Deputy Chief Inspector Raymond V. Martin.

By Tuesday morning every paper in the city had its own overwrought profile of the three suspects. The *Post* quoted Jerry's mother as pleading with a pack of reporters to go away and leave her alone. "No one can help me now," she told them. "No one can ever help me again." Another reporter reached Jerry's father at the office. "The neighborhood is bad and it made my son bad," Lou allegedly told him. "I wish I had broken both my arms and legs before I ever bought that house." Other reports quoted detectives who had had dealings with Jerry in the past. "Even if he lived on Sutton Place he would have ended up with a rap like this," one of them told the *Post*'s Anthony Scaduto. "Jerry was the kind of kid who'd go along with anything. I can remember locking him up when he was still just a baby—for possession of a starter's pistol in a local movie house."

That same morning a seventeen-state alarm had been issued for the two remaining suspects, all the bridge and tunnel crossings were being watched by eagle-eyed patrolmen, and a squadron of Texas Rangers was even dispatched to the little house in Texas City. But still no sign of the fugitives.

At his next briefing Martin tried a new approach and attempted to spook the two of them into voluntary surrender. "These men have no friends left," he growled. "All their buddies are turning on them in droves. In fact, we're closing in on Delvecchio right this minute. And as for Rosenberg, we have information that he's hiding out somewhere in Greenwich Village, dressed in women's clothing and wearing a wig and heavy makeup. Police have a standing order to pick up anyone, male or female, answering his description."

The pressure got to Delvecchio first. And on Wednesday morning Seedman received a call from an attorney in Norwich, Connecticut, named Savino Tamborra, who identified himself as Delvecchio's brother-in-law and said that his client would be willing to surrender in Norwich at twelve o'clock. Seedman quickly arranged to have him picked up there by a covey of Connecticut State Police, who turned him over to city detectives at the state line.

At 3:15 that afternoon a trio of unmarked police cars snaked along Ditmas Avenue and came to a halt in front of the Sixty-second Precinct House, where Delvecchio would be booked and held overnight pending his arraignment in Brooklyn Felony Court on Thursday morning. Waiting for him at the curb were Captain Al Seedman and a huge crowd of reporters, photographers, and furious bystanders, pushing and shoving and screaming vindictively behind double rows of gray-and-black police barricades.

And once again there was a major discrepancy between what police claimed Delvecchio told them in private and the frantic statement he made on his way into the building. The police version, as reported by both the *News* and the *Post*, had Delvecchio admitting that he "drove the killers to the scene of the holdup." But Delvecchio himself, when he finally emerged in handcuffs from the middle car, pointed to Seedman and other top police brass and shouted, "I'm innocent, and you know it. I have two witnesses who can prove where I was." He then turned and headed for the steps, holding his head so low that nobody could get a picture. There was an immediate roar of outrage from the photographers, and Seedman obligingly grabbed the suspect by the neck and twisted him around for the benefit of the press. The picture showed up in half the papers in the city the next day—Delvecchio's face contorted with pain and surprise, Seedman chomping impassively on the stub of a slimy-looking cigar.

The American Civil Liberties Union and several other watchdog organizations promptly demanded disciplinary proceedings against Seedman. But Police Commissioner Michael Murphy waited a full week and then finally responded with a terse, one-sentence announcement that Seedman had been privately "admonished." It was, however, the first public smudge on Seedman's record, and it no doubt slowed his otherwise rapid climb up the departmental ladder.

The *Daily News* headline for Thursday the twenty-fourth read: 2 DOWN, 1 TO GO, IN COP KILLER HUNT. The story summarized the case to date and then quoted Martin as saying, "It's only a matter of time. Jerome Rosenberg has been sighted as late as last night in both Upper and Lower Manhattan." And yet the story went on to explain that:

> Police in Houston and Texas City are also still on the alert, where it is thought the fugitive may have sought refuge using the aliases Jerry Rosenberg, Samuel J. Rosenberg, or Edward Arnold. Each alarm relayed to police departments across the nation has warned that the slow-talking, scar-faced killer "has sworn that he will not be taken alive."

In fact, at the very moment that the *News* early edition first hit the streets, Jerry was dozing fitfully on a couch in a tiny, cluttered apartment just off the Grand Concourse in the Bronx. He'd been there since the morning after the shoot-out, hoping, at least in the early stages, that the whole thing would blow over. The apartment belonged to his myopic, eighty-three-year-old aunt, and so far she had accepted his explanation that he had business in the neighborhood and simply couldn't face the long subway ride back to Brooklyn.

That, for sure, was a lie. Right from the beginning Jerry certainly must have realized that his yellow sheet and neighborhood reputation would make him at least a peripheral suspect in the case. And he also knew from the early newspaper and TV reports that the cops were moving heaven and earth to pin the rap on somebody. And so, guilty or not, he had obeyed the same self-protective impulse that had gripped almost every other known criminal in the city. One hundred and forty-eight of them had gotten caught up in the police dragnet. But Jerry, along with hundreds of others, had successfully managed to elude the manhunt and to drop out of sight completely. Why this "largest single police operation in the city's history" had been unable to trace him there is a question that no one in the department has ever attempted to explain. But as Jerry's friends are quick to point out, if he truly felt that his life and freedom were in jeopardy, he would surely have chosen a more secure hideout than his aunt's ground-floor apartment, just around the corner from one of the busiest streets in the Bronx.

Not that he hadn't had a number of close calls, the most serious of which took place on Tuesday morning, the day after Portelli's arrest. Jerry had gone out for breakfast at the Bickford's Cafeteria on the corner of Tremont Avenue—cautious, but still unaware that his name had been publicly linked with the shoot-out. He took his tray to a corner table, red-eyed and strung out from a night of intermittent sleep, and practically choked on his scrambled eggs as a weary-looking blue-coated patrolman sat down directly opposite him and opened up a copy of the *Daily News*. There on the front page were two huge, smirking mug shots of Jerry and Portelli and a headline that read:

KILLERS SOUGHT IN DOUBLE COP MURDER. Jerry was armed, as he had been since the night he left Brooklyn, and the incident could very easily have turned into the third cop killing of the week. But for the moment this particular cop was far more interested in the racing charts at the back of the paper than he was in the identity of his tablemate. Jerry forced himself to linger for a few more bites, then got slowly to his feet and headed as casually as possible for the front. He pushed through the revolving door, his heart in his mouth, and glanced desperately back through the window. But the cop hadn't moved a muscle. Jerry spun around toward the street, spotted his picture again on the newsstand at the corner, and frantically ducked into the nearest doorway. And then he called his parents.

His mother, Rose, was pacing helplessly in the living room, tears of abject despair streaming down her cheeks, having just received word of her son's horrendous predicament via Frank Blair's newscast on the *Today Show*. And yet her remarkable loyalty held up even in the face of this latest, devastating accusation. She finally whirled on her husband, who was clicking desperately through the channels. "How could they think he did such a thing, Lou?" she groaned. "There's nothing vicious about him. He's not a killer!"

Jerry's father shook his head in numb despair. He, too, was positive that Jerry could never have done the shooting. But he couldn't bear to tell her what he knew of the law—that under the state's Felony Murder Statute, the thin bandit was every bit as liable for the murder of the two policemen as the man who had actually pulled the trigger.

And so when Jerry's frantic call finally came through from the basement of a Tremont Avenue bar and grill, the only thought on both their minds was how to get their son out of the Bronx in one piece. Perhaps, in retrospect, it might have been wiser to hire an experienced criminal attorney and let him negotiate with the police directly. But Lou had another inspiration—a plan that would not only guarantee

Jerry's safety but would also make sure that he had a chance to get out his side of the story.

"I know a guy who works for the *Daily News*, Jerry!" Lou shouted, thumbing one-handed through his vest pocket address book. "His name's Gary Kagan, and he's a big-time staff photographer over there. Now what I'm going to do is try and get him on the phone and see if he can arrange the whole thing through their office."

"Arrange what?" Jerry shot back, dishes clattering wildly in the background. "Hey, it wasn't *me*, Pa!" he yelled. "You've gotta believe that. They got nothin' on me, so let's just try and relax."

They talked around in circles for the next few minutes, Jerry at first imploring his father to go down to the *Daily News* without him and try to straighten things out as he had always done before. But even Jerry finally had to accept that the situation was far more ominous than anything he had faced in the past, and he finally agreed to call them back with an answer sometime that afternoon.

In fact, it would be two full days before he called again—forty-eight hours that he spent holed up in the tiny apartment, reading every newspaper he could get his hands on. He read every line of those stories. He read about the "ten other tobacco store holdups" he'd never committed, about the preposterous vow he'd supposedly made never to be taken alive, the descriptions of himself as a slow-talking, round-shouldered, scar-faced killer. And yet, despite the mounting hysteria against him, despite the fact that Marty Flanagan eventually traced the black fedora to a haberdashery shop where Jerry was an occasional customer, the decision he finally made was far more consistent with innocence than it was with guilt. He had clung to his freedom for close to five days, hanging on out of fear and stubbornness and a rapidly growing sense of indignation, perhaps in some dark and private way even enjoying the unparalleled notoriety. But on Thursday morning he returned to the pay phone in the basement of the bar and grill, and he made the last free-world telephone call of his entire life.

"Okay, Pa," he finally whispered. "Go ahead and make the call. And tell that guy Kagan to bring his camera, awright?"

He gave his father the number from the dial and hung up to wait. He was to remain in the basement there, hiding behind the cartons of soup cans, for another five and a half hours.

At 6:45 that evening a dark blue Daily News delivery truck jolted over the curb at Forty-second Street and Third Avenue and disappeared down the ramp into the bowels of the Daily News Building. Jerry and Lou were huddled anxiously in the back, perched on stacks of yesterday's papers. They waited until the motor cut off, then pulled back the heavy canvas tarpaulin and jumped down to the pavement—and were immediately surrounded by a small knot of photographers, newspaper executives, and hustling reporters. For this was a genuine exclusive, and the *Daily News* would be boasting editorially for weeks about the key role the paper had played in bringing in this dangerous fugitive.

There was time for only a few shouted questions from the reporters before the little group whirled around in confusion, startled by the sound of running feet thundering down the ramp from the direction of the street. It was a squadron of grim-faced police sharpshooters, and they quickly took up positions around the truck, their sniper's rifles trained on Jerry. Jerry's response was immediate, indignant, and hopelessly unrealistic. "Get your goons outta here, dog face," he shouted to the lieutenant in charge, "or I'm calling this whole thing off right now!"

Fortunately Paul O'Neill, the paper's associate managing editor, had the presence of mind to step forward before Jerry could antagonize them any further. "We worked out a deal with Chief Martin, Lieutenant," O'Neill shouted. "The man's agreed to surrender at nine o'clock, as soon as we take some pictures and give him the chance to make a statement."

The lieutenant nodded grimly. He was well aware of the ground rules, having left Martin's side in a police-communications van around the corner only moments before. "You've got exactly two hours and fifteen minutes, Rosenberg," he shouted back. "Then you belong to us."

The pictures were Jerry's idea. He had been beaten by cops off and on all his life, and he was determined to emerge from this encounter unscathed. He and Kagan disappeared into the men's room off the loading-dock floor, and Jerry stripped buff naked, then posed for a series of color close-ups of every square inch of his anatomy—a portfolio whose existence he flaunted at the cops on his way up to the newsroom. But before he answered any questions, he told Kagan, he wanted a big steak, a Caesar salad, and a bottle of Valpolicella. "Send the bill to slob-face Martin," he chortled. "It's the least he can do for causing me all this aggravation."

A small group of reporters, meanwhile, had escorted Lou to the paper's executive offices on the seventeenth floor, peppering him with questions and finally extracting the following statement. "Jerry is an average boy," Lou told them. "I didn't want him hounded around like an animal. He's innocent. He's a good-hearted boy, and I can't believe he's done anything wrong."

But the center of attention, obviously, was Jerry himself. "Surprisingly self-assured," the *News* described him in a front-page article the next day. And while he managed to keep his head through it all, he must have been well aware that his natural flamboyance and roguish humor would make wonderful copy for the paper's two and a half million readers. "I'm no innocent babe," he told the circle of reporters clustered around his makeshift dinner table in a corner of the newsroom. "But this is one job I didn't pull." And although he readily admitted knowing both Portelli and Delvecchio "from the neighborhood," he vehemently insisted that he'd never done a job with either one.

"In that case, can you tell us why you decided to surrender like this?" one of the reporters asked him.

"A guy could get hurt out there," Jerry grinned, waiting for the laugh. "I gave myself up for one reason," he added quickly. "Because I'm innocent. If I'd done it, I'd be in Mexico or someplace. I sure as hell wouldn't be schmoozing about it with the *Daily News*." He paused for a moment, pouring himself another glass of wine. "The fact is," he told them, "I was framed."

"By whom?" the reporter wanted to know.

"Who else?" Jerry answered, a smile that the *News* described as "cryptic" pulling at the corners of his mouth.

And then he glanced up quickly as Raymond V. Martin himself strode triumphantly through the door, his driver toting a carton full of sandwiches and coffee for the cops who were already in the room. Martin took one look at the steak and the bottle of wine and whirled furiously on the lieutenant in charge. "What the hell is this, a party?" he roared.

"That's exactly what it is, Fatso," Jerry shot back. "I got fifteen minutes yet, then you take me in." Martin turned grimly on his heel and disappeared in the direction of the men's room. "Save me the turkey sandwich," he growled at his driver on the way out. "The brown wrapper. I don't like this kind of ham."

Jerry watched him go—then stretched luxuriously in his swivel chair, deftly reached back for this very sandwich, and took a huge, unobtrusive bite. Whether this prank was wantonly self-destructive or whether it merely reflected innocent confidence in his eventual acquittal, he was to pay for the bite in spades just fifteen minutes later.

The questioning finally turned to the issue of his whereabouts on the afternoon of the shooting, a question that Jerry adamantly refused to answer no matter how cleverly the subject was broached. "Have you got an alibi or not, Jerry?" one of the reporters finally asked in exasperation.

"I've got one, all right," he answered, jabbing his fork in the direction of Chief Martin, who had just returned from the men's room. "But I ain't gonna tell this mutt—he'll go right out and destroy it!"

Martin ignored the taunt, rummaging in vain through the carton for his sandwich. "Where's the turkey?" he shouted at his driver.

"Right here, slob face," Jerry chortled. "I don't like ham, either!"

If Jerry had deliberately set out to goad the cops into a rage, he couldn't have done a better job of it. He was finally dragged from the room in chains ten minutes later, his ankles and wrists shackled together, cops totally out of control, jostling and spitting at him on the way to the waiting elevator. And the beating he received, pictures or no pictures, as the doors glided shut behind him would come as a surprise to no one who had been in the newsroom at the time.

Martin's own participation in the beating was to become the subject of a bitterly contested lawsuit almost ten years later. But the statement he made to the feverish knot of reporters and photographers who were waiting for them downstairs is a matter of public record. He squinted into the eerie glare of the TV floodlights, then glanced over at the block-long convoy of police cars idling and flashing at the curb. "We've got him," Martin shouted, grabbing Jerry by the hair and twisting him around viciously for the cameras. "Here's the cop-killing bastard. He's gonna burn!"

6

Try as they might, Martin and Seedman and a rotating platoon of roughhouse interrogators at the Sixty-sixth Precinct could extract absolutely nothing from Jerry in the way of a confession or information that might link his fellow suspects to the crime. They kept him up the rest of the night and all the next day, holding the specter of the death penalty over his head, grimly confident that he would have to crack sooner or later. He was spat upon, kicked, rabbit-punched, and physically harassed for close to fifteen hours, with his left ear still bleeding intermittently from the beating he had received in the elevator and his hearing on that side at least temporarily impaired.

They were working on all three suspects simultaneously now, hinting to each one that the others had broken and were spilling the beans, counting on fatigue and hunger and the inhuman pressure to finish off the job. And yet all three of them held fast, perhaps drawing strength from their innocence, perhaps just grimly aware as time went by and the pressure never slacked that the case against them might be weaker than they thought.

The district attorney's office entered the case the following day in the person of fifty-four-year-old Thomas D. Selzer, one of the brightest stars in the Brooklyn DA's office. And yet four full weeks would go by during which the suspects were held incommunicado in the maximum-security wings of three different city jails, without indictment or the opportunity to make bail. Four full weeks during which any one of them could have saved his neck simply by parroting the scenario that had by now become so familiar to even the most casual reader of the daily press.

The main reason for the delay was that the harder Selzer looked at the evidence, the more convinced he became that they'd have a devil of a time making the charges stick. And for most of those four weeks, a furious battle had raged back and forth between the district attorney's office and the police, Selzer arguing heatedly that they had nothing whatsoever linking anyone to the actual shootings, Martin repeatedly assuring him that the department was developing testimony from several new and more reliable witnesses.

Meanwhile the papers were still very much alive with the case, speculating wildly about a fourth suspect who was now being sought in South Carolina, shrieking hysterically about witnesses vanishing and round-the-clock police guards for several others.

There was also a long and dubiously constitutional delay in getting lawyers certified for Jerry and Portelli, both of whom had requested court-appointed counsel. In 1962 there was still no formal legal aid system in the city courts, private lawyers being appointed to handle the defense of indigents on a case-by-case basis. In a capital case such as this one, the custom was to appoint two attorneys for each defendant—one of them reasonably experienced, the other a political or personal crony of the presiding magistrate, who was expected to do little more than initial the documents. It took a full week, but a pair of attorneys named Joseph Darienzo and Samuel Goldstein finally presented themselves at the gate of Jerry's cell. And while they were both well intentioned and reasonably competent, there's no question that they had been intimidated by the avalanche of negative publicity in the case and that they saw their job as virtually hopeless.

Delvecchio, on the other hand, had made a much shrewder choice, retaining a young former assistant district attorney named Jacob Evseroff, who was known around the Brooklyn courts as a clever man on his feet. But even more significant was the fact that Evseroff had a reputation for defending *cops*, having recently won acquittals for two policemen who had gotten caught up in a complex bribery and extortion scheme. Understandably, then, his decision to defend Delvecchio had some interesting courthouse resonance to it even before he'd filed a single motion.

Finally, on the third of June a grand jury was convened to hear the evidence—a process that required an astonishing two and a half weeks and that finally drew a stern warning from Kings County Magistrate Harris Malbin: Indict the three suspects by the nineteenth, Malbin told the DA's office, or set them free on their own recognizance.

What was taking so long was that Selzer had apparently decided to compensate for what he lacked in the way of hard physical evidence by overwhelming the grand jurors with detail. And he had also decided to ask for the indictments under an obscure provision of the New York State Penal Code known as the Felony Murder Rule, which mandates first-degree-murder charges for *all* participants in a felony (in this case armed robbery) during which a murder occurs.

It was an approach that eliminated the necessity of proving that any of the three had actually killed *anybody*. All the state had to prove was that Rosenberg, Portelli, and Delvecchio were part of a conspiracy to commit armed robbery and that Finnegan and Fallon had somehow been killed during the commission of that crime. There was no necessity to prove premeditation or intent to kill and no requirement that the state link the murder directly to any one of the accused. And yet the penalty—even though the prosecution freely admitted that Jerry and Delvecchio, at least, had never fired a shot at anyone—was still death.

And so on Tuesday, June 19, the three suspects were led into a Brooklyn courtroom swarming with detectives and were finally indicted before Judge Hyman Barshay. Portelli kept muttering "No, no" as the three murder indictments were read off, and he shouted a vociferous "Not guilty" when the judge asked for their pleadings. But the six defense attorneys unanimously requested a two-week postponement before entering pleas for their clients, charging that they had been "obstructed and hampered at every turn by both the police and the district attorney's office," that they had been refused permission even to visit the Boro Park Tobacco Company, and that they had been unable to make a proper investigation of their clients' side of the story. It was but the first of a long series of adjournments and delays that would push back the start of the trial for another seven months.

Jerry spent most of that time at the Queens County House of Detention, a primitive and overcrowded lockup where the suicide rate was among the nation's highest. His lawyer, Darienzo, saw him regularly every few weeks, mostly to convey a running series of cop-out offers from the prosecution. The final offer was made just before Christmas, at a time when both sides fully expected the trial to get under way within a matter of weeks. In the past Darienzo had simply relayed the offers without expressing an opinion one way or the other. But this time he strongly urged his client to accept. "Give them Delvecchio and place the murder weapon in Portelli's hand," Darienzo told him, "and they'll let you plead guilty to armed robbery." As Jerry knew very well, armed robbery was worth a piddling five to eight years under the penal code at the time. But his answer was an immediate and unequivocal "Never!"—an answer that was full of contempt for a system of criminal justice that relied on lies and sellouts and official betrayal.

Darienzo looked over at him with a total lack of comprehension. It was for sure the oddest case he'd ever been involved with, the first capital case within memory in which none of the defendants had made a confession or statement of any kind. But the final piece of news that, in Darienzo's mind, made Jerry's refusal to talk such a risky decision was the announcement several days before of the judge who would be presiding at the trial. His name was Samuel S. Leibowitz, and he had a reputation as one of the toughest, shrewdest, least compassionate, and most overbearing judges on the felony court bench.

At sixty-three years of age Mr. Justice Leibowitz, as he liked to be called, was nearing the end of what amounted to a second illustrious career. He had first made a name for himself as a defense attorney nearly forty years before, as an outspoken civil libertarian with a penchant for taking on unpopular causes and cases and a track record that was the envy of his colleagues on both sides of the ideological fence. In 1933 he had won an acquittal for the Scottsboro Boys at their second trial in Decatur, Alabama, successfully challenging the systematic exclusion of blacks from southern juries under the due-process clause of the Fourteenth Amendment. He had taken the case *pro bono* (without a fee), and he had had to withstand telephoned death threats on a daily basis as well as the jeers and taunts of racist mobs who spat upon him and reviled him as a "New-York-Jew-Nigger-Lover." But the victory he achieved not only saved the lives of the nine defendants, it amounted to a revolution in southern justice—and it also earned Leibowitz a permanent place in American legal history. "I hear many people calling out, 'punish the guilty,' " he had told the jury in a murder case in 1943. "But very few are concerned to clear the innocent." He took his greatest professional satisfaction in doing just that. And sometimes—at least in the opinion of his critics—he had used his prodigious energy and legal acumen to clear the guilty as well.

In 1954, at an age when most lawyers' thoughts are beginning to turn to winters in Florida and long, lazy afternoons in the sun, Leibowitz accepted an appointment to the New York Felony Court bench, at which point his attitudes and opinions—and his fundamental judicial philosophy—began to undergo a radical shift. Perhaps he knew from personal experience just how easy it was to manipulate the criminal-justice system on behalf of a guilty client. Perhaps as a judge, he finally became nauseated by the steady stream of human desperation that paraded in and out of his courtroom. Perhaps it was advancing age or a volatile temperament that was not ideally suited to the bench. Or perhaps it was a deeply felt and very genuine change in his personal belief system.

Whatever the explanation, his behavior as a judge thoroughly confounded most of those who had supported and admired him throughout his long and distinguished career as a criminal lawyer. He became aloof and imperious and short-tempered and demanding. Father Time, they called him—a judge who was known for his ruthless sentences, a judge who would cut off a lawyer and take over the cross-examination himself if he didn't like the drift of the questions, a judge who prided himself on "knowing how to be tough with tough people." He also knew the law. Cold. But the qualities of empathy and compassion and generosity and hope that had animated the first of his two careers now seemed almost totally missing from the second.

Darienzo was not the only one of the defense attorneys who was upset at the news of Leibowitz's appointment. Even more concerned was Delvecchio's lawyer, Jacob Evseroff, who at one time had served a five-month stretch as the prosecutor on permanent assignment in Leibowitz's courtroom. And so he knew from firsthand experience just how tough on the defendant the Leibowitz treatment usually turned out to be. Evseroff had prosecuted twenty-six cases in that courtroom, and in twenty-five of them the jury had quickly returned with a verdict of guilty.

"I don't think Leibowitz presided over more than one or two acquittals a year," Evseroff recalled many years later. "I've never met a man who had as great an insight into the manner in which jurors react. He could look at a juror during the selection process, and he could ask him one or two questions, and he could predict with a great degree of certainty just how that person would vote. And then once the jury was impaneled, he was a genius at conveying to them, using facial expressions and vocal intonations that never showed up on the trial record, exactly what he thought of the case."

Evseroff also knew that Leibowitz was in the habit of working hand in glove with the prosecutor. "When I was working in his courtroom, he would have me in his chambers incessantly," he recalled. "He would discuss the manner in which the case should be tried, what I should do, how I should elicit the testimony, how I should attack the witnesses for the defense. There was a standing joke between us that pretty much summed up his attitude. 'If the guy isn't guilty,' he'd ask me, 'who in the hell told him to get locked up?' "

Clearly not the kind of judge Evseroff wanted to be going up against in a murder case. And after talking things over with his client, he thought he saw a way out. For Delvecchio had come before Leibowitz once before—an armed-robbery case in 1946 in which he had taken a plea of guilty and had been sentenced to a six-and-a-half-year prison term. Evseroff hastily located a copy of the trial record. And there staring up at him from the page was a statement by Leibowitz that struck Evseroff as highly prejudicial. "You are just kids now," Leibowitz had told Delvecchio and his youthful co-defendant sixteen years before. "But the finger on that trigger can be mighty itchy. You are potential holdup killers." Evseroff was elated. And he confidently drew up a motion in which he argued that the remark had hopelessly compromised Leibowitz's objectivity and that the old man had no choice but to disqualify himself from the case.

But Leibowitz didn't see it that way. "There is no question in my mind that I can give this defendant a fair trial," he replied testily. "What happened in that case or the expression of the court in that case all those years ago has not the slightest bearing on whether this defendant will get a fair trial. Motion denied."

Leibowitz also batted down a long list of other defense motions, including a request from Portelli's lawyer, Lawrence Wild, for a change of venue. In his motion to the court, Wild had quoted extensively from a *New York Times* editorial that spoke of the "evident violations of the civil rights" of those who were arrested. "In the first place," the editorial lamented, "various statements made by police authorities prior to and after the arrests have led to what was, in effect, the public trial and conviction of these individuals in the newspapers even before their indictment."

But the judge was not impressed with the argument, and Wild turned in vain first to the appellate division and then to the state court of appeals. In the brief he submitted Wild vividly described the treatment his client had received at the hands of police. "He was placed on public display like a wild animal," the attorney charged. "Photographs were disseminated showing him manacled, held in various wrestling holds, and held for photographers by the hair. In reading the clippings, one can understand why huge crowds surrounded the precinct stations where these men were held. And I can readily remember calls from the crowd of 'kill the dogs,' while the police displayed them at will. A lynching of Portelli would certainly have occurred had not the police brought armed reinforcements to the scene."

* * * *

On January 14, 1963, the trial finally got under way, with two special squads of policemen patrolling the courtroom and the halls and an unusual ruling in effect that forbade anyone from sitting in the first five rows of the spectators' section. True to form, Leibowitz jumped into the jury-selection process with both feet, conducting all the initial questioning "in order to save time." Evseroff objected repeatedly but without success, charging that Leibowitz was systematically excluding Jews, blacks, and Italians from the panel. In all, close to four hundred prospective jurors were called and dismissed over a three-day period, and the atmosphere in the courtroom quickly became thick and poisonous, and very tense.

Jerry in particular was highly sensitive to the nuances and subtle maneuvers that Leibowitz was using to undermine their defense. It was the little things that bothered him the most, such as Leibowitz's insistence that each of them stand silently with his head held high in the time-honored mug-shot posture, while each of the potential jurors was asked if he had any personal acquaintance with the accused.

The tension finally erupted into full-blown hysteria the next day, when Leibowitz stormed back into the courtroom after the lunchtime recess and announced that a secretary in the building had overheard Jerry muttering in the hallway that "before this trial is over, chairs will be flying around the courtroom." Leibowitz turned to the defense table, his heavy jowls quivering with rage. "If this defendant throws any chairs," he roared, "or if any other defendant causes a distraction in my courtroom, he will be put in handcuffs, in a straitjacket and, if necessary, in leg irons." The judge then returned obsessively to his favorite topic. "These defendants are going to get a scrupulously fair trial," he said, "fair one hundred percent from the bench. But let any defendant try any roughhouse tactics and he will see what will happen to him. I have had plenty of experience in roughhouse tactics, and I am fully capable of handling anything that will occur. No one is going to rough up this trial. And if anyone thinks he is, he is crazy." Leibowitz went on to order additional security precautions for the courtroom. And on the nineteenth of January, he ordered the jury sequestered as well, claiming that he had received an anonymous tip that the wife and children of one of the witnesses had been threatened repeatedly by phone.

From that day on the trial sessions often ran as late as 11:30 at night in an attempt, Leibowitz said, to free the jurors from their onerous chore as quickly as possible. But the unmistakable subtext of every one of these unusual measures was that, in Leibowitz's view, the defendants would stop at nothing in their attempt to thwart the machinery of justice.

The question of protection for the witnesses had originally come up months before, when Seedman was first coaxing a mug-shot identification out of the Goldberg brothers. Martin's statement that the perpetrators were members of "the top hoodlum element in Brooklyn" had just appeared in the press, and the Goldbergs were suddenly acting very concerned about the possibility of reprisals. "Help us out on this, and we'll put a detective in your store for as long as you think you need him," Seedman had assured them. "He'll work alongside you, only he'll be carrying a loaded thirty-eight." Sure enough, Detective Philip Kissel had showed up for work at the tobacco company the next day. And he would remain there eight hours a day, hauling cigarette cartons and filling orders, until his retirement from the department four and a half years later.

In return for that kind of cooperation, Seedman expected two extremely convincing witnesses at the trial. And that's exactly what he got. Both Goldbergs insisted that it was Portelli and Rosenberg who had pulled the job. And David Goldberg, in response to a prosecution request to identify the perpetrators, got to his feet, stepped down from the witness stand, and firmly placed his hands on Jerry's and Portelli's shoulders. Under cross-examination by Darienzo and Wild, he admitted that the masks and handkerchiefs and dark glasses had made identification impossible during the early stages of the holdup. But he insisted that he had caught a glimpse of both bandits as they dashed for the door after the shootings—a story that he stuck to no matter how fiercely the two attorneys attacked and ridiculed and derided his claim. Unfortunately, neither Darienzo nor Wild had researched the press clippings in the case. If they had they would certainly have been able to make good use of the statement Martin had made to reporters eight months earlier in which he admitted that the Goldbergs "had been too shocked to remember much of anything."

Richie Melville finally had his day in court on January 23, and he glumly ran through his account of Portelli's escape to Chicago and the explicit confession he said Portelli had made to him the night before—a confession, as Melville recalled it, that also implicated Rosenberg and Delvecchio.

On cross-examination Evseroff was ready and waiting. He had told reporters outside the courtroom that morning that "two hundred detectives had gone into Boro Park right after the killings and had unmercifully beaten up anyone who had ever been arrested in order to make them implicate these three suspects. A cop-killing never goes unsolved for very long," he had said. "Someone always has to take the heat." And now with Melville on the stand, he had a chance to make the jury understand as well. He carefully elicited every ghoulish detail of the beating Melville had received in the station house seven months before.

"I was taken there by force," Melville whispered. "I was put in the ground floor squad room, where eight or nine detectives questioned me. They twisted my arm behind my back. They hit me about the ear, they smacked me around the head. Then they took me to the bathroom and stripped me naked. They laid me face down on the floor, wouldn't let me get up, and hit me with a rubber hose and a wooden stick. They beat me on my private parts. I was crying. You can imagine I was scared to death. They said they would kill me. Then they touched lighted cigarettes and matches to my back. I held out for almost eight hours, but I couldn't hold out for any longer."

There was dead silence in the courtroom as Melville finished his account. Evseroff slowly turned to the judge and solemnly requested that Melville's entire testimony be stricken because it had been extracted by violence and threats.

Leibowitz looked over at the witness, his enormous bulldog face registering shock and horror at the story he'd just heard. "Mr. Melville," he said. "These beatings you have described would do credit, if I can call it credit, to a Gestapo wretch in Hitler's concentration camp. And the officials involved deserve the most utter condemnation on the part of every citizen in this community. This isn't Russia. This isn't Castro's Cuba. This is America. This is a glorious country where we don't tolerate things of that nature." He glanced around the courtroom, his eyes sweeping the jury for just a fraction of a second.

"Now, Mr. Melville," he resumed, his voice softer, as if he'd finally managed to get his emotions under control. "You say you decided to tell the police your story because of these beatings?"

"That's right, Your Honor," Melville whispered, his expression more frightened than it had been at any time during his testimony.

"I want you to forget about the beatings for just a moment," Leibowitz told him gently. "And I want you to focus instead on the testimony you gave to Mr. Selzer earlier today, especially as it concerned the three defendants who are seated here in the courtroom. And I want you to tell the jury, Mr. Melville, was that testimony true or false?"

"True," Melville finally whispered.

"I can't hear you," Leibowitz shot back.

"True," Melville said, a little louder this time.

Leibowitz glanced up at the clock at the back of the room, banged his gavel, and smiled beneficently at the jury. "We'll take a little fifteen-minute break now," he purred in his folksiest manner. "And we'll resume these proceedings at ten minutes till four."

But Richie Melville refused to return to the courtroom after the recess, sending in a note via the clerk that one of the spectators had pointed a trigger finger at him as he was leaving the stand. Leibowitz furiously sealed off the room, ordered Melville brought out again under armed guard, and demanded that he identify the spectator who had made the threat. Melville looked around fearfully and said he wasn't sure anymore, that maybe he'd made a mistake. Furious now, Leibowitz promptly called Lieutenant Domenico Carranante to the stand to confirm the authenticity of the note. Carranante was in charge of the Sixty-sixth Precinct House, where Seedman and Martin had established their command post, and he had been waiting in the witness room with Melville, expecting to testify later in the day.

"What did this man tell you during the recess?" Leibowitz roared at the cop as soon as he had been sworn in.

"He said he was threatened during the course of his testimony," Carranante replied. "He said he couldn't see very well, but he thought it might have been either a man named Joseph Franolina or it could have been John Delvecchio, the brother of one of the defendants."

At which point Delvecchio himself jumped to his feet, his voice trembling with rage, his finger pointed straight at Carranante's nose. "This is the guy who's trying to frame me," he shouted. "He told me I was innocent. He knew it! And now he's trying to frame my brother."

"Keep quiet, mister," Leibowitz shouted back.

"You liar!" Delvecchio yelled at the cop. "This is the guy who swore I was innocent. He tortured me to get me to testify. And when

I refused, he said, 'I will frame you!' Him and Seedman, the bastards. They're framing me, judge, I swear. Give me a lie-detector test, give me anything! And now they're trying to frame my whole family, the lying bastards."

Leibowitz finally gaveled the man down and restored a semblance of order, but he was flustered and erratic in his comments, overwhelmed in a way that many courthouse regulars could never remember seeing him before. "If witnesses are going to be threatened," he said, "if their lips are going to be sealed, then this whole thing is a farce. Heaven knows I want to conduct a fair trial. I locked up the jury because I was afraid of what might happen from either one side or the other or both." He paused for a gulp of water and then looked over at the defense table. "Is there any objection to my clearing the courtroom for the balance of the trial?" he asked. There was a chorus of objections from all six attorneys, and Leibowitz uncharacteristically backed down.

"Many a witness has been sealed by the code of *Omerta*," he rambled. "It is my belief that this witness was scared to death of somebody in this courtroom." And then he scratched his head, banged his gavel, and adjourned the trial for the rest of the afternoon.

7

In the days ahead the jury would hear from Richie Melville's wife, Fernanda, who confirmed a part of her husband's story but only as it related to Portelli. She had not heard the alleged confession, she said, or the references to Rosenberg and Delvecchio. But Portelli *had* spent Saturday night at their apartment and had asked her to go out to a drugstore and purchase a color comb, which he had used to dye his hair from sandy brown to black.

Twenty-four hours later Portelli's attorney, Lawrence Wild, produced a witness named Anna Gandolfo, who described herself as a close personal friend of Melville's wife. Mrs. Gandolfo testified that she had not seen her friend since the robbery but that she had received a total of five telephone calls from her, in which she had sounded agitated and distraught. "She told me that detectives were hounding them night and day," Mrs. Gandolfo testified, "and that the cops had warned her that unless she appeared at the trial and told a story implicating Portelli, her children would be taken away from her and she herself would immediately be arrested for prostitution." In one of the phone calls, Mrs. Gandolfo said, Melville's wife had begged her to help her find a lawyer she could trust. But then she had called her back the next day and told her she had made a big mistake, that they had no need of a lawyer, and that she hoped Mrs. Gandolfo would forget about the entire affair.

The saga of Richie Melville was to take two more bizarre turns, the first of them in March of 1965 when he walked into the Bath Avenue police station, his elbow shattered by a bullet from a .38-caliber revolver. He told police that he had been walking near his home at Bay Twenty-second Street and Cropsey Avenue at about eight P.M. when he felt a sharp pain in his arm. He said he had seen no one around, but that a neighbor had told him he thought he had heard the sound of three shots being fired.

And then nine years later, in an affidavit notarized by a guard at the Mattewan Correctional Facility in Beacon, New York, where Melville was then serving time, he recanted his entire testimony. "Every element of the story I told at the trial was a lie," he swore in the affidavit. "The story was told to me by the police, and I was rehearsed by them and told exactly what to say. The reason I said on the witness stand that my testimony was the truth was because the cops assured me they were going to kill me and my wife if I did not cooperate." The recantation formed the basis of an appeal that Jerry submitted to the State Supreme Court in Westchester County later that same year, an appeal in which Jerry grimly quoted Leibowitz as having told the jury that "perjury is a crime second only to murder." The court denied the appeal three months later, claiming that it was up to the original jury to have weighed the credibility of Melville's testimony.

For Jerry and his co-defendants the most agonizing part of the trial was the unanimous decision by their attorneys *not* to put them on the stand. For as long as they refused to testify, the law forbade the prosecution from disclosing their prior criminal records to the jury. For Jacob

Evseroff it was an especially difficult decision because not only was he genuinely convinced of his client's innocence, he was also certain that Delvecchio could have been very eloquent about the pressures that had been brought to bear during the interrogations—and about the series of increasingly desperate deals that had been offered to him right up until the start of the trial. But since it was their clients' prior records that had first attracted the attention of the police in the case, none of the six defense lawyers, Evseroff included, wanted to give the jury the opportunity to leap to the same damaging conclusions.

There was no similar obstacle to the mounting of a strong affirmative defense, however—an attempt, at least, to establish that their clients were elsewhere at the time of the shootings. And yet no such attempt was ever made on behalf of either Jerry or Portelli. Evseroff, who was not directly involved in the decision, speculates that the alibi witnesses they would have had to call were probably known criminals themselves, knockaround guys whose testimony would have introduced an element of guilt by association and who probably would have been disbelieved by the jury in any case. Others have theorized that Jerry and Portelli simply knew too much and that whatever alibi they might have been able to establish, they would have had to betray so many underworld confidences that their lives on the street would have been virtually impossible.

And so Jerry sat there at the defense table, mute and helpless and increasingly enraged as the long parade of prosecution witnesses came and went. Some of them were total strangers; others, like Louis "The Geezer" Ferrara, were acquaintances from the neighborhood. And one of them, an angelic-looking seventeen-year-old business-school student named Linda Manzione, had been his closest friend.

Linda had spent the past six months closely guarded by detectives in a room at the St. George Hotel, Seedman and Martin both fearful that she might recant if she were reexposed to the Bath Avenue candy-store milieu where she and Jerry had first met years before. She had been hauled in on a hunch right after the shootings, and for a cumulative total of twenty-four hours of intensive questioning spread over several days, she had vehemently denied any awareness of the crime. Of course she knew Jerry and the two Anthonys, she said, but she knew nothing whatsoever of their activities on that Friday afternoon.

By the fourth straight day of interrogation, her spirits had begun to sag and she had begun to wonder if she might actually have to spend the rest of her life in a filthy police lockup. At which point Seedman pulled a ruse on her that finally elicited the story she would later repeat at the trial. He answered the phone in her presence and pretended at first to be trying to get rid of the caller. And then all of a sudden his face lit up and he whirled away from Linda, lowering his voice but still careful to talk plenty loud enough for her to overhear. "Yeah," he said, "no kidding? Why the hell didn't you say so in the first place?" There was a brief pause, and then Seedman said, "Jeez, I was hoping for something like this." He snuck a glance over his shoulder at the girl and then terminated the conversation with a terse, "Don't worry, she's going to be right here when the guy comes over."

Ten minutes later two detectives escorted a seedy-looking little man with dandruff on his shoulders into the room—a man who was in fact a civilian employee of the police department, a teletype operator from the Centre Street headquarters in Manhattan. He squinted at Linda for a moment, then turned and nodded at Seedman. "No doubt in my mind, Captain," he said. "That's the girl." The man left quickly, and Seedman pretended to ignore the incident for a few moments. Finally Linda could contain her anxiety no longer, and she begged him to tell her who the man was.

"I'll come straight to the point, Linda," Seedman told her. "That guy's a salesman from Philip Morris, and he was parked outside the tobacco store—just across the street, he says, from where you and

Delvecchio were waiting in the car. He heard the shots just like you and Tony did, he saw the two of you pull away and squeal around the corner, and his testimony is all we need to indict you as an accessory after the fact."

Linda was not indicted, of course. She agreed to testify, instead. And as she was led into the courtroom on the seventh day of the trial, Jerry would swear that he saw the two little words *forgive me* forming themselves upon her lips. Her testimony was glib and beautifully rehearsed, and it also filled in virtually every remaining gap in the prosecution's case.

She had seen Jerry at the Delvecchio candy store on the afternoon of the shootings, she told the jury. And she had watched as he went around behind the counter, crouched down, and took a newspaper from the shelf. As he lifted it up, a gun slipped out of the paper, she said, a gun she blithely identified as the weapon that later was found in the shrubbery around the corner from New Utrecht Avenue.

Later that same day, she claimed, she and Jerry and the two Anthonys got into John Delvecchio's red Pontiac convertible and drove to within a few blocks of the tobacco store, where Jerry and Portelli got out of the car and put on the now-famous sunglasses and wide-brimmed Borsalino hats. "Don't they look a little obvious?" she had allegedly asked Delvecchio. "No," he told her. "They always look like that when they're going to pull a job." She and Delvecchio had driven around for a couple more minutes and had then parked directly across the street from the tobacco store, Linda claimed, at which point they heard a barrage of gunfire, and Delvecchio pulled away from the curb in a panic.

She paused for a moment, glanced over at the defense table, and then concluded her testimony with a final burst of beautifully remembered dialogue. As he squealed around the corner onto Twelfth Avenue, Linda said, Delvecchio was muttering under his breath: "He never learns, he never learns." And when she asked him who he meant, he said, "Jerry, who else? I just hope to God nobody got hurt."

Delvecchio himself had been listening to her testimony with a mounting sense of outrage and incredulity. And as soon as the last of the jurors had disappeared into the jury room for a ten-minute break, he once again jumped to his feet, his voice ringing with a sense of righteous indignation. "Judge," he said, "you are on the bench for almost twenty years. Nobody can fool you. I didn't fool you sixteen years ago when you sent me up for armed robbery. Wouldn't I be crazy to take a seventeen-year-old kid in an open convertible car, with the top down, to go pull a job? I'm only thirty-five years old, and I've spent fourteen of those years in jail. This man [pointing at the district attorney] can fool the jury. They're simple people. But nobody can fool you, Judge. I didn't do this thing."

Sitting next to Delvecchio at the defense table, Jerry waited in vain for the tough old judge to cut him off or humiliate him or slap him down. And yet Leibowitz did none of these things. It was Delvecchio's fourth sustained outburst of the trial, and the judge was hearing him out now, listening carefully and then administering only the mildest of rebukes when his tirades were over. It was as if the old man's rigid preconceptions of the case were slowly being realigned. It was a startling example of the power of simple eloquence, persistence, and a marvelous sense of timing—an example that would serve as an inspiration to Jerry in the dark and hopeless years immediately ahead.

Louis "The Geezer" Ferrara was the last significant prosecution witness, and he was now willing to go far beyond the simple statement that he had loaned Jerry his sunglasses—a statement that had originally been fed to him by Al Seedman. Louis now recalled a car trip to a neighborhood doughnut shop with Jerry and Delvecchio on the day of the shootings, during which the two defendants were discussing a score. (A *score,* he patiently explained to the jury, is a "planned robbery.") When they reached the doughnut shop, Louis said, a man walked out with a bag of doughnuts and handed Jerry an automatic pistol through the open window, at which point Jerry turned around, handed the pistol to Louis in the backseat, and told him to put it under the floor mat. Later that same day, Louis recalled, he overheard Delvecchio asking his brother for the keys to the red convertible. "I gotta go pick up Jerry now," he quoted Delvecchio as having said.

The cross-examination of Louis Ferrara was especially vigorous, with Jerry's lawyer Joseph Darienzo hammering away at Ferrara's story and finally causing Leibowitz to intervene on the witness's behalf. And while Ferrara stoutly denied that he had been beaten or physically harassed at the station house, he did admit that he had been "frightened by screams" from other suspects who were being interrogated at the same time.

And then Darienzo had an idea—a piece of inspired courtroom dramaturgy that marked his finest moment in the course of the entire trial. He had been struck by the physical similarity between Jerry and Ferrara—the same build, the same rounded shoulders, the same wavy hair and delicate features. And he now turned to the bailiff and requested People's Exhibits 7 and 19—the hat and the sunglasses. "Louis," he said, "I'd like you to put these back on, and I'm going to ask you to hold this white handkerchief over your face." And then he recalled several of the "eyewitnesses" to the stand and elicited from them the admission that Louis Ferrara, dressed in his own sunglasses and a hat that seemed to fit him to a tee, was a dead ringer for the thin bandit in the back of the store. "Ladies and gentlemen," Darienzo told the jury, "I would submit to you that if Louis Ferrara's photograph had happened to be in Captain Seedman's pocket on the afternoon of the shootings, that *he*, rather than Mr. Rosenberg, would now be on trial for his life."

Jerry turned around in his seat, his eyes locking with his parents', who were sitting in the fifth row of the spectator section. And it seemed to him as if the last vestige of suspicion and uncertainty had suddenly fallen away from his mother's face. Years later Rose would say that it was at that moment that she first realized how easy it would have been for Jerry to save himself by ratting on Ferrara, whatever the actual merits of the case. And it was at that moment, too, that she first began to feel a fierce and paradoxical sense of pride at the way her son had handled himself throughout the arrest, the long incarceration, and now the trial.

"How well do you know Louis Ferrara?" a reporter shouted at Jerry as he was led from the courtroom in chains at the conclusion of the day's proceedings. Jerry looked up at the guy and just shook his head. "I'd like to wring his fuckin' neck," he said.

The next day was a Friday, and Jacob Evseroff finally had the opportunity to begin the presentation of his defense for Anthony Delvecchio. The first witness he called was Delvecchio's brother-in-law, Savino Tamborra—the attorney from Norwich, Connecticut, who had arranged for Delvecchio's surrender to the state police. Tamborra's importance to the defense was his testimony that Delvecchio had been at a birthday party in Connecticut on the day he was alleged to have bought one of the holdup weapons in Aberdeen, Maryland. But on cross-examination Selzer seemed far more interested in the circumstances surrounding Delvecchio's surrender. Had Tamborra discussed the matter with anyone in Hartford, the state capital, Selzer wanted to know. "No," Tamborra told him. And then he corrected himself, retracting the denial and dropping a piece of highly prejudicial information. "Wait a minute," Tamborra said. "By telephone, I did have several conversations . . . one of them, I believe it was, with his parole officer."

"I object to that," Evseroff roared, leaping to his feet in an instant. Indirectly Tamborra had just disclosed his brother-in-law's criminal background. And in so doing, Evseroff argued, he had irrevocably tipped the scales against him.

"Overruled," Leibowitz said. "He was not asked that, he volunteered it."

"I will ask Your Honor to instruct the jury to disregard it," Evseroff continued.

"No, I shall not," Leibowitz shot back.

"At this time I respectfully move for the declaration of a mistrial," Evseroff told him, "on the grounds that the witness's statement was so prejudicial as to preclude the possibility of my client's receiving a fair consideration from this jury."

"Your motion is denied," Leibowitz told him. "And if you keep this up, I will hold you in contempt."

But by Monday morning the judge had reconsidered. Perhaps it was simply a recognition of the legal validity of Evseroff's argument. Perhaps Leibowitz had finally been swayed by the cumulative weight of Delvecchio's outbursts and impassioned denials. Or perhaps his finely tuned antennae had detected that the jury was leaning toward an acquittal for Delvecchio, and he didn't want the doubts they were feeling to spill over to Rosenberg and Portelli as well. In any case, he called Evseroff and Selzer into his chambers, announced that he had spent the weekend going over the entire record of the trial, and told Evseroff that if he renewed his motion for a mistrial, he was now prepared to grant it. "A judge must have courage regardless of his opinion as to the defendant's innocence or guilt," he observed. "A judge who does not have that courage does not belong on the bench." And then, looking Evseroff straight in the eye, he said: "I am *not* a patsy for the district attorney's office."

Several minutes later Delvecchio himself was confronted by reporters on his way back to the Raymond Street jail. "How's it feel, Tony?" one of them shouted. "I don't want a mistrial," Delvecchio told him. "I've been locked up for eight months. I want to get this over with."

The defense table was far less crowded but nonetheless extremely agitated when the trial finally resumed that Monday morning. Darienzo and Wild were on their feet in a second, both of them moving for a mistrial on behalf of Jerry and Portelli as well, arguing vehemently that the jury could not now avoid drawing the inference that the two remaining defendants must somehow be guiltier than the man who had been severed from the case. But Leibowitz denied the motions out of hand, adding that he now expected to send the case to the jury by the middle of the following day.

There was one final piece of testimony to be heard before the summations, and it concerned a single thumbprint on one of the checks that littered the floor of the Boro Park Tobacco Company in the aftermath of the shootings. It was the only piece of physical evidence directly linking either defendant to the scene, and Selzer had produced an FBI fingerprint expert several days before who had testified that the print was definitely Portelli's. Wild now produced an expert of his own, a former Treasury Department Enforcement Bureau chief named Buck Greene, who had assured him in private that the print was too small for positive identification. But now, from the witness stand, Greene unaccountably changed his story. Yes, he said, the print fragment *was* large enough for identification. And in his opinion it matched the left thumbprint of Portelli's that was on file with the FBI.

Wild's shoulders sagged in disbelief. And although he promptly took the stand himself and told the jury of his earlier conversation with Buck Greene in private, the impact of this self-inflicted wound was still profoundly detrimental.

Selzer's summation took nearly two hours: a meticulous witness-by-witness restatement of the entire case. Toward the end he erroneously referred to Portelli's fingerprint as having been left on the murder weapon—a slip, incredibly enough, that none of the defense attorneys managed to detect. "We have proved their guilt beyond a reasonable doubt," the DA roared in conclusion. "And I demand that you return a verdict of felony murder in the first degree with no recommendation for mercy."

Wild and Darienzo in rebuttal took less than an hour each. Wild sneered at the coerced testimony from Richie Melville, attacked the eyewitness identifications as "wishful thinking," and told the jury that Portelli had fled to Chicago "simply in order to avoid a police beating." As for the fingerprint, he emphasized that the check itself had not been stolen, that it had been included in a batch of evidence that was stored at the Sixty-sixth Precinct House, and that the fingerprint could very easily have been placed there after Portelli's arrest. "For all we know, they may have handed him the check during the interrogation and asked him if he'd ever seen it before," Wild told the jury.

"Please be merciful," he concluded. "A guilty verdict," he said, "would be like sending a man to the electric chair on the basis of surmised speculation and suspicion."

Darienzo came next and spent a great deal of time on the possible eyewitness confusion between Jerry and Louis Ferrara. "Is there any doubt in your mind that this Ferrara would not hesitate to hang it on anyone as long as it wasn't himself?" he asked. As for Richie Melville, Darienzo said, "given the beatings and the pressures that were brought to bear on his wife, no one should even attempt to convict a *dog* on the basis of that testimony."

But then, undercutting most of what he had said before, he reminded the jury that even if Jerry *had* been a part of the holdup, his active role had ended well before the shootings. Darienzo had had one eye on the death penalty throughout the trial, and he felt an obligation now to do everything he could at least to save Jerry from the chair. "In this case the law makes no meaningful distinction between armed robbery and first-degree murder," he told them. "Should you people, in your wisdom, elect to return a guilty verdict against my client, it will be your responsibility to make that distinction. A recommendation for mercy, although not binding on the court, will put you all firmly on record as having recognized the difference between what my client is alleged to have done on that Friday afternoon in May and the crime of murder, which—by no stretch of the imagination—did he ever commit."

It was a very thin line that the attorney was attempting to tread, the trickiest part of any murder defense in which the death penalty is even a remote possibility. But to many of the jurors that Tuesday morning, his elaborate plea for mercy may well have sounded like an out-and-out admission of guilt.

The jury went out right before lunch. It was a hellish interval during which Jerry and Portelli remained shackled in the bull pen directly behind the courtroom, trying desperately to keep their spirits up and complaining, as they had all during the trial, about the quality of the food that was brought up for them from the holding tank across the street.

The knock on the door came just two hours and forty-five minutes later, and as they were led back into the courtroom, they noticed that the jury box had been screened from the spectator section by a line of movable blackboards and that the room was jam-packed with detectives and uniformed police. They watched as the clerk got the nod from the court officer at the door of the jury room, and they peered under the blackboards as twelve pairs of shoes shuffled slowly up the steps into the box. “Mr. Foreman,” Leibowitz whispered, his voice hoarse from the incessant arguments and long hours on the bench. “How do you find as to the defendants Anthony Portelli and Jerome Rosenberg?”

“Guilty under the felony-murder statute, Your Honor, with no recommendation for mercy,” the foreman croaked, provoking a bloodthirsty cheer from the cops in attendance and a furious outburst from Portelli’s mother, who was then forcibly ejected from the courtroom. “They framed my boy,” she screamed on her way out the door. “God will punish the judge!”

The New York *Post* concluded its coverage of the trial with this final paragraph:

> Jerome Rosenberg’s mother and father bowed their heads and wept in the aftermath of the verdict. Two sisters and a brother of slain detective John Finnegan looked on grimly. And Judge Leibowitz whispered his thanks to the jurors for their twelve days of deliberations and told them that arrangements would be made for each of them to be escorted safely home. As to the defendants, Portelli belched, and Rosenberg smirked.

Although the death penalty was now mandatory for both of them, Leibowitz waited almost three full weeks before pronouncing sentence. Finally, at a hearing on February 18, 1963, he denied perfunctory motions by both Darienzo and Wild to set aside the verdicts and also revealed his own thinly disguised view of the proceedings. “The evidence against Rosenberg was so overwhelming it was a moving picture case,” the judge observed. “There’s no question that he got a fair trial.” And then he turned to Jerry and asked him if he had anything to say before he pronounced sentence.

Jerry got slowly to his feet, his leg irons rattling and clanking under the table. And then he made what amounted to his first public statement in a court of law. "You keep saying this was a fair trial," he told Leibowitz, his voice soft but steady as a rock. "It was not. It was a lynching. And the fact that you keep repeating those words only means that deep down in your heart—"

At which point Leibowitz banged his gavel and shouted him down. "Jerome Samuel Rosenberg," he said, "I hereby sentence you to be executed in accordance with the law during the week of March 31, 1963."

"You're the murderer," Jerry shouted back. "You and the DA and the police department all know this."

"Get this killer out of my sight," Leibowitz roared. "The order for his transfer to the Sing Sing Death House will be signed this afternoon."

Anthony Delvecchio was retried three months later before Judge Julius Helfand, with Evseroff once again handling the defense and Linda Manzione once again the principal witness against him. As before, she told of riding around in the convertible with the three suspects and then waiting outside the tobacco company until she and Delvecchio heard the shots. Only this time when Evseroff got her on cross-examination, she broke down and admitted the ruse Seedman had used in order to get her to testify. She became highly emotional and began raving about threats she had received not only from the police department but from the district attorney's office, and then explicitly retracted all her testimony linking any of the three defendants with the crime.

In his redirect examination Selzer strongly implied that it was the Delvecchio family and not the police and the DA's office that had made the threats and frightened her into a recantation. But the all-male jury was not impressed with Selzer's claim. And on June 5 they returned a unanimous not-guilty verdict after ten hours of deliberation. Delvecchio jumped to his feet, thanked the judge effusively for giving him a fair trial, and promptly dropped out of sight. He has never again run afoul of the law and is now reportedly the owner of a small retail liquor business on Staten Island.

PART 2

The quality of a nation's civilization can be accurately measured by the methods it uses in the enforcement of its criminal law.

—JUSTICE LOUIS D. BRANDEIS

8

Sixteen years later, in November, 1979, forty-three-year-old Jerry Rosenberg would once again be going up the river. The verdict had finally gone against him in his Byzantine nine-million-dollar lawsuit against former State Special Prosecutor Maurice Nadjari. And while Jerry had laid the groundwork for an eventual appeal, any further legal work was out of the question for the moment, preoccupied as he was with the transfer upstate that he knew was coming.

It was a transfer, he was sure, that would mean an end to the luxuries he had begun to take for granted at the MCC in lower Manhattan—an end to his phone calls and frequent visits and smuggled-in goodies. And a major upheaval, for sure, in his relationships, especially with his girl friend and sometime legal assistant, Arlene.

Theirs had never been an easy relationship, and it was growing rapidly less so now. Jerry was frequently petulant and demanding, as if he were attempting to store up feelings of being cared for against the long winters of neglect that he knew lay ahead. Perhaps, too, he was struggling to put his infatuation with Arlene into some kind of more reasonable perspective. For they were clearly *not* an ideal match, Arlene every bit as erratic and mercurial as Jerry—and still bogged down in the middle of a protracted and highly emotional divorce.

One of Jerry's closest friends at the MCC, a man called Augie, recalls sitting up with him for hours at a stretch one night early in his relationship with Arlene. Jerry was frantic and raving because he couldn't reach her on the phone as they had planned, and his mood was swinging wildly from despair to rage to fear of losing her altogether. Augie finally grabbed him by the shirt and shook him back and forth like a little kid. "You're in *love,* my man," he yelled at Jerry. "It *always* feels that way. You been off the streets so long you must've forgot!" Augie had been in and out of prison himself dozens of times since the middle sixties, and he patiently tried to lay out for Jerry the realities of modern life. "The world has changed a lot in twenty years," he explained. "By Arlene going out like that sometimes, she don't mean no disrespect," he said. "Believe it or not, a woman can be a regular person these days if she wants. She's got a *right* to her own life, understand?"

In the end, perhaps, the message finally sank in. In any case, Jerry's near-tyrannical demands on Arlene's time and attention gradually began to abate. Perhaps, too, he had simply moaned and groused about the transfer enough that he was finally able to turn his attention to the future, to a life of diminished contact, toward making the best of a circumstance he had always been able to rise above in the past.

While Jerry had no choice in the matter, he certainly knew exactly what the possibilities were. For over the previous sixteen years he had done time at all four of the maximum-security institutions in the state: Greenhaven in Dutchess County, Dannemora up near the Canadian border, Attica near Buffalo, and Sing Sing, less than an hour from the city and located in a beautiful, parklike setting on the banks of the Hudson River. Dannemora was the absolute worst—cruel and remote, with a climate, they said, that knew only two seasons: winter and July. If he landed there he'd be lucky to see Arlene twice a year. Attica would also be hell because of the many guards who would remember him from the rebellion; likewise Greenhaven, where Deputy Superintendent Joseph Keenan was an implacable foe, Jerry having drawn him into court on several occasions and roughed him up every time.

That left Sing Sing as his clear favorite. "Over there you can kiss and love it up," he told Arlene one night in the Attorneys' Conference Room. "No problem whatsoever."

And then he was off and running, elaborating a baroque jailhouse fantasy of the free and easy life he'd be enjoying just thirty miles up the river. It was utter nonsense, and they both knew it. But it said a lot about his newly rediscovered ability to cope with an uncertain and oppressive future. "Pretty soon I'll be out on the grounds till eleven o'clock at night, then twelve o'clock like it was before, then two o'clock!" he told her. "It's gotta be the best connection joint in the state . . . any kinda special food or luxuries. In fact, my old friend Nicky DeCicco practically runs the place. Right away he'll fix me up with a job as A-block porter. That's nothin'. I'll pick up a mop around noontime, five minutes later I'll put it down. And as far as long-distance calls is concerned, I wouldn't be surprised if my man Wiggins is still on the phones. Sing Sing," he concluded, "without exaggeration, is just like being on the streets!"

He got to his feet and glanced through the barred window at the twinkling lights of the downtown cityscape in the distance. "I do pretty good in jail," he said finally. "I'm no king, I'm just Jerry. But I do the best I can."

They came for him at six A.M. on the twelfth of October, 1979—a pair of U.S. marshals with handcuffs and leg irons and chains. He had spent the previous day packing and had filled three huge cartons with books and legal papers, one of them containing all the materials he would need for his appeal in the Nadjari case as well as notes and trial transcripts on his current cases.

He was going to Sing Sing all right, the marshals told him, and the cartons would be sent up later, after the hacks had had a chance to check them for contraband.

They whisked him downstairs and into an armored cruiser, where Jerry's leg irons were shackled to a set of special fittings on the floor of the backseat. More prisoners are lost during transfers and other trips outside the walls than in any other way, and the Marshal's Service has a special set of precautions for lifers and other prisoners on especially long sentences. The precautions include unannounced departures, circuitous routes, and the presence of a second car that would tail them at a distance of several hundred yards. Jerry would remain handcuffed for the entire trip, and every one of the several dozen cigarettes he consumed would have to be smoked two-handed.

They took the East River Drive north to the Cross Bronx Expressway, then cut across to the Henry Hudson Parkway, scudding along easily ahead of the rush-hour traffic clot that would begin building up within the next twenty minutes. Jerry's eyes were glued to the window for the entire time, feasting on the tiniest details of ordinary life: cars, billboards, a string of oil barges barely moving upstream against the current. He had been at the MCC for close to two years and had seen nothing in all that time but drab prison and courthouse interiors. And so the thing that surprised him the most was how bright and vivid everything seemed in the early autumn light, how crisp and brittle—and above all, how complex. They continued on past the Tappan Zee Bridge, past the prosperous commuter towns of Dobbs Ferry and Scarborough and Ardsley-on-Hudson. Jerry leaned back and closed his eyes, giving himself over to the journey. He was safe in this car, far safer than he ever felt in prison, surrounded as he always was by scores of wackos with seething grudges and violent imaginations. Here in this car he didn't have to front anything off, hide his fear, pretend to be anything that he truly wasn't. The marshals in the front seat meant nothing to him. He'd probably never see them again. They were robots, anyway: anonymous and spiffy-looking and probably only semiliterate. His thoughts roamed ahead of the car. He saw the ancient, pitted concrete wall that ran around the prison, the old New York Central commuter line curving close alongside. He saw the main entrance, saw one huge gate closing behind the car before the other one opened up in front. He knew exactly which way the marshal would steer the car, could see the upper roadway alongside the hospital and the gym, the grunting clusters of inmates working out with jail-made weights inside. He heard the music from a dozen Christmas concerts, the laughter from a hundred witless movies, the roar of a thousand tasteless meals in the enormous mess hall. He could feel the shock of the ancient Van Dorn cell gates clanging shut, the scratch and sting of the harsh state-issue soap grating against his cheek. He knew the boredom of the commissary line, the gut-clenching fear of a sudden shakedown, the warmth of the feed-up room where he hoped his old friend Nicky DeCicco would still be cooking up a storm. But most of all he smelled the smell of the Death House.

He had arrived that first time at 9:30 A.M. on Thursday, February 19, 1963. Not in a station wagon but in a van—a black-and-white Department of Corrections van—straining against the shackles, his old friend Anthony Portelli chained to the bench on the other side. Finally, as the van lurched and bucked through a hard right turn at the foot of the hill, they were able to catch a glimpse of their destination—an ultrasecure two-story blockhouse, squatting on an open patch of barren soil about fifty yards from the riverbank.

Waiting for them as the van rumbled to a stop in front of the building was a gauntlet of jeering corrections officers that stretched from the edge of the roadway all the way up the steps to the main gate. For, however unjustly it may have been applied, the cop-killer label was to haunt Jerry for his entire prison career. And his initiation onto Death Row was no exception.

He and Portelli staggered out of the van and made their way inside as scores of bloated, angry faces hurled curses and prodded them with batons. For in many respects these guards were cops themselves. They were called cops by the prisoners, they identified with cops and often aspired to their salary and prestige—and in those days they even dressed like cops as well: dark blue trousers and caps, light blue shirts with flap pockets and a shiny silver badge.

Watching it all from the top of the steps was a lithe, uncomfortable, fifty-three-year-old correctional lieutenant named Louis V. Rauch, a man who already had nineteen condemned prisoners under his direct personal supervision, only three of whom were even close to an execution date. For a curious thing had begun to happen on Death Row: There was still plenty of new blood coming into the facility, but very little old blood going out. Over the past seventy-four years the State of New York had executed 695 of its citizens—close to ten a year and far more than any other state. But there had been no executions at all in 1962 and none so far this year. And somewhere down the line, Lieutenant Rauch was beginning to worry about running out of room.

He had assigned Rosenberg and Portelli to a pair of cells in the West Wing, where they would be the responsibility of a tough, fair-minded day-shift watch officer named Reggie Wiggins, one of the first black guards on the Sing Sing staff and the man who first swung the gate of Cell 9 West shut in front of Jerry's face. The cell itself was nothing more than a steel cage eight feet wide and twelve feet deep with a cot, a backless stool, a small writing surface attached to the wall, a toilet, and a cold-water sink. It would be Wiggins's job to pass Jerry a quart of hot water and a razor through the bars every morning, to watch him shave and then collect the razor as soon as he was finished (suicide was the main "security problem" in the Death House), to light his cigarettes one at a time (matches were strictly forbidden), to supervise his visits, to escort him to the tiny exercise yard for a half-hour every day, and to listen to his endless complaints about the noise, the food, the heat, the cold, the cardboard slippers they were required to wear, and the total lack of medical attention for his chronically infected left ear.

Always screaming and yelling or raving about something. Never seemed to get worn down by the routine, never got humble or depressed or down on himself like the others. One of the most antagonistic little guys Wiggins had ever seen behind bars. "What a fight that kid had to put up," he recalled many years later, now comfortably ensconced behind a desk in the administration wing. "What Jerry accomplished for himself is something truly amazing—something you can't even begin to appreciate unless you know what he was up against. Screaming and yelling was just about the only weapon the little bastard could use. And God knows he had to fight us for every inch."

It was the cop-killer label, Wiggins realized, that really made Jerry's life impossible, that inspired the highest degree of hatred and contempt on the part of the rest of the staff. Portelli somehow managed to shrug most of it off with a laugh or a giggle or a stupid remark. But Jerry seemed determined to give as good as he got. And for every time that his mail was held up or his yard time was canceled arbitrarily or his dinner tray was delivered cold, he always managed to scheme something in return. Little things. Like he'd call for a match and then grind out the cigarette as soon as the hack had turned his back. "Hey, dog face," he'd yell after the man. "Come back here. I didn't get it lit." Or he'd leave his cap out on the yard after exercise and the hack would have to go back and get it, through four sets of double-locked gates. Somehow Jerry just never seemed to accept his status as a person who was about to be physically destroyed.

In fact, what was about to happen was still not entirely clear. For in capital cases an appeal was mandatory under the law. And Jerry's parents had taken out a second mortgage in order to hire one of the best-known appeals lawyers in the state—a dapper, pink-faced attorney named Maurice Edelbaum. At least the man inspired confidence. And while he wasn't promising miracles, he was definitely able to assure them that his ten-thousand-dollar fee would buy their son a lot of time.

In the old days, of course, these things were handled much more expeditiously: A man was sentenced to death, the court of appeals rubber-stamped the conviction, the governor routinely passed up his opportunity to commute the sentence, and that was that. But in the early 1950s a wave of underworld hit men had come onto Death Row with a new attitude. They were determined. They had access to outside money. And for the first time sophisticated legal manpower was brought to bear on the question of how to keep a Death Row inmate alive. In fact, it turned out to be quite simple, the trick being to get the cases into federal court, raising procedural and substantive issues that would then have to be readjudicated in the state courts—a process which, if it was skillfully orchestrated, could be dragged out almost indefinitely.

Now, less than ten years later, there was a peripatetic little organization called the Committee to Abolish Capital Punishment, staffed by a handful of volunteer law school professors, which had succeeded in getting thirteen separate stays of execution over the past three years and which was prepared to step in as soon as any Death Row inmate began to approach the point of no return. They weren't invincible, of course: Two men were in fact executed within nine months of Jerry's arrival. But they were very smart. And they were largely responsible for the rising population on Death Row about which Lieutenant Rauch had grown increasingly concerned.

And yet, despite the overcrowding and the long delays, Rauch's job really hadn't changed that much over the years. His prime responsibility was still what it had always been: to keep them all alive until, every once in a while, one of them would finally run out of appeals. And then on the fourth Thursday of the month at ten o'clock in the evening, he would call in the anonymous civilian employee who actually pulled the switch, he would take his seat in the simple oak pew along with the four other witnesses and the prison doctor, and he would watch as a human life was snuffed out by 2,000 sizzling volts of direct current. Rauch, of course, knew all the statistics. He knew that the executee's blood reached the boiling point within a half-second after the switch was thrown and that the proximate cause of death was the effect of this boiling liquid upon the heart muscle itself. He also knew that the victim's brain function ceased within another second or two, and that every muscle in his body went through a cycle of violent contraction and then eternal relaxation. The only thing he didn't know for sure was whether or not it hurt.

For the first few months Jerry spent most of his energy dreaming up endless schemes to *get over* on the system, smuggling in contraband and disrupting the Death House routine in any way he could. It was a strategy of denial—an attempt to assert that he could still live some tiny piece of his life on his terms rather than theirs. And for the first couple of months, at least, the strategy got him through.

His ally in many of these schemes was a spunky young Brooklyn hood named Frankie Cutrone, who was doing seven years for forgery and whom Jerry had come to know on the Bath Avenue candy-store circuit years before. Cutrone was locked in Seven Building, a medium-security cell block located several hundred yards away on a bluff overlooking the river. But his job assignment was lead man on the Death House feed-up crew, and he quickly beame Jerry's main link to the outside world—bringing in sausages and creamed herring and jailhouse gossip and handling all Jerry's outgoing mail to avoid the arbitrary restrictions, long delays, and extra-heavy censorship that were part of the carefully calculated agony waiting for him on Death Row.

When I first hit the Death House, I was considered pretty dangerous. I was a wild kid, a cop killer in their eyes—plus I had an escape attempt from Kew Gardens on my jacket. And the result was I got a steady diet of buckwheats. *That's what we call the little things they do to harass you, to make you miserable. Several times during those first few months they would come into my cell at night and begin tearing down my stuff. They didn't need an excuse. And then when I started up with them, which I usually did—I'd throw a punch or something—before you know it, the whole fuckin' cell would be in a shambles.*

The Death House was a vicious-looking place, and the pressure, the mental anguish, was always with you. It was a bad scene. It's not the scene where you crumble. It's never that. It's just the pressure. Never knowing when you might be next. Seeing your neighbors going one at a time. It was real easy to slip into a form of self-pity. In fact, it was irresistible sometimes, even though it would be days of sheer agony trying to snap yourself out. Now try and imagine putting twenty guys in that situation under the same fuckin' roof.

To be honest with you, that's where me and Baldy made a helluva difference. Single-handed, we introduced humor into the Death House. We got the guys pepped up. To me humor is always the best thing when you're facing danger. It helps you hang onto the difference between fearing something *and being* afraid. *Of course I feared death—every day for two and a half years. I was suffering like a bastard. But I wasn't* afraid *of it. I wasn't afraid to deal with it or go after it if I had to. And in terms of our day-to-day survival, that was the biggest fuckin' difference in the whole world.*

* * * *

As far as his legal predicament was concerned, Jerry resolutely chose to look on the bright side. Not that the ins and outs of it made a great deal of sense to him, but he knew enough to be sure that they hadn't gotten him *right.* He also had a great deal of confidence in his new, high-priced attorney, and his hopes soared even higher on June 5, 1963, when Delvecchio was finally acquitted—Jerry and Portelli following the case in the newspapers that Wiggins would bring in for them every evening when the shift changed at 7 P.M.

"Fortunes of war," Portelli shrugged when Jerry finished reading him the article announcing the verdict. But Jerry saw quite a bit more to it than that. In the first place, he just couldn't get over the fact that Delvecchio had jacked himself out of the situation pretty much on his own. No question he had a good lawyer. But the only reason his case got severed was the sustained impression he had made on Judge Leibowitz during the course of the original trial. It was Delvecchio himself who had planted the seeds of doubt in the old man's mind, simply by standing up at the table and yelling his head off until the message finally began to sink in. The first double police homicide in twenty years, the toughest judge on the county court bench, and this guy Delvecchio gets himself off with sheer lung power. And in the second place, with Linda Manzione's testimony against them now discredited, their appeal, Jerry hoped, would now sail through without a hitch.

Their next-door neighbor on the right wasn't so sure of that, however, and he certainly knew a lot more law than Jerry did. His name was Gene Probst, and he was in for a string of robbery-murders in Rockland County—a homicidal spree that had received even more than the usual amount of sensational publicity. Probst had been widely vilified in the press as a cold-blooded killer, a man with an unshakable belief in the necessity of eliminating *all* the witnesses, a man who even felt obliged, on one occasion, to whack out the family cat. He had a platoon of fancy lawyers working on his case, however, and they would eventually succeed in having his conviction thrown out on the grounds of prejudicial pretrial publicity. He was retried in June, 1964, at which time he became one of only two men in Sing Sing history to be convicted twice for the same murders and to be sentenced to die on both occasions.

He was a huge, bald-headed man with thick, Coke-bottle glasses, a fondness for roasted peanuts, and a fierce hatred for the lone sex offender in the group, a guilt-ridden twenty-eight-year-old rapist named Roland Fillmore, who was housed in the cell nearest the Watch Office. Probst was convinced that Fillmore received all kinds of preferential treatment from the hacks, and he liked to keep an eye on that cell with a small, stainless steel "mirror" thrust between the bars, shrieking at the top of his lungs whenever he saw anything unusual going down between Fillmore and the guards.

And then in the next breath Probst would be spouting law. He had a couple of law books in his cell, including the *State Code of Criminal Procedure,* and he spent a lot of time and lung power analyzing the legal chances of those around him. As far as Linda Manzione's retraction was concerned, he assured Jerry and Portelli that it wouldn't make a damn bit of difference. "Forget about it," he told them. "All they've got to do is find that the weight of the evidence still favored conviction beyond a reasonable doubt. They aren't going to monkey around with a cop-killing case," he chortled. "It's the unwritten law."

9

The general living conditions in the Death House were truly horrendous. They had all-steel cells in there, and believe me, there's nothing hotter in the summer or colder in the winter than an all-steel cell. The noise was another big problem rattling down them metal corridors. There was a big loudspeaker for the radio, and every day in the summertime they used to have the ball games on real loud. I hated the fuckin' Dodgers. All that chitchat about change-ups and batting averages used to drive me wild.

We got thirty minutes' yard time a day, supervised one-on-one by some hack in a cage. Tiny little yard. You could throw a basketball around if you had one, otherwise just sit on the ground. Plus you had to do your laundry on the way in and out. There was a clothesline right by the shower, and by the end of the day, everybody's underwear would be lined up there drying. We used to tell Baldy his shorts looked like a tent. "They must've been made by Omar the Tentmaker," Probst would tell him.

At first, all I really cared about was keeping the day moving for myself. I guess that's the main reason me and Baldy played a lot of cards. We couldn't see each other, but we could see the cards if we placed 'em face up on the floor between the bars. Only problem was, Baldy used to cheat. He used to have extra cards socked away, and I'd be watching as they came out onto the pile. Every once in a while I used to catch him red-handed, and he'd say, "So what? What's the difference? It's only a game." Sonofabitch used to cheat in the Death House!

I played cards with Wiggins a lot, too, especially when he worked the late shift. To tell you the truth, I liked fuckin' Wiggins even though he was a cop. Mostly 'cause he showed concern for people under the circumstances.

One night he came on and he said, "Listen, we're gonna have a new game down here. I'm gonna donate the cigarettes, and whoever wins at bingo is gonna walk away with five packs of cigarettes tonight." Turned out to be a very popular game. Wiggins would make up the cards, the regular bingo cards, and he would shake them in a shoe box and call out the numbers. Whoever won, won. Out of his own pocket, he'd slip the guy five packs. The funny thing is he'd never let Baldy win. He used to let him hang on one number all the time, and Baldy would go nuts. "I gotta win, I gotta win, I almost got it," he'd be screaming. And then all of a sudden somebody else would call out "Bingo," and drive Baldy up the fuckin' wall.

We had another guy used to work the midnight shift we called the Genius. I was pretty good at card tricks in those days—still am, as a matter of fact—and one night the Genius comes over and starts hanging around, watches me practicing there in the cell. Must've been around the middle of July of that first year. After a coupla minutes he says, "Jerry, do that last trick again, willya? Real slow. I got some people comin' over to the house next week, and I wanna show off a little bit, y'know?" "Why should I show you a fuckin' card trick?" I told him. "You never do any fuckin' stuff for us in here." "Whatta you got in mind?" he asks. "How about some fuckin' sandwiches or cold cuts," I told him, "a couple of pizzas?" "Oh, no," he says, "it's against the regulations." "Well, it's against the regulations to show you a fuckin' card trick," I said. He just walked away.

Five minutes later he's back. "Tell you what," he says. "You show me that card trick and I'll bring you in a meatball hero, awright?"

Anyhow, that's the way it got started. For six months straight we were getting food like that. I used to score for everybody. We'd get together and plan the order in advance—baked clams, eggplant parmigiana, you name it.

One night he even brought in a couple of bottles of J & B strapped to his leg. It was Mother's Day, and I guess he was feeling a little compassionate. Believe me, we all went fuckin' nuts, wasted everybody. Six A.M. *Lieutenant Rauch comes stalking down the gallery, sees everybody draped over the bunks with their tongues hanging out. "What the hell is going on in here?" he roars, and me and Baldy barely got time to smash the bottles and flush them down the toilet. Anyhow, Rauch cracks my cell, starts sifting through all my stuff, and finally comes up with a clam shell from the night before. "Where'd this come from?" he roars. "A sea gull dropped it on the yard," I told him. "I use it for an ashtray sometimes, you mind?" "A sea gull dropped this?" he says. "That's right," I told him. "I seen it with my own eyes." "There aren't any clams in the Hudson River, Rosenberg," he says. "And there aren't any sea gulls, either." "Well, maybe he flew with it all the way from Long Island," I told him. "How the hell do I know?"*

You better believe that was the last we ever saw of the Genius. Rauch had him transferred to one of the gun towers and that was the end of it.

On September 12, 1964, just as Gene Probst had predicted, the New York State Court of Appeals denied Jerry's appeal, dismissing Edelbaum's arguments in a tersely worded, three-page opinion. Jerry's reaction was one of disgust, disbelief, and sheer desperation. But what made it especially difficult to swallow was a newspaper clipping that Wiggins had shown him several weeks before, a society-page photograph of Edelbaum in Florida, smiling broadly at a racehorse in the saddling paddock at Hialeah.

"Where'd you get this piece of garbage, Pa?" Jerry shouted at his father when he and Rose made an emergency visit the following day.

Lou eased himself down on the seat in the visiting cell, his top-of-the-line B. Altman's suit beautifully fitted and pressed as always. "This is a famous lawyer, Jerry," Lou told him wearily. "We just received a letter here where he says—"

"Famous for what?" Jerry shot back.

"He's still filing motions, Jerry," Lou told him gingerly, "still fighting for time. He's going to take it straight up to the Supreme Court, he says. Meanwhile he's got some other issues he wants to raise in the Court of Appeals, and he still thinks you've got a helluva chance."

"Terrific," Jerry said. "How come he blew the appeal?"

"I'm not a lawyer, Jerry . . ."

"You're going to have to talk to him, Lou," Rose interjected, unable to reach out and touch her son because of the metal screen and the four-foot gap between them. "And if he won't listen—"

Lou whirled on her in exasperation. "I can't tell the man how to practice law," he said.

"Well, you can certainly inform him that we expect a little more effort," Rose told him heatedly.

And so it went for most of the visit, a round robin of mutual recriminations and despair, all three of them dizzy and wrung out from the futile bickering.

"Did they set a new date yet, Pa?" Jerry finally asked as he struggled wearily to his feet.

"It's just a technicality," Lou told him quickly. "As soon as Edelbaum gets the papers in, they'll grant you an automatic stay."

"I asked you for the date!" Jerry roared, furious at being treated like a child.

"February third," Lou told him in a whisper. "But I swear to God, Jerry, it's nothing to get upset about."

Wiggins escorted him slowly back down the gallery, past the shower stalls and the varnished oak door that led to the execution chamber; past the tiny exercise yard, where Portelli was stretched out on a bench in the thin December sun.

Jerry glanced into the cell next to his own and stared at Probst for a moment. "Lemme take a look at one of the law books, willya, Gene?" he said. "I think I'm gonna fire my lawyer."

The law book that Gene Probst furtively slipped through the bars that afternoon was entitled *Volume 66, Part 2* of the *Consolidated Laws of the State of New York.* It ran to 612 densely printed pages, and along with four other volumes of roughly equal length and complexity, it set forth a body of law known as the New York State Code of Criminal Procedure.

It was a grim-looking, badly printed volume with a mottled black cover and flaky gold lettering on the spine, full of bewildering cross-references, strange-looking symbols and index numbers, and reams and reams of archaic legal gibberish. The reason Gene Probst had it in his possession, however, was that it contained everything the state had to say on two subjects of vital interest to every prisoner on Death Row—a chapter entitled "General Provisions in Relation to the Punishment of Crimes" and another chapter entitled "Of Appeals."

If Jerry was looking for easy answers, he certainly didn't find them here. He opened at random to Section 505 of Title XI ("The Death Penalty—Infliction by Current of Electricity") and read through the dense, convoluted prose with a sense of absolute mystification. He set the book down in frustration and bounced around the cell for a few minutes, razzing the guard on duty down the hall. But he couldn't get a rise out of the guy, and he finally picked up the book again, looking for anything that at least made a little sense. He chuckled his way through a section entitled "If female convict is pregnant, warden of state prison to impanel a jury of physicians." And then, in the "Appeals" section that followed, he hit a long, relatively straightforward passage that truly piqued his interest:

> Every person accused of a crime is entitled to have a fair and impartial trial before an unbiased court and unprejudiced jury, regardless of any preconceived opinion that may exist as to the conclusiveness of the evidence against him.

A little further on he found another passage, this one underlined in red pencil.

> Where it appears that there is a strong probability that bias exists throughout the community, defendant shall not be compelled to take the risk of a trial before a jury whose members might be influenced by adverse sentiments—sentiments which the jurors may not even be cognizant of themselves. In such a case, defendant shall be granted a change of venue.

The main problem here, of course, was the legal vocabulary. And while Probst was willing to fill him in on the meaning of *cognizant* and *venue,* he was no help whatsoever with a seemingly contradictory passage several pages deeper into the book.

Clearly the first thing Jerry needed was a legal dictionary, and Wiggins managed to sneak one in for him several days later. In the meantime he had continued to pore over the law book, mostly at night when things were quiet, every once in a great while extracting some morsel of legal reasoning that seemed to bear on his chances for survival. He underlined practically every third word in the homicide section, and soon he had filled most of a spiral-bound notebook with definitions and cross-references to other sections of the book. But all he was really able to absorb were isolated bits and pieces, many of them seemingly contradictory. And like most of the tens of thousands of other prisoners who at one time or another have picked up a law book in hopes of finding a way out, he quickly found himself face to face with the bottomless pit of his own ignorance, instead.

It was a view that Jerry had been forced to contemplate many times over the years, a view that frightened and upset him and that he had devised a vast repertoire of psychological devices in order to avoid. But this time his response was totally out of character. Instead of distracting himself with delinquent schemes and defiant ranting as he always had in the past—instead of sinking into passive acceptance of the fate that now seemed all but inevitable—he set a goal for himself unlike any he had ever dreamed of before. "I accepted the fact that I was going to die," he says. "But still I was going to fight. Never too late for that. And the way I was going to fight was the law."

On one level I guess it was a way of convincing myself that they could never hurt me. Like religion or body building, which a lot of guys were into. A way of strengthening myself, trying to gain some leverage over this force that was slowly eating me alive.

On another level, of course, it was just something to keep your sanity, something to do—like a giant crossword puzzle to occupy your mind. Always with the hope of getting out. A one-in-ten-million shot.

Knowing me, if the administration had made it easy, I might never have taken it up. Fortunately, a lot of it turned out to be either against the rules or an insult to their authority—or both. It also turned out to be a pretty good way to keep from living in the past. Otherwise I was just thinking about the streets all the time—food and broads and parties. All the different people and holidays you wish you were out there for. It could drive you crazy in a week.

But with the law I began to turn my mind toward getting even in court. I could lose myself in a law book for hours at a time, almost like a form of self-hypnosis. And for those hours, at least, I began to believe I had a future.

My parents were terrific. They came through for me with everything I needed, especially encouragement. They made it seem possible. Not only that there could be a way to beat the case legally but that I could actually study hard and make something of myself. That I still had a chance.

During the day Jerry lived and breathed for his yard time. When the weather was good, he would spend most of those thirty minutes stretched out flat on his back in the sun, positioned in such a way that he could almost lose sight of the concrete cage that surrounded him.

He also spent a lot of time talking through the bars to the guy in the other yard alongside. More often than not it was a slender, fifty-two-year-old former alcoholic and strip-joint cashier named Freddie Woods—an accused holdup murderer who had been in the Death House longer than anyone and who was only now beginning to run out of appeals. Woods was an intense, thick-featured man with curly, graying hair, a high forehead, and a pair of incredible blue-green eyes that gave him an immediate silent advantage in almost any encounter. But over a period of several months a gentle and curiously intellectual friendship slowly began to evolve between them.

Freddie Woods had spent well over half his life in one kind of lockup or another. And over the years he had arrived at a rather remarkable set of firsthand conclusions. "All the brutalization and dehumanization you see in these prisons is for a reason," he would tell Jerry as they sat back to back with the wall between them, their voices carrying easily through a small barred window nearby. "It's part of the system to take these young guys and break them down, and then to send them back into society so crazy and violent to where they're gonna commit even worse crimes than they did before. That's why there's nothin' prison officials like better than a crime wave," he would laugh. " 'Cause that's the only way they're gonna get more guns and more money."

Woods also kept a scrapbook of articles and clippings on the inner workings of the criminal-justice system, one of which had a headline that read, U.N. COMMISSION FINDS AMERICAN PRISONS FALL BELOW STANDARDS OF GENEVA CONVENTION. But his favorite article had been given to him by his lawyer—a clipping from *The New York Times* that reported on a study conducted by two sociologists from Cornell University. They had carefully analyzed the crime rates within the State of New York over a seventy-year period from 1890 to 1960. And they had found that on the average there had been two *additional* homicides committed somewhere in the state during the thirty-day period following each of the 695 executions at Sing Sing. The real message conveyed by an execution is one of lethal vengeance, the sociologists had concluded. The death penalty clearly has a brutalizing effect on the entire society, they said, *provoking* violence in some hideous way rather than deterring it.

By the middle of that first summer, Jerry had acquired a small stack of law books, most of them flopping around without a binding since Death House suicide regulations required that all staples be removed before the books were actually delivered. One of them was an eight-hundred-page textbook on criminal law written by Herbert M. Cummins, a professor of law at the University of Virginia. And it was to the section of Cummins's book entitled "Offenses Against the Person" that Jerry understandably directed his closest attention—locking himself in nightly combat with those private demons that had always crippled his endeavors in the past.

The brainpower had no doubt been there all along, though pathologically misdirected and underutilized. What was new was an insatiable appetite for some kind of legitimate accomplishment. Something he could point to with a little pride, something other than a batch of headlines and a death sentence—and the dubious distinction of having kept his mouth shut when it really counted, a distinction that no one outside his own little circle of Brooklyn reprobates could even know about or comprehend.

And so, slowly and painfully—and with the benefit of many hours of spirited colloquy with Gene Probst down the hall—Jerry finally began to organize a few of the isolated bits and pieces of legal esoterica he had been collecting into something that began to resemble a piece of the whole.

The more he read and understood, the more outraged he became. For one of the most basic precepts of the Anglo-American legal system—and one that Cummins hammered away at over and over—was that for a crime to have been committed, the state must first be able to establish some connection between the criminal act itself (the *actus reus)* and the state of mind *(mens rea)* of the perpetrator. "No one," Jerry read over and over, "can be convicted of a crime he did not *intend* to commit."

One of the few exceptions to this fundamental principle, Jerry came to realize, was the felony-murder rule—the statute under which he had been sentenced to death for a pair of homicides that the prosecution freely admitted he hadn't even known were taking place. Clearly they could never have established a connection between his *mens rea* on the eighteenth of May and the *actus reus* that was splashed all over the front pages of the *Daily News*. But in his case—because of the felony-murder rule—they didn't even have to try.*

It was a doctrine, he discovered, that had originated nearly a thousand years ago in Anglo-Saxon common law, at a time when virtually *all* felonies were punishable by death and the prevailing judicial philosophy was that criminals might as well be hanged for stealing a sheep as a lamb. But in England itself, the rule had fallen into disuse by the end of the nineteenth century. And it had been abolished outright there in 1957, on the grounds that it necessarily resulted in cruel and unusual punishment and that it "eroded the relation between criminal liability and moral culpability." Even Cummins couldn't hide his contempt for this particular law, concluding his discussion with a quotation from Oliver Wendell Holmes: "It is revolting to have no better reason for a rule of law than that it was laid down at the time of Henry IV," Holmes wrote in 1897. "It is still more revolting if the grounds upon which it was laid down have vanished long since, and the rule simply persists from a blind imitation of the past."

Jerry, of course, had his own theory about why the statute remained on the books. In his view, it was a stool-pigeon law, pure and simple. And he knew from personal experience that cops and prosecutors were totally dependent on the leverage it provided in breaking suspects down and eliciting testimony—often perjured testimony—in cases that might otherwise be too difficult to crack.

"This fuckin' law ain't even constitutional!" he told Gene Probst one day after a week-long struggle with the Bill of Rights. "It's an

* The felony-murder rule simply states that all persons convicted of a felony during which a murder takes place are responsible for that murder as if they had pulled the trigger themselves. In one celebrated case in Rhode Island in 1958, a holdup man was actually sentenced to death for the murder of his crime partner, who had been shot through the heart by the owner of the liquor store they were attempting to rob.

abridgment of my constitutional rights to due process and equal protection under the Fifth and Fourteenth amendments."

"Good for you, Jerry," Probst told him with a patronizing chuckle. "I guess they're just gonna have to cut you loose."

"I'm serious," Jerry shot back, fumbling through his stack of papers. "I got a law-review article right here where it says, quote, 'the irrebuttable presumption of malice inherent in the felony-murder doctrine does not comport with the constitutional requirement that the state prove every element of the crime beyond a reasonable doubt,' unquote!"

There was a derisive chorus of laughter from both ends of the tier. "Shut the hell up, willya, Jerry?" Portelli called out to him from the cell next door. "Every fuckin' word out of your mouth these days is nine syllables long."

But underneath the laughter and the put-downs, there was a growing sense of appreciation for Jerry all up and down the line. Here was a guy who was actually doing something with his life, who was getting *stronger* rather than *weaker*—a man who was choosing to light a candle rather than curse the darkness.

And sometimes when he couldn't study and he yelled and screamed about the noise, they'd even hit the locks and tell the hack to turn off the radio for a little while. "Atta boy, Jerry," they would call out to him. "You need anything else, you just give a holler." For on some level they all realized that through the law, Jerry was also discovering a brand-new way to create some distance between himself and the day-to-day grasp of the system that was slowly destroying them all. *You can keep it!* he was saying. *I didn't ask to come here! It ain't my fuckin' prison!*

And even the most hopeless and guilt-ridden of his neighbors had to respect him for that.

* * * *

Freddie Woods went to the chair on April 15, 1963. He had spent the previous twenty-four hours in a state of remarkable fatalistic calm, joking quietly as he sat on a shiny oak stool in the middle of the tier, submitting to the last haircut of his life. Jerry watched in awe-struck silence, wincing in spite of himself as the barber gouged out the three little bald spots that would be greased with electroconductive salve and to which the electrodes leading from the helmet would later be attached. But Freddie Woods never even batted an eyelash. "Gentlemen," he told his captive audience with a smile, "tonight you will have the opportunity to witness an experiment designed to measure the effect of electricity on Woods."

They were all hanging on every twist and turn of the preparations, listening carefully as Woods ordered his final meal and specified his final request. And later, as the afternoon wore on, they watched as a steady stream of official visitors paraded nervously in and out: a doctor, a priest, the warden himself—and finally Woods's closest relative, a cousin from South Carolina who'd been traveling all night on the bus.

Through it all Freddie Woods's composure never cracked. As the afternoon wore on, he wrote a few letters and nibbled at the pot-roast dinner they'd ordered for him from a restaurant in town. And then with less than an hour to go, he gathered together his personal belongings in the time-honored Death House tradition, and he began passing them through the bars all up and down the tier, any of the inmates free to keep what he wished.

I was five cells away, and by the time the stuff got to me, all that was left was a shoeshine kit and the scrapbook full of clippings. Both of which got trashed in the Attica riot.

They came for him at nine fifty-five on the nose, and I watched every step he took. You could hear the generators revving up and the exhaust fans in the ceiling roaring to carry away the smoke. But Freddie never looked back. There was a tremendous sense of dignity about him all the way, and I'll always carry with me the sight of him disappearing through that door—with the chair just waiting for him and the leather straps coiled neatly on the arms.

A few minutes later the lights dimmed for twenty seconds. There was a brief pause, and then they dimmed again—this time for the full two minutes.

It was a terrible night. And that's when I finally realized the state wasn't playing games.

10

Despite all his blustering and legal bombast, Jerry, of course, had not actually gone out and fired his lawyer. But as the months went by and still no word from the Court of Appeals, he had begun to pepper Edelbaum with letters full of suggestions and reminders and advice. One week he'd see the long delay as a hopeful sign, and his letter would be nothing more than a euphoric, convoluted analysis of that possibility. But the next week gloom would have descended once again, and his letter would be full of procedural questions as well as new strategies he'd just dreamed up and drafts of appeals language on points he was sure Edelbaum had overlooked.

Jerry never received a single reply. But once on a visit his father proudly told him that he'd gotten a phone call from Edelbaum that week, who'd said that he was receiving the letters regularly and was very impressed.

"Impressed!" Jerry roared back at him across the four-foot gap. "Well, maybe Mr. Edelbaum don't realize it yet, but I've been working on this fuckin' case full-time!"

The Court of Appeals finally bestirred itself, rose up on its elderly, conservative haunches, and issued a new opinion in the case of *People*

v. *Rosenberg & Portelli* on March 11, 1965. And as Jerry opened the letter, sitting there hunched over on the backless stool, this, in part, is what he read

COURT OF APPEALS OF NEW YORK
15 N.Y. 2d 235

William Sonenshine and Maurice Edelbaum for appellants. Aaron E. Koota, Dist. Atty. (Aaron Nussbaum, Brooklyn, of counsel) for respondent.

PER CURIAM:

1) We find the proof adduced upon the trial is more than sufficient to support the jury's verdict that the defendants are guilty of felony murder and, since we find no errors of law, we would have no occasion to write were it not for the testimony of police brutality which the record before us contains.

On May 18, 1962, two police officers, Detectives Luke Fallon and John Finnegan, were shot and killed in Brooklyn during the course of a hold-up when they sought to apprehend the robbers. Upon the trial, held in January of 1963, one of the principal witnesses against the defendants was a small-time criminal by the name of Richard Melville. On cross-examination, Melville testified that detectives had picked him up several days after the shootout and had taken him to a police station for questioning. He stated that, although he first denied knowing anything about the crime, he later told police substantially the same story that he had just recited in court. But he also declared that he had done so only after he had been held in custody overnight and had been severely beaten and tortured—and that he would never have cooperated with the police had they not abused him in this manner. It is the defendants' contention that Melville's testimony should have been stricken once it appeared that his statement had been coerced by police.

2) Although we deprecate official lawlessness with all the emphasis at our command, we do not believe that such conduct warrants a holding that Melville's testimony should have been stricken and excluded from the record. Testimony given from the witness stand by a witness who was, some eight months earlier, compelled by police brutality to give a statement implicating a defendant stands on a different footing from an out-of-court confession coerced from a defendant. While the latter will be excluded as a matter of law, the testimony of a witness like Melville—who, although previously forced to make a pre-trial statement, now asserts that his testimony at the trial is truthful—is for the consideration and appraisal of the jury. The requirements of law are met if the fact of such earlier coercion or other official lawlessness is disclosed to the jurors so that they may pass upon the witness' veracity and credibility and determine whether the testimony given in open court is truthful and worthy of consideration.

In reaching the conclusion we do, we cannot condemn too strongly the shocking and reprehensible conduct on the part of the police about which Melville testified and we simply note that an appropriate forum is available for these charges of misconduct.

Judgments of conviction affirmed.

DESMOND, C.J., and DYE, FULD, VAN VOORHIS, BURKE, SCILEPPI and BERGAN, JJ., concur.

Jerry folded the papers back up and stuffed them in the envelope. "Hey, Baldy," he called out quietly. "You still there, buddy?"

"What's our next move, Jerry?" Portelli asked him, his voice overheated and barely under control.

Jerry unfolded the papers and read through the first paragraph one more time. The phrases "proof . . . more than sufficient" and "no errors of law" seemed to fly off the page and scream at him, taunting him with their utter falseness.

He got to his feet and stared out the window, where a ratty-looking Sing Sing blue jay was pecking in the frozen dust. "The law is a rotten science, my man," Jerry said.

Maurice Edelbaum came in to see him ten days later—energetic and very busy and once again sporting a recent Palm Beach tan. "Well, Jerry," he said as a pair of guards ushered his client into the second-floor conference room, "I guess we didn't have much luck with the Court of Appeals, did we?"

Jerry said nothing, flipped a thick folder full of notes and legal ideas down on the worktable, and waited until the guard withdrew. He was pissed off at Edelbaum already—at his suntan and his Florentine leather briefcase and his chitchatty style. But he had spent a week of sleepless nights preparing for this meeting, and he didn't want to blow it with an angry remark right off the top.

"From a strictly legal standpoint, Jerry, I just want to make sure you realize there's nothing to be terribly concerned about." Edelbaum smiled, motioning him to a chair alongside.

For Maurice Edelbaum the visit was strictly *pro forma.* He knew exactly what he needed and where he was going with the case. For the thing that had attracted him in the first place had been the Melville question. And he was determined now to take it straight up to the United States Supreme Court.

He even planned to use much of the same language he had used in his brief to the Court of Appeals—lovely, round, Holmesian language

Jerry, age twenty-four, on his release from state prison in 1961, after serving four years for third-degree robbery. He was to remain on the streets for less than a year. (NY Daily News Archive via Getty Images)

DAILY NEWS

NEW YORK'S PICTURE NEWSPAPER ®

5¢

Vol. 43. No. 286 New York 17, N.Y., Thursday, May 24, 1962★ WEATHER: Mostly cloudy, windy, warm.

3D MAN GIVES UP TO NEWS

Rosenberg Surrenders in Cop Killing

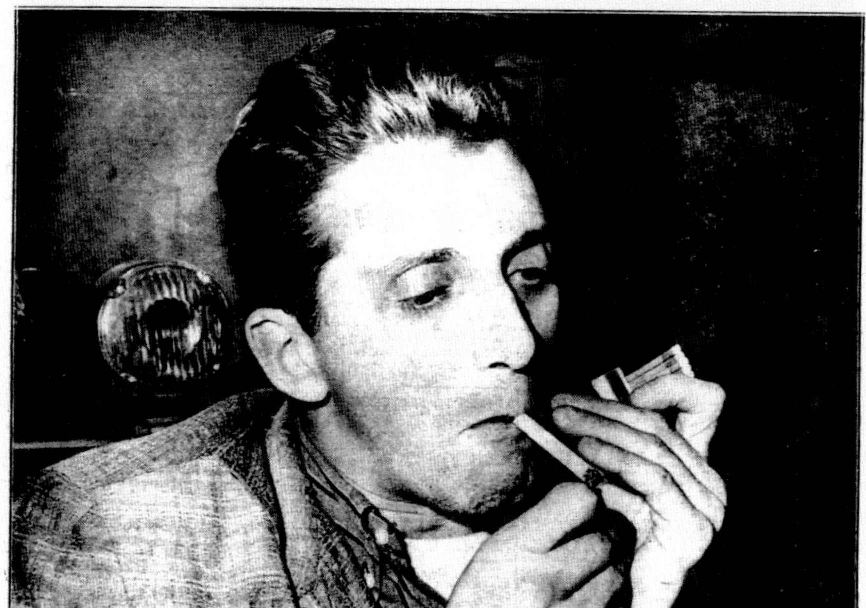

Jerome Rosenberg lights a cigaret after giving himself up to THE NEWS last night.—*Story on page 3*

Jerry "surrenders" in the *Daily News* offices on Forty-second Street. He gives his story to reporters Sidney Kline (right) and Nathan Kanter. (John Duprey / NY Daily News via Getty Images)

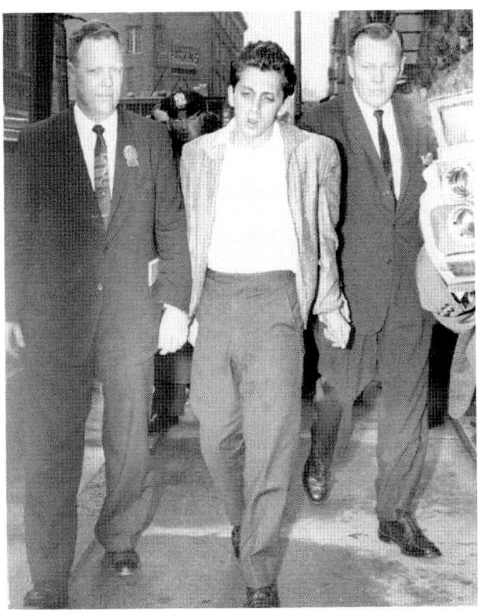

Handcuffed to two detectives, Jerry is perp-walked into the Sixty-sixth Precinct in Brooklyn. (New York Post Archives / Contributor / Getty Images)

Jerry is booked for felony murder as a *Daily News* photographer records the scene. (Harry Ransom Center / The University of Texas at Austin.)

Jerry and his co-defendants, Anthony Delvecchio (left) and Anthony Portelli (right), May 24, 1962. (Alec Byrne)

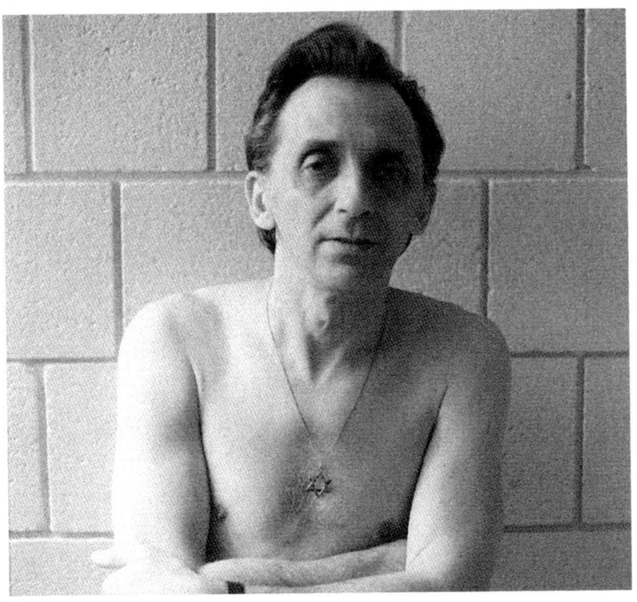

Jerry at the Metropolitan Correctional Center, New York City, 1982. (Alec Byrne)

Jerome Rosenberg, Esq. The first New York State prisoner to earn a law degree. (Alec Byrne)

Jerry in his cell, Auburn Correctional Facility, 1988. (David Grunfeld)

Jerry, still wearing waist chains from the prison van, represents himself in court, June 23, 1988. (David Grunfeld)

that he was as proud of as anything he'd ever done. "While precedent may be lacking in this case," he had written, "principle most assuredly is not. The entire history of our jurisprudence, as distilled from reported opinions, militates against condoning judgments like this one that rest upon official violence and disorder." Several pages later he had delivered himself of another ringing paragraph in which he staked out the basis for his constitutional claim:

> There are fundamental and over-riding considerations which rip asunder the very underpinnings upon which Rosenberg's conviction now rests. We refer, of course, to the vibrant frontiers of the Due Process Clause in our State and Federal Constitutions which embody not only the ancient English view but the more current and broader concept that official brutality in any form is tainted by its own self-defeating poison.

Edelbaum, of course, had good reason to feel that the high court might be receptive to these arguments. For in recent years it had substantially broadened the rights of suspects and defendants in many areas that he found far less compelling than this one.

To Jerry, on the other hand, it just didn't feel right to be staking everything on an issue where they had already been beaten once. But even more important was his newfound legal certainty that the trial had been full of *dozens* of substantive errors—errors that he was sure Edelbaum should now be raising in the state courts on a writ of collateral attack.

"What about the fact that they brainwashed the eyewitnesses?" Jerry asked him heatedly. "What about Linda and the recantation? What about the bias against me from the bench?"

Edelbaum really didn't want to get into this. He had better things to do than argue criminal procedure with some flake on Death Row.

Besides, he simply had a gut feeling about which way the Supreme Court was headed. And his gut feelings, he liked to think, based as they were on years of study and specialized legal practice, were very often right on the money.

"Jerry, Jerry, Jerry," Edelbaum sighed. "You're just going to have to take my word on this, okay? Believe me, I've been through that transcript a million times." He clicked open his briefcase and handed Jerry a sheaf of papers, one of which called for a twenty-five-hundred-dollar supplement to his original retainer.

"Yeah? Well, what about the cover-up of the skin test where they proved I didn't have none of that tax-stamping ink on my hands?" Jerry asked him heatedly, tossing the papers down in the middle of the table. "How come you never raised that?"

It was an excellent point, and one that Jerry would come very close to winning on his own years later. For his face and hands had been swabbed meticulously right after his surrender in an attempt to find particles of the indelible tax-stamping ink with which the thin bandit's getaway towel had been soaked. No traces of the ink had been found. But, as Jerry had pointed out to Edelbaum in one of his recent letters, Martin and DA Selzer had hushed up the tests and had failed to divulge this exculpatory evidence, as the law required, at the "discovery" hearing six weeks before the trial.

"That's called passive nondisclosure, Jerry," Edelbaum told him wearily. "It's almost never sufficient to overturn the verdict."

"It was plenty sufficient in *Simmons* v. *Kentucky.*"

"That was a civil case. Look, Jerry, I know you've been reading some law books. I can understand your impulse to get involved . . ."

"But I don't know nothin', is that what you're trying to say?"

"I'm saying I'm thirty years and two legal degrees ahead of you," Edelbaum told him, his patience finally beginning to wear thin. "And

I'm also saying that a little knowledge can be a very dangerous thing!"

Jerry just glared at him, fighting off the impulse to tear up the new retainer agreement that lay in front of him.

"You're in a very dangerous legal situation, Jerry," Edelbaum finally told him, his tone suddenly stone-cold sober.

"That's not at all what you said when I walked in here, is it?" Jerry asked him grimly.

Edelbaum said nothing and then finally averted his gaze.

"Didn't you tell me that from a legal standpoint there was nothing to be terribly concerned about?" Jerry insisted. "Isn't that what you said?"

Edelbaum took a breath, groping for a way to placate this lunatic. But he certainly hadn't gotten where he'd gotten by backing down in the heat of battle or indulging his clients' fevered egos.

"I must have misspoken myself, Jerry," was all he finally said.

Jerry stared at him for a long, uncertain moment, his fate dangling palpably in the balance. And then he bowed to the odds, unscrewed the top of Maurice Edelbaum's fancy Mont Blanc fountain pen, and signed on for his final appeal.

A couple of months earlier I'd started following a case in the papers that would ultimately affect every one of us in the most amazing way. Of course, we didn't realize that until much later. At first it was the way the cops made the arrest that intrigued me, and some of the legal issues that came up in the pretrial maneuvering. Probst was following the thing, too, and we'd often strategize about it back and forth.

It was the case of an eighteen-year-old black kid named George Whitmore, who had been accused in a highly publicized murder case in Brooklyn and who had been more or less brainwashed into confessing by the same kind of Brooklyn cops who'd gone after me and Baldy. This kid was like half-retarded, and they just flat-out lied to him—they told him the murder victims were still alive and had identified him. They totally fucked with his mind, and he ended up confessing to a whole string of murders and sex crimes. It was outrageous. Some cops even came down from Boston hoping he might be the Boston Strangler.

Anyhow, he gets convicted at the first trial, which was a rape case, and right before he's about to go on trial for murder, his mother switches lawyers. She gets some storefront guy from Brownsville who puts her in touch with one of the biggest and most politically connected-up criminal lawyers in Brooklyn: a guy named Stanley J. Reiben, whose law partner happens to be a Brooklyn assemblyman named Bertram Podell.

Suddenly, mostly because of Reiben, the press starts to pay attention to the Whitmore case again, and when it eventually turns out he spent the entire day of the shootings at his sister's house in Cape May, New Jersey, the editorial writers start to go crazy. Before you know it the indictment gets dropped, some other guy gets arrested and convicted, and right away Podell introduces a bill to abolish the death penalty. Lots of luck, right? A bill like that's been introduced for the past eighteen years, it gets nowhere.

But to me there was always that chance. And the difference this year was the Whitmore case.

"I don't have to highlight for you the terrible effect that Whitmore's execution would have had if the falsity of his confession and the tactics used in securing it had come out after the switch had been pulled," Podell said when he introduced the bill. And a New York Times *editorial said, quote, "The ease with which the city's police used duplicitous methods in coercing a totally false confession has raised fresh doubts about the wisdom of capital punishment," unquote.*

Of course, what the papers and Podell and all the other politicians failed to take into account was the political weight of the law-enforcement pressure groups in Albany—especially the city cops, the PBA. They were beautifully organized, and they quickly got involved in the issue in the most destructive and irrational way.

About this same time I started working on a criminal law course by mail from the Massachusetts Department of Education. I saw an ad in the back of a Mechanix Illustrated *that had been kicking around for close to a year, and as far as I know, it was the first time it had ever been done from the Death House. They covered the basics pretty good, but to tell you the truth, I knew most of it already. In fact, I did the first four lessons in one night. At that point I think all I really cared about was the certificate at the end, just to prove to myself that I could still accomplish something, that it wasn't over yet.*

He was even learning something, too. For the textbook they sent him, though simplistic in its theoretical approach, was crammed with examples and case summaries—stuff that he'd need hundreds of hours in a fully stocked law library to pull together on his own. Of course, very little of it bore on his own predicament in any direct way. But more and more he was finding himself fascinated by the law in its own right. Suddenly it wasn't mumbo-jumbo anymore, and he was actually beginning to savor the delicate balance between all the legal oddities and exceptions and anachronisms on the one hand and the tightness of the definitions and the overall sense of logic and certainty on the other. And—most significant in terms of his long-range chances for survival—he was also beginning to understand how a skillful attorney could manipulate and exploit this delicate balance to create totally unexpected results.

I had to fight like a bastard for that course. In fact, the only way I found out I got in was from Wiggins. "Rauch clamped your letter from Boston," he told me one day, real hush-hush. "You do what you gotta do," he said. "Just don't put me in the middle of it, y'hear?"

I waited twenty-four hours. And then the next day when I was out on the yard, I caught sight of that sonofabitch Rauch moving real fast by the cage where the hack always sits.

"Hey, Rauch," I called out to him, "ever hear of the United States Constitution?" "Not in quite awhile," he said. "Well, you better look into it, buster," I told him. "'Cause under the First, Sixth, Eighth, and Fourteenth amendments, I got the constitutional right to take that fuckin' course."

He knew I was on solid ground, because I'd beaten him on an Article 78 in Westchester County Court a couple of months before. And sure enough, the next day the warden himself came down and gave his permission.

That first time I beat them in court, they couldn't believe it. In fact, as far as I know, it was the first time anyone had ever filed a lawsuit from the Death House. Basically what happened was they refused me a visit with my daughter on the grounds that she was underage. Now there was no such regulation in the Manual of Procedures, and I filed what's called a writ of mandamus under Article 78 of the Civil Practice Law to try and compel them to stick to the rules. It's a standard legal remedy I found in a law book my parents brought in for me, and I've used it a lot over the years. In certain situations it's the quickest, simplest way to force a public official back into line.

Anyhow, at the time I was doing ten days in a strip cell for choking a fuckin' hack through the bars. I'd been in a lot of pain from a toothache—my jaw was like all swollen up and they refused to call the dentist—and this big fat piece of shit waddled down from the Watch Office, a hack named Bernheimer. He steps up to the bars, flips a letter through the tray slot, and starts laughing when he sees the size of my jaw. "Pretty soon you won't have no more pain in your tooth, Rosenberg," he tells me. "Twenty-five hundred volts is the answer to all your problems."

I was so fuckin' furious I grabbed him by the throat. It wasn't easy, because you can only fit through so much. But I got him. I got him by the fuckin' throat. I tried to kill him. Choke him. And two other hacks ran down, they pulled him away.

Anyhow, I spent ten days in a strip cell for that—with my toothache and no clothes, just a blanket. And that's when I filed the writ of mandamus. I mailed it right out, had the papers served on the warden and everything. And ten days later he conceded to let her in before the court ruled on it.

It's the little victories like that that keep you sane.

By the middle of March 1965—more than two full years after Jerry's arrival on Death Row—the legislative ball that Bertram Podell had set in motion was slowly beginning to gather speed. On March 11, six weeks after introducing his bill to abolish capital punishment, Podell announced at a press conference that he had already lined up fifty-seven of the sixty-eight votes needed for passage in the State Assembly. But the situation in the State Senate was a good deal less hopeful, he admitted, partly because of its rural bias and partly because of the fierce opposition of the chairman of the Codes Committee there, a staunch law-and-order man from Queens named Thomas J. Duffy.

And so although the odds against its final passage were still substantial, repeal of the death penalty had finally taken a serious place on the legislative agenda. Clearly there were a number of special factors at work this year that made the legislators uniquely receptive—factors that had far more to do with politics than with the morality or legality of the issue. For one thing, there had been a bitter and very petty leadership fight in the Assembly several months before, a self-serving and convoluted squabble that many lawmakers felt had seriously damaged their credibility with the public. "This [capital punishment] is exactly the kind of issue we need right now," one anonymous legislator told the *Times,* "to make people forget all about the mess we got into last fall."

Also at work was a growing awareness that because of the possibility of indefinite appeals, the death penalty was rapidly falling into disuse anyhow, and that it had also begun to create some very serious internal problems for law enforcement. This view had been most candidly expressed by the chairman of the State District Attorney's Association in his testimony before the Codes Committee on February 23. "Most of the recent Supreme Court decisions that have hurt us," he told the panel, "particularly in the area of confessions, have resulted from cases where the death penalty was involved. In my opinion, it's just not worth it anymore," he said, "particularly when you consider that the law seems to create a morbid sense of sympathy for the defendant."

In the weeks that followed, a swelling brigade of establishment heavyweights began to fall into place behind the issue of repeal, with the *Times* eagerly trumpeting each new addition to the list: New York City Mayor Robert F. Wagner on March 4; former City Commissioner of Corrections Austin McCormick on March 8; the 3,500-member New York State Trial Lawyers Association on March 12; the board of directors of the American Civil Liberties Union on March 22. They all struck very much the same notes: that capital punishment does not protect society, does not deter crime, and does not mete out justice fairly—that innocent persons like George Whitmore might very well be executed for crimes they never committed—and that most of all, as Commissioner McCormick put it, "The death penalty is a barbaric practice that is every bit as evil as the crime it punishes."

On March 25 the subject received another heavy dose of journalistic attention when the *Times* front-page coverage of a Rockefeller news conference prominently featured a series of questions and answers dealing with Rocky's nonposition on the issue ("It's entirely up to the legislature") and whether or not he planned to stay the executions of those prisoners whose dates might come up in the meantime ("No").

Finally, on April 1, a blue-ribbon commission appointed by the legislature announced the results of its own year-long deliberations, voting 8 to 4 in favor of repeal. Their vote, of course, had no force of law in itself, but as a formal legislative recommendation, it was still expected to swing a good deal of political weight. For Podell and his law partner Stanley Reiben, however, it was a major disappointment. Not only had they been hoping for near-unanimity on the question, they were also deeply troubled by the tone of the minority report, an angry and often-fearful document announcing in unequivocal terms that the powerful law enforcement interests in the state—and their spokesmen in the legislature—would not be going down without a fight.

"There is more crime in the State of New York than anywhere else in the world," the minority report had shrieked. And it went on to say:

> The nature and complex make-up of our population, the ugly moods and attitudes which now appear to prevail among varying ethnic groups in the state, and the boldness with which atrocious crimes are committed, with less and less effort at concealment, make it entirely possible that any movement toward abolition of capital punishment at this time may be taken by the lawless masses as a signal for even further outbreaks of lawlessness—despite what statistics from other jurisdictions may or may not show.

It had come down, then, to a classic political standoff—two diametrically opposed and deeply entrenched positions, neither one with a coherent majority. It was exactly the kind of situation in which the fertile political mind instinctively turns to the possibility of compromise. But how in this particular case, the fertile minds were wondering, would it be possible to compromise with death?

It was Thomas J. Duffy, the archconservative state senator from Queens, who eventually came up with the answer six weeks later—an answer so evasive and yet so broadly acceptable that it immediately propelled the repeal bill through the State Senate by the astonishing vote of 47 to 9. The answer was *exceptions.*

11

"Exceptions!" Anthony Portelli roared when Jerry finished running the situation down for him several days later. "How come we can't get nothin' in this fuckin' joint? How come everybody gets everything but us?"

It did seem like some kind of hideous conspiracy. For the exceptions that the vote had been predicated on, Jerry quickly realized, would apply to only two of the twenty-one men on Death Row. The first exception, which had a kind of primitive logic to it, retained the death penalty for prisoners on a life sentence who killed a guard or another inmate while in prison or during the course of an escape, the argument being that something beyond life imprisonment was required in order to keep psychopathic lifers in check. But the second exception had no such judicial rationale behind it and was in fact an undisguised political handout to the powerful law enforcement pressure groups within the state. The second exception retained the death penalty for anyone who killed a *cop.*

Governor Rockefeller's reaction was only slightly less incredulous than Portelli's was. "To me it doesn't make any sense at all," Rocky announced at a news conference the following day. "If you kill a policeman, you get sent to the electric chair, if you kill a prison guard you get sent to the electric chair—but if you kill a priest or a minister you get life." He went on to say that the exceptions "torpedoed" the intent and moral principles of the bill, contradicting both the moral argument that the state has no right to take a life as well as the statistical argument that capital punishment has never been proved effective as a deterrent. But, significantly, he refused to make any statement at all on the question of whether or not he would veto the bill if it passed the Assembly in its present form.

The chances for that happening began to seem increasingly remote, however. For once the idea of exceptions had been injected into the debate, there was nowhere to draw the line. Manhattan District Attorney Frank O'Connor, for example, promptly came out in favor of repeal except for the crimes of first-degree murder, kidnapping, and treason. And with the vote in the Assembly scheduled for less than a week away, the politically potent New York State Council of Law Enforcement Officials took a position in favor of two further exceptions: murders in sexual assaults and murders of persons in a lawful occupation (for example, shopkeepers).

The debate in the Assembly finally took place on May 20, drawing near one hundred percent attendance and lasting almost five and a half hours. Each of the proposed exceptions had its own band of die-hard supporters, and as the afternoon wore on, it began to look as if the issue was so thoroughly fragmented that no possible consensus could ever emerge. There was a brief flurry of enthusiasm for a new amendment that had been offered by Assemblyman Daniel Lowenthal—an amendment that would have gotten everyone off the hook by requiring that the issue be submitted to the voters in the form of a referendum. But then a growing awareness began to set in on the floor that after months of deliberation and discussion and debate, they would all look pretty silly if they decided to duck the issue now. And so at 8:35 that evening, having sent out for supper, as they often did, the assemblymen finally voted 78 to 67 to enact the bill in exactly the same form as it had passed the Senate, with the same two exceptions, thereby ridding themselves of responsibility for the whole issue and dumping it squarely into Governor Nelson Rockefeller's highly political lap.

It didn't stay there long. "The governor will have no comment whatsoever," a spokesman pointedly told reporters the following day, "until he's had a chance to seek the advice of prominent legal and religious leaders throughout the state."

He was also, no doubt, consulting prominent political leaders as well. And if so, they were doubtless pointing out to him that many polls were showing a definite shift in the direction of repeal. The latest Gallup poll, for example, had shown a 50–50 split, a gain of 10 points within the year. And with Rocky once again casting a quadrennial eye in the direction of the Presidency, the polls were something he couldn't altogether afford to ignore. Of course, his personal instincts may well have been in sync with this trend—certainly his stated objection to the bill in the past had always been that the exceptions destroyed the sense of moral authenticity that the issue required.

But that was all beside the point now. For the issue had reached his desk in such a murky form that there was no way to predict how either course of action—signing the bill or vetoing it—would be perceived by the press, by the party leadership, and ultimately by the voters themselves. And so the decision was quietly made for Rocky to attempt to shun the spotlight on the issue altogether—to create the fewest waves possible and above all to prevent his name from becoming attached to this peculiar legislative solution one way or the other.

A week later, on June 1, Rocky announced at a general press conference that he intended to act on the death penalty bill that same day. But he deftly checkmated any questions on the subject by refusing to say what he was or was not going to do.

And then an hour later his press office announced that the bill had been signed. That wasn't the bombshell. The bombshell was that he had also decided to commute the sentences of all those currently on Death Row to life imprisonment—all those, the press release explained, except for the two who would still have been subject to capital punishment under the *new* law: Jerome Rosenberg and Anthony Portelli.

"There was no demonstration, no cheering, no yelling at each other," Warden Wilfred Denno told *The New York Times* by telephone a few minutes after the announcement. "In fact, there was no discussion at all. In my opinion life imprisonment is the greater punishment than death," he said, trying to account for the phlegmatic attitude of the inmates. "From seventy-five to eighty percent of the men who have gone to the electric chair would have preferred death to spending the rest of their lives in prison," he said. "In one sense your troubles are over when you go to the chair."

The ball game was on, as I remember, and the guys just took it nonchalant. It wasn't like you see in the movies, where everybody's happy when they get the news. It was nothing like that. In fact, they almost didn't believe it. Like it could be turned around again in another hour. Guys were relieved; don't get me wrong. The reaction was like, "Hey, look at this fuckin' break, now we can deal with it."

It was a helluva big change, though, and the day after the announcement was the only truly quiet day I ever spent on Death Row. Me and Baldy were on a fuckin' yo-yo. It was as if suddenly anything could happen, and yet for some fuckin' reason it wasn't happening to us.

The weirdest part was that on the surface nothing had really changed. The other guys were still there, every one of them, waiting for their appeals to finalize before they took the commute.

* * * *

Nevertheless, the atmosphere on Death Row had changed precipitously. For one thing, the preoccupation with suicide prevention vanished almost overnight. For another, the prisoners were allowed out on the yards two at a time now, the guards supercautious at first, watching through the bars like zookeepers introducing a pair of wild donkeys.

Jerry and Portelli, of course, were still subject to the old rules and still had to take yard time by themselves, with the devastating pressures at work on them intensified now by the fact that all their neighbors were out from under it, were going through a totally different kind of crisis, and often seemed to be regarding them with a sense of ill-disguised pity. Only Wiggins retained his ability to kid around. "What'sa matter, Jerry?" he'd ask him. "You feeling sorry for yourself today?" And then he'd burst out laughing, ducking away from whatever thrown object might be headed in his direction.

Characteristically, Jerry's reaction to this hellish situation was most definitely not one of terminal despair. Even in his legal work the pace he was setting for himself was every bit as ambitious as it was before. And there's no question that his ability to lose himself in legal abstractions must have brought some measure of relief from the relentless day-in-and-day-out compression.

In any case, he now had a small, unframed certificate from the Massachusetts Department of Education proudly taped to the wall of his cell—a form letter, really—that barely hinted at the extent of his knowledge and legal awareness, but that somehow seemed to be giving him the incentive to reach for more.

By far the most vivid proof that his mind had begun to function in a truly lawyerlike fashion, however, was his decision to send away for a copy of the repeal bill. Certainly there had been nothing in the press coverage to suggest that the wording or legal premises of the bill were anything but solid as a rock. And he also knew that the statute itself had no direct bearing on him one way or the other—that it was

Rockefeller's retroactive extension of the law that either applied or it didn't. Nevertheless, the lawyer within him had to see it in black and white. And so on July 3, 1965, he sent off a handwritten note to the Honorable Bertram Podell, c/o the State Assembly, Albany, New York, asking for a copy of the final text of the bill.

The idea that he might actually find a loophole may well have been percolating just below the surface—too dangerous to contemplate openly and too ridiculous, certainly, to talk about with anyone he knew. And yet loopholes were definitely on his mind. For his first impulse when he had read the account of the bill's passage in the State Senate was that there might possibly be some room for maneuver in the use of the term *peace officer.* Were Finnegan and Fallon in fact recognizable as *peace officers* when they burst into the store in plainclothes with their guns out? Did the term specifically include undercover agents, he wondered, or wasn't there some underlying connotation of public identifiability? He had feverishly riffled through his copy of the *Code of Criminal Procedure.* But the term *peace officer,* he found, included not only harbor masters and Onondaga County Park Rangers, but also "sworn officers of any authorized police department or force of a city, town, village, or police district"—a definition, Jerry realized with a sickening nose dive, that was clearly inclusive of undercover cops.

And so when the thin manila envelope from Podell's office finally arrived sometime during the last week of July, Jerry was determined not to get his hopes up. The only way he could handle it was to pretend that it was just another scrap of legal busywork. And so he stuck it under a pile of law books and pretended to be too tired to think.

And yet when he finally got around to opening it and found the relevant passage several days later, his entire body began to pulse with hope. For the text of the bill contained one medium-sized extra word that had never been picked up in any of the press or radio accounts that Jerry had seen or heard. The language of the exception—and he must have read it over a million times that morning—inexplicably referred to the *premeditated* murder of police officers: an offense that no one in his right mind would ever commit and a crime of which Jerry and Portelli had most definitely *not* been convicted.

Portelli heard him out in silence, taking his cue more from the excitement in Jerry's voice than from the ins and outs of the legal situation, which he had never completely understood to begin with. "Well, then, you fuckin' well better get a hold of that lawyer, Jerry," he finally said.

But at this point Jerry knew exactly where he stood. And he wasn't about to relinquish control over his destiny to *anyone*—certainly not to Maurice Edelbaum, who had already squandered so many of his best ideas in the past. And so he sat down and wrote three drafts of a letter in less than an hour, pointing out in crystal-clear legal syntax that he and Portelli had been convicted of *felony* murder—that no element of premeditation had ever been proven or even alleged—and that since they would both, therefore, *not* be subject to capital punishment under the new law, they were clearly eligible for executive clemency under the terms of the governor's official announcement of June 1.

Ten days later he received an emphatically noncommittal reply from Robert R. Douglass, Rockefeller's newly appointed chief counsel. The governor, Douglass wrote, had received Jerry's letter—but would not have an opportunity to consider the matter until a later date.

Three full months would go by before the appropriate executive opportunity would finally present itself, and another three full months beyond that before word of Rocky's decision would finally come to public attention. But when the story broke, it broke with a vengeance. Representative of press reaction was the January 27, 1966 headline, COP KILLERS SPARED; COMMUTATION TO LIFE BAFFLES LEGAL CIRCLES; SECRET ROCKY ACT KEPT D.A. IN DARK, in the *Journal-American* which devoted its entire front page to the news:

Gov. Rockefeller, under circumstances that baffled law enforcement officials closely connected to the case, has commuted the death sentences of two gunmen who shot to death two honor detectives in the 1962 holdup of a Brooklyn tobacco store, the *Journal-American* exclusively learned today.

Warden Wilfred L. Denno of Sing Sing confirmed that the pair of cop killers were removed from the Death House and transferred to other prisons "several months ago."

His statement substantiated the rumors that stunned Brooklyn legal circles yesterday—that killers Jerome Rosenberg and Anthony Portelli were saved from the electric chair last Oct. 27 by a secret document issued by the Governor.

But what remained unexplained today were these four questions:

1) Why did the Governor commute the death sentences of two cop killers when the new state law that abolishes capital punishment makes specific exceptions for cases where police or prison guards are victims?

2) Why did the Governor take the equally unusual step of acting while the U.S. Supreme Court was in the process of considering an appeal?

3) Why did the Governor not only shun the usual process in commutation applications of calling in the affected District Attorney, but actually kept the Brooklyn D.A. in the dark?

4) Why was the commutation kept secret?

Brooklyn court observers, amazed that news of the October commutation had drifted down to top officials only within the past day or so as rumor, reacted sharply to the mercy shown the slayers of Dets. Luke J. Fallon and John P. Finnegan. "I can't understand this," declared Surrogate Judge Edward S. Silver, the former head of the Brooklyn D.A.'s office at the time of the Rosenberg/Portelli trial.

"It was as brutal a killing as could be," he stressed. "They shot those two cops down in cold blood." He said that cop killers now "stand a better chance of escaping the chair than was previously believed."

Judge Silver said he "didn't attend the hearing" that traditionally takes place in the Governor's executive chamber, with the district attorney and defense lawyers presenting their arguments, and with the Governor reserving decision before making his final judgment.

However, that traditional hearing never took place, according to Brooklyn D.A. Aaron Koota.

"There wasn't a hearing," he said flatly.

Mr. Koota recalled that only yesterday he had called in assistants to discuss what position to take in consequence of the U.S. Supreme Court decision last Monday to let the Rosenberg and Portelli death sentences stand.

"It was only then that one of our assistants told us about the rumors that there had been a commutation in October," he said. "It struck me as highly unusual because as a rule the Governor would consult us. I asked the assistant to check with Albany. He later told me that the Governor had in fact commuted the sentences and that the Governor would write to me about it."

Kings County Judge Samuel S. Leibowitz, who sentenced the killers to death, noted that Gov. Rockefeller had adhered to pre-commutation custom at least to the extent of asking the sentencing judge for a recommendation.

"The Governor asked me for my recommendation and I sent him a letter," Judge Leibowitz said. But the Judge, whose unspoken views against the abolition of capital punishment are well known, declined to disclose the nature of his recommendation.

Quietly sitting out the controversy today were the two young killers, both in their twenties. Anthony Portelli, who was nabbed three days after the shooting in a Chicago motel room, is now in the Maximum Security Wing of Dannemora State Prison.

Jerome Rosenberg, who surrendered voluntarily several days later, has been transferred to Attica.

The New York Times cleared up at least some of the confusion in a front-page story the next day, pointing out that a "little known facet" of the eight-month-old repeal bill restricted the use of the death penalty to those convicted of the *premeditated* murder of police officers or prison guards. And then the story went on to quote a windy and somewhat confused statement by Podell's colleague, Brooklyn Democratic Assemblyman Joseph R. Corso. "We definitely never intended that a killer of a police officer or a prison guard should be limited to premeditated murder," Corso said. "If there's a problem here at all, it was just a slip-up on the part of the staffer who drafted the legislation. Our intent was clearly expressed in both the Senate and the Assembly—that anyone who killed a police officer in pursuit of his duty while attempting to apprehend a person during the commission of a crime should get the death penalty. Our intent was clear, positive, and unequivocal," he said. "And if there is any doubt about the so-called felony murders of a police officer or prison guard, we will make sure that any such doubt will be cleared up."

The *Times* also reported that the city's three-thousand-man Detective Endowment Association "angrily protested the clemency accorded to Rosenberg and Portelli, and urged remedial legislation to close the loophole."

Three weeks later a bill to that effect shot through both houses of the state legislature and was quietly signed into law by Governor Rockefeller on March 30.

It wasn't happy or sad, believe me when I say this. In fact, for the first couple of days it was like a complete unknown—an empty feeling, really. It was just too big to deal with all at once. I mean when he opened his letter, all Baldy said was, "Oh, shit." It was like they gave us back our future and then threw us in jail all over again.

The weirdest part about it was we left the Death House before everybody. They were all still waiting on their appeals, but I'd say most of them were happy for us. They understood what we'd been been through better than anyone.

As you can imagine, just walking out of that nutcracking place was a tremendous boost. We got vanned up the hill and put in regular solitary for ten days' mental observation, and for those ten days I was just floating.

Right away my mother came up and she could touch me on a regular visit. All those years we couldn't touch in the Death House. Plus she brought me my first food package in more than two and a half years. I must've gained ten pounds that first week.

I knew I was going to Attica by then, but it didn't concern me. I felt invincible. I felt like I'd finally done something good for myself. And for obvious reasons I was now totally hooked on the study of law.

12

We made it up there pretty fast. About seven hours. Stopped once. I had coffee and a sandwich at one of them joints where you pull off the highway. There were four hacks in the car with me, upstate hacks—Canucks, we call 'em, all potbellied and out of shape. They made a few remarks, innuendoes, really. Stuff like "They should've juiced him," and "If he fucks around up there, they'll kill him." But they didn't say nothing directly. They always play that shit, you know, real quiet. You're supposed to be scared if they don't talk too much.

We got there around four o'clock, four thirty in the afternoon. It's a gruesome-looking place from the outside, looks like a fuckin' castle. One of them says, "I don't think he's gonna like it here," or something to that effect, real sarcastic. I told him, "They're all the same to me."

They pull up at the front. I had a chain on—handcuffs and leg irons—and the steel door opens and they walk me in. There were maybe five guys there, local hacks, and they took the chains off and escorted me to a cell on the second tier of the Reception Block, which at the time was C-block. Reception's a regular two-week procedure: forty-two guys at a time, special rules, no yard time, no commissary. You're locked up twenty-one and a half hours a day.

Soon as the hacks are gone, I hear someone calling out to me. So I jump up on the bars and I look down and there's my old friend Fat Fungi Giambino way down there on the flats. "Hey, Jerry!" he's yelling up at me. "What's happening?" "What's happening!" I tell him. "I'm in this fuckin' place!!" "Just hang in there, awright?" he says. "I got a load of stuff comin' up for you from the Officers' Mess." Fungi's a helluva cook, forget about it—which surprises a lot of people, 'cause the cops always say he was like half a boss on the streets. "Don't worry about nothin'," he yells up. "Soon as you get out, we want you on our spot, c'peche?"

Anyhow, that night I got the sandwiches and stuff. Delicious. Plus a carton of cigarettes. And a tab, like a card, really, signed by all my friends. A dozen of 'em at least. "Hang in there, Jerry," it says. "Give 'em hell." Made me feel pretty good to get something like that on my first night.

Six A.M. *the next morning we get called out four at a time for physicals. These prison doctors are really something. You got a heart condition? You got diabetes? You got this? You got that? Then the nurse comes over, she takes out blood, pricks your finger, takes a hammer, hits you on the fuckin' knee, looks in your eyes, puts a thing in your ears, and that's it.*

Around 12:30 you go for lunch in the mess hall. You go in a special line. That's another thing—when you walk in on the Reception line, you're the last. And of course a lot of guys have never been in jail before and they see this big fuckin' mess hall with big pillars and twelve hundred guys in it and hacks with guns—gas guns—watching the whole thing from catwalks overhead. These new guys coming in aren't used to it. They're petrified. They see it and they get scared.

Built over a three-year period from 1928 to 1931, Attica at the time of its construction was the largest, most secure, and most expensive nonfederal prison in the country. There are four huge, autonomous cell blocks, each one designed to house five hundred inmates in single cells, each one enclosing a self-contained yard and linked to the others by a network of underground tunnels. The entire fifty-five-acre facility with its nearly two dozen separate structures is surrounded by a gargantuan thirty-foot poured-concrete wall, for which the materials alone cost one and a half million 1929 dollars. The labor was provided gratis by inmates from Auburn Prison, forty-five miles to the south.

Despite the fact that the winds of social change were swirling furiously outside, Attica in 1965 was still being run along the same harsh penological lines that had been laid down thirty-five years before. Inmates were locked in their cells fifteen hours a day, and no talking was allowed from the 8 P.M. silence bell until 6:30 the next morning. Each of the cell blocks was divided up into ten *companies* of approximately fifty men each, who were grouped by job assignment and almost invariably by race. Whenever the companies moved through the prison, they marched in lockstep and total silence, punctuated only by the sound of the officers rapping the walls with their sticks. One knock meant forward; two knocks, stop; three knocks, shut up.

The grooming code was rigid and strictly enforced. Shirts and sweaters had to be tucked inside the pants; shirts had to be buttoned except for the top button. On the third day of the Reception procedure, each new inmate was issued one hip-length gray coat, three pairs of gray pants, two gray work shirts, three pairs of underwear, six pairs of socks, and a belt. He was allowed to keep his street shoes as long as they were not two-toned, zippered, or steel-toed, did not have large buckles, and were not over six inches high. All the clothing was made by inmates in the prison tailor shop, using antiquated machinery, and many sizes were in short supply.

The food situation was even worse. There were two mess halls, each one seating 768 prisoners, who were "run" down from the cell blocks in groups of two companies at a time. They ate at metal tables, seated on immovable metal stools. Tables had to be filled in sequence as men came off the food line, and it was forbidden to get up or turn around once you were seated. According to documents subpoenaed by the McKay Commission after the Attica riot in September, 1971, the food budget at that time worked out to exactly 63 cents per inmate per day—a figure that fell far below federal minimum dietary standards.

"The food was nothing short of unbelievable," one inmate told the commission. "It was so bad you had to supplement your diet any way you could, and for most guys that meant scheming and hustling. There was no way you could survive in that joint without breaking the rules. During the summer the mess hall was hot and dusty and blanketed with flies and roaches. The floors were mopped with dirty water. The food was served on dirty metal trays. Even the chairs you sat on were filthy. The whole place smelled foul, and it was like an oven."

Next day we got marched through the tunnel to the Psych Unit, where some nitwit gets up and starts asking questions. Have you ever been in a mental home? Did you ever have sex with your mother? "With your mother," some guy yells out to him from the back. Anybody homosexual? Shit like that. The homos you can spot, anyway. They come in like broads, you know, swishing. They don't give a fuck.

The kid sitting next to me was really petrified. I could see he was sweating—his eyes were like that. "It's no big thing," I told him. "Just go along with it, make believe you're in the army." "You got a cigarette?" he asks me. He was short 'cause we couldn't get to the commissary, so I gave him a pack and lit one for him. All of a sudden this big fuckin' goon walks over and crashes his bat down on the kid's shoulder. "This is Attica," he says. That was the line, like it was supposed to scare somebody. "Over here we do things our way," he says. "And the next guy who lights up a cigarette in here, I'll crack his fuckin' skull open."

Now there was no sign or nothin' or I would never have put the kid in that position—I mean it was obvious the hack was just selling him a ticket. But the kid don't know that, and he's really shaking now. So me, I started to laugh—it was real laughing, but I did it to make a point. "You think it's funny, Rosenberg'?" the goon asks me. "Everything is funny in this fuckin' place," I told him. I'm only there two days and I'm starting up with these people already. I can't help it. It's just something that happens to me when they start pulling that phony shit or picking on some guy they shouldn't.

Anyhow, the hack says, "You won't think it's so funny when we get through with you." He turns away, and I lean over to the kid and I say, "Watch this," and I blow a huge cloud of smoke in the hack's face. He whirls around and says, "I'm lockin' you up, Rosenberg." "I'm locked up already," I told him. Everybody's laughing now, including this kid who was so petrified just before. "Everybody who's laughing out into the hall," the hack screams—I mean, the guy's really hot. "You think you had it bad in the Death House?" he yells at me. "Well, we're gonna make you so fuckin' miserable you'll wish you were dead!" So I told him, "All right, sucker, you do what you gotta do. Just save that scary shit for these new guys; don't tell it to me." So he grabbed me and called two other hacks and they took me back to the cell block, the three of them, and locked me in. Stopped the whole fuckin' Reception for the rest of the day. Everyone was laughing that night, it was beautiful, sending me tabs and messages. By the next day the whole prison knew about it. The grapevine in that fuckin' joint was unbelievable.

The collision between Jerry Rosenberg and the nineteenth-century penal system at Attica was both spectacular and highly protracted. No doubt the officials up there had never seen anything quite like him before, and their hope at first was that he was still just a little batty from the Death House. On the contrary, as they would soon discover, with Jerry Rosenberg confrontation was a way of life. He knew for sure that he would be spending a good chunk of his life in this place, and he also knew that for him to spend those years on *their* terms would be downright suicidal. "If I hadn't used my mind and kept fighting those people," he says, "all that hard time upstate would've killed me, just like it killed Baldy and a lot of other guys. There's only two ways to live in jail, and take my word for it, the other way is even worse."

The testimony of another inmate at the McKay Commission hearings sheds some light on this issue from the other side. "The only way to survive up there was to stay invisible," he told the panel. "And the only way I found to stay invisible was to become a non-entity—to just go along with their bullshit so they'd put me on the *pay-him-no-mind list*."

Hardly the kind of list Jerry Rosenberg wanted to spend the rest of his life on. And so he became one of the first inmates Attica officialdom had ever encountered who simply said no. You can't do this to me, he would tell them, in actions as well as in words. This infringes on my civil rights, he would be saying—on my manhood, on my human dignity. In the years ahead a large percentage of the prison population would be taking these same positions. But by then it would be a collective action, and in prison there is always safety in numbers.

Perhaps the most remarkable thing about Jerry, then, was that he did all this strictly on his own. Not out of any grandiose political or social theory like so many of the rebels in years to come, but out of a growing and very private sense of his own self-worth. He was, after all, a man who had literally fought his way back to life by dint of his own wit and fortitude and belief in himself. And as he came to understand Attica more clearly over the next few weeks, he quickly found that he had nothing but contempt for an institution that operated on the basis of scarcity, ignorance, prejudice—and above all, fear.

When we got back to the cell block that day, it turns out they'd moved the young kid in right next to me, the kid that was petrified. Now I'm not knocking him for that. He came into something he never seen before. He felt lonely, he misses everything, he lost all sense of reality with the outside. Anyhow, he says to me, "Boy, you got a real problem." I said, "No, they got a problem." He says, "What do you mean?" I said, "Well, as you start to go along, you'll get to understand how to deal with things. For now, just don't go putting your head in something where you're gonna get beat or killed or put in the hole." He says, "Well, you did it." I said, "Yeah, but it's a little different with me, y'know? I got some powerful friends here," I told him. "When you're doing life, it's a whole different game." But I guess he didn't understand what I meant, so I didn't go into it. I became pretty friendly with this kid, by the way. He died of cancer in Attica.

Next morning I got called in to see the deputy warden—the PK [Principal Keeper], they used to call him. A big fat red-neck type of guy, cigar ash all over his belly. A real farmer. He's wearing one of them clip-on ties so you can't strangle him and a big high trolley-car hat with a badge on it. "Oh, Rosenberg," he says. "We understand that you just came out of the Death House, that you've been in prison before, and that you're nothing but a vicious hoodlum. But this is Attica, and in Attica we kill people that don't abide by our regulations. Now, what you did yesterday was a very bad thing," he's talking to me like a child now, "but nevertheless we still try to get along with people in here. Sure you've got a stigma on you that you're a cop killer and a troublemaker, but we're willing to overlook them things. We're gonna give you a new chance, and we hope you conform to our policies."

And I says, "Well, before we go any further, I'm not a conformist and I couldn't give a fuck less about your prison or your policies, because they're all unconstitutional anyhow." Don't forget, I'm in the bag now, you know, with the law. "And furthermore," I says, "you do not scare me. These assholes you got running around with bats this long do not scare me. I know I can't win because you got the odds, but I'll sure cause you problems. And if you kill me, things happen on the street." "Are you threatening me with the outside mob?" "If that's the way you heard it,"

I told him. "Go ahead and report it to whoever you want—the government, the police, I couldn't give a fuck. But don't mess with me like you're messing with one of these new turkeys, because it's never gonna work. I may die, but you'll die, too."

He started to get real red in the face. "Well, I can put you in the hole for what you just said, you threatened me." "That wasn't a threat," I told him. "That was a promise. You leave me alone, I'll leave you alone. Just don't come up to me with these petty fuckin' rules." Meanwhile he's shaking and looking at me with those so-called vicious eyes that are supposed to penetrate me and make me crumble. And I'm just smirking at him. I don't smirk intentionally. It's just something that happens when there's danger: It automatically comes to my face.

"Well," he finally says, "in the circumstances, I know you just came out of the Death House, you've got a lot of hostility, so we're going to give you a suspended sentence on that smoking pinch. Does that show fairness on our part?" I looked at the guy for a minute, and I can't believe he totally backed down.

"Nothing could be fair in prison," I told him.

Perhaps the cruelest aspect of imprisonment at Attica was the sense of total isolation. Incoming and outgoing mail was censored by the correspondence office. English was the only permissible language, and the Spanish-speaking population, which numbered well over 250, was forced to buy the services of an inmate translator. All outgoing letters had to be written on coarse prison stationery. Each sheet listed the grounds on which prison censors could reject the letter, including:

It contains criminal news.
Begging for packages or money not allowed.
Correspondence with newspaper or newspaper employee not permitted.

You did not stick to your subject.
Cannot have a visit with the person named in your letter unless approved by the Superintendent.
Must confine your correspondence to your own personal matters.
Institutional matters and other inmates are not to be discussed.

There was no way, then, that inmates could let anyone on the outside know what was really happening to them. They lived in a closed, totalitarian world. And prison officials had devised a number of effective techniques to make sure each new inmate knew exactly where he stood:

The end of the first week they brought all forty-two of us down to the auditorium for the Murder Game. That's actually what they called it. First the captain gets up and starts breathing into the microphone. "I'm Captain So-and-So," he says. "We are here today to give you the rules and regulations that must be followed in Attica State Prison. This prison is the roughest prison in the world. We are not here to rehabilitate you, we are here to punish you. And if you want to see the streets again alive, then you will follow our procedures. If you don't, we have ways to do things and no one will ever know. When there's a place where you're not supposed to talk, you don't talk. If you talk, you'll be disciplined. If you do it twice, you'll be put in a strip cell—no clothes, one meal every four days. If you commit an act of violence, you will be put in solitary, which is dark, nothing. No cigarettes. And if you really get outrageous you'll be in the morgue. We have ways to do it, and nothing can be done about it. Because you are in our prison—Attica. And this is a world of its own."

Now the lieutenant gets up and gives his speech. The mail routine is you're allowed to send out three letters a week. One is for free; you've got to pay for the other two. If you violate any rules you will be reduced to two letters, and so forth—another letter, another grade. "Now on the visits," he says, "you get two a month. We allow English-language conversation only, no smoking, no physical contact, and no contraband of any kind. Break any of those rules and you lose your visiting privileges for a month. Break 'em twice, you go to the hole for thirty days. After that, God help you." Then he comes up with their famous phrase: Do your own time. *In other words, keep to yourself, don't get involved with nobody, and you'll make life easier for yourself while you're here. The whole thing was to keep us separate, to keep us from seeing each other as part of a group.*

An inmate's wages at Attica in the late sixties averaged 25 cents a day, half of which was held back in a special account and given to him on the day of his release. If he was a smoker he was in debt already. "It's very expensive to live in jail," one prisoner told the McKay Commission in 1971. "A man has to have coffee, sugar, toothpaste. And this is an adult. And nobody cares. He walks up there and he has a list in his hand. He gets to the commissary. Maybe they are out of peaches or maybe they are out of sardines. So he has to make that whole list over again, trying to squeeze pennies. Can you imagine how degrading that is? This man worked all week long. He ran a punch press or worked on the spot weld or on the shaper all month long and he made $3.05 or something. And he goes to the commissary. Maybe he can get a jar of coffee. 'I better not,' he thinks. 'I will get a smaller jar of coffee so I can get some sugar. Maybe I can get two packs of cigarettes and a can of Bugler [tobacco].'

"He gets up there and maybe they are out of Bugler. He has to go over there and make that list. I seen guys take up that list and tear it up and throw it on the floor."

Yard time—or the lack of it—was another major grievance. The four outdoor yards were small and crowded and almost completely unequipped, and from November to March they were usually covered with several feet of snow. And yet there was no gymnasium or indoor recreation area of any kind.

Beginning in 1970 a new recreational officer was appointed who made a number of improvements and changes, including the construction by inmates of handball and basketball courts in each of the yards. This was accomplished only over the protests of most of the other yard officers, who felt that several dozen inmates working together at one time constituted a threat to security. A request for plumbing supplies necessary to construct four outdoor showers for use after strenuous exercise was rejected on budgetary grounds.

Prisoners were allowed one indoor shower a week plus two quarts of hot water a day for shaving, which was delivered every evening by an inmate water boy pushing a rusty fifty-gallon oil drum on wheels. The water boy also carried with him a typed "catalog" that listed a smattering of the books available from the prison library. The library was funded exclusively from the profits of the prison commissary and was physically off-limits to prisoners for security reasons. Despite the fact that they spent close to half their waking lives in their cells, inmates were allowed only one book and three magazines a week and were required to fill out a request form, also available from the water boy, listing no fewer than thirty alternate choices. Censorship was in the hands of the prison's educational director, a civilian employee who selected and ordered new books once a year. "I never approved books on psychology, physics or chemistry," he told the McKay Commission, "because our policy was to discourage inmates from becoming amateur psychologists or using their chemistry books to make bombs."

Fourteen days later they open the doors bing, bing, bing, *and I go out onto the yard. I walked out—this was in the winter now, but even so the yard is packed. Guys are scrimmaging with footballs, guys are shooting basketball. Other guys are at the picnic tables playing dominoes or chess. There's a TV out there under the rain shed and a couple of fires going in metal barrels to keep warm.*

Now don't forget three spots want me on their spot. A spot *is like a unit of friendship—five or six guys at a table. Already I got friends on all the spots, so before you know it there's gonna be a conflict. A little fuckin' animosity. "How come you didn't come to my spot?" So right away I go with my people, which is the Organization spot—strictly Organization. I knew Fungi, of course, and a huge moose of a guy named Red Hot Gentile. As a matter of fact, I knew most of the guys at the table before I even sat down. "Fellas," Fungi says, "say hello to Jerry the Jew."*

Anyhow, I look around, I see that they're actually playing dominoes. *"What is it with you guys," I said. "You becoming institutionalized or something?" They look over at each other, real sheepish. "Cards is a big pinch in here," Fungi tells me. "It's a box lockup." "Whatta you mean it's a box lockup?" He points over to the hack on the yard platform nearby: "That retard over there can practically* smell *the goddamn things," he tells me. "They say you can take the red ink off a deck and make a bomb with it."*

"You ought to be ashamed of yourselves," I told them. "Out on the streets you're killing people. Over here you're worried about dominoes with some fuckin' hack in prison!"

They all started laughing, even the old-timer, Joey D. "Yeah, you're right," they said. "I guess we gotta deal with it." So I grabbed a doughnut box they had there at the table and I set all the dominoes faceup on the bottom, and I started marking the suits—eleven is jacks, twelve is queens, and so forth. Then I dealt 'em facedown so nobody couldn't see. Wasn't as good as real poker, but I swear to God the hacks never caught on.

That same day I got my regular cell assignment on the second tier of C-block, right alongside Fungi and the others. The hack up there was a guy named Cramer—a mild, curly-headed guy, always reminded me of Red Buttons. He was a good guy, a fatherly type of guy. Later on he'd even let people come up on the gallery and talk to me about their cases. He thought it was only right. He never held no animosity toward me, even after the riot.

But it was Red Hot who really had this guy's number. In a funny way I think Cramer idolized him, y'know? "I don't want no fuckin' trouble from you, Cramer," he'd say. "Open up the cells, we want to cook." And then Red Hot would get him in a hammerlock and pull the lever himself. Sometimes Cramer would wander down the gallery when he had nothing better to do, just to shoot the breeze. "All right, you guys," he'd say. "You're all pinched." That was his favorite line.

To tell you the truth, Red Hot practically ran that cell block for him, kept everybody in line. And from his end Cramer would try and tip us off about shakedowns and stuff in advance. Sometimes he'd even let us hide our cooking stuff in his locker. You better believe there was a lot of laughing on that gallery, scheming how to rob food and all that, regular line of stuff.

Joey D. didn't go for it, though. He was an older guy, and I heard he was sick. Maybe he was just more conservative, more rational in his ways. Like he wasn't the type of guy to tell a hack, go fuck yourself. He figured it didn't pay, y'know? And in a way he's right. He always used to try and tell us, like me and Fungi, "Why don't youse calm down? They'll kill you and they'll fuckin' destroy you. You can't beat 'em. Try to get out, that's the main purpose. Why make it more complicated for yourself while you're here?"

But then you say, after you yes him to death: fuck him.

13

My first job assignment was the metal shop. A terrible place. In the summertime guys would literally pass out from the heat and fumes. They made lockers in there, mostly, the big heavy steel lockers. They had heat processes and welding equipment and a big oven to bake paint in. Made a nice profit, too, I understand: a couple hundred thousand dollars a year. Lotta guys called it slave labor, and they were absolutely right.

The place was run by a sergeant named Cunningham—stocky, bald guy, hair on the sides, real Irish face. This guy was probably the most hated man in the whole institution. A real tyrant. The only sergeant I ever seen who carried a bat. And he used it. "I've been in this prison for fifteen years," he used to tell us. "And what I say, they go by"—meaning the higher-ups.

Fungi was in the shop, too, at that time. He'd never work. He'd always be laying up, drinking coffee. You gotta picture this guy, two hundred and forty pounds and a face like a squashed marshmallow. Never had a crease in his pants. Red Hot used to tell him he was so ugly bricks would fall down when he walked by. But loyal. One of the absolutely best friends I ever had. You become very attached to people in jail, no matter what their educational level or their moral level. Everybody has something good about him. A guy could be a moron, for example, or could get very violent when he's angry. But he might have another area of awareness where he'd be the first guy to come through for you when the chips were down.

Anyhow, Fungi was a beautiful guy. Good sense of humor, didn't give a fuck about nothin'. They gave him five to seven years for extortion, and he did the full seven. They never parole a guy like that—he gives 'em too much trouble. But in a way it's better, 'cause when you max out you're a United States citizen again, free and clear.

In any case, me and Fungi were actually the first ones to draw up a petition at Attica. See, you weren't allowed to smoke in the metal shop. If you wanted a cigarette you had to sneak a break, you had to go in the bathroom to smoke. But if you smoked in the bathroom, you were locked up for goldbricking—getting out of your job. Either way you were trapped. So me and Fungi wrote up a petition and got everyone to sign. Well, not everyone, 'cause in those days a lot of guys were still just trying to do their own time. Maybe they were in a program, or had a parole date coming up, or a conditional release. They didn't want to jeopardize nothin'. It's understandable.

So we got the signatures, as many as we could, and we sent the petition over to the PR's office. But the PK don't want to deal with it. He turns around and sends it right back to Cunningham. My name was on the top, Fat Fungi's name was second. So when Cunningham got the list, he called us all in his office, about sixteen of us, and he lined us up. And believe it or not, this is the way they used to deal with grievances.

"I got a petition here," he says. "You boys are complaining you can't smoke, and when you do smoke, you get locked up?" He looks around, and we all nod. "Well, it so happens we also got a rule against circulating petitions in here," he says, "so either way, you're still gonna get locked up."

"That's fine with me," Fungi told him, "anything beats the fuckin' metal shop." So they keep-locked me and Fat Fungi and one other guy—

only three of us out of the sixteen. We got out ten days later. But every day after that Cunningham would always throw me and Fungi up against the wall and frisk us.

In fact, that's how he found the legal papers on me the first time—a couple of pages from some other guy's trial transcript, just some guy we knew, I told him I'd take a look. Anyhow, Cunningham shakes me down, sees the other guy's name on the papers, and confiscates them on the spot. "That's a pinch, hotshot," he tells me. "A big one. You just bought yourself a lot of trouble real cheap."

I must've done a year total in the hole up there, and always for the same fuckin' thing: possession of another man's legal papers. Thirty days at a shot. It was insane. The only reason they fought it so hard was they knew in the long run the law was gonna bring in outside scrutiny and interference. It threatened their sense of total control. They even used to stamp the law books so you couldn't loan them around. I had a couple dozen of them at that point, mostly from my parents. The stamp used to say: "If found in the hands of anyone else this book will be considered contraband and destroyed." And they would write my name in it. They would stamp it like eight times so you couldn't erase it off—on the hard cover, back, front, middle, every fuckin' place.

Anyhow, the hole up there was the worst I ever seen. The box, the guys used to call it, and that's exactly what it was. I never went quietly. I always gave 'em a fight. After a while they got smart and started coming for me with mattresses. The goon squad. They crack your cell and the first guy comes in with a mattress in front of him and pins you against the wall. Then they shoot gas at you and drag you over to the HBZ [Housing Block-Z]. A sick fuckin' piece of work, every one of 'em.

From C-block there's two ways to go: You got the spiral stairs and you got the elevator. As soon as you get in the elevator, you get a couple of punches in the head, kicked in the ass, dragged by the throat. You walk up the spiral stairs, they kick you down the stairs a few times before they drag you back up. Either way it's the same as far as the psychological impact of it.

This bastard Cunningham tormented me for six years straight. I lost my visits from my mother. My packages. No mail of any kind. But when that riot jumped off, fuckin' Cunningham was begging on his knees. He went on TV and told Rockefeller to grant all our demands. "These are reasonable people," he said, meaning us. This same guy who'd been beating and torturing prisoners for fifteen years. "I'll be dead in the morning if you don't come and negotiate," he said. And the strange thing is he was right. He was the first one killed by the assault force when they came over the wall. Shot by his own kind. The troopers killed him, and I was glad.

By the middle of that first summer, Jerry was working on his regular law degree, by correspondence, from the Blackstone School of Law in Chicago. Founded in 1895, Blackstone is a relic of a less sophisticated but nonetheless highly effective system of legal education. For in many states up until quite recently, it was still possible to qualify for the bar examination by means of three different methods of study: accredited three-year law schools, clerkship, and correspondence.

Today only California still accepts correspondence study like Blackstone's in fulfillment of the educational requirement. And yet many Blackstone graduates from the 1950s and 1960s are still practicing successfully throughout the country, having passed even the most difficult of the state bar exams, including New York's.

There's no question, then, that the course is thorough and ingenious and remarkably effective in conveying both a body of knowledge and a set of skills. Of course, it isn't Yale Law. But as Jerry likes to point out, he really didn't have much of a choice.

* * * *

I saw an ad for the course in one of my regular law books, and right away I knew I was going to do it. I was still feeling pretty good about myself. I figured if I can beat the chair, I can do anything. I sent away for the catalog and a trial lesson, which looked pretty good when it arrived. This is a solid outfit, by the way, not one of them get-rich-quick schools. And I signed up the next day.

I did the whole course in fifteen months—seventy-seven different subjects, and exams in each one. The whole idea was to get credentialed, and I think I set a record for speed. Don't get me wrong, I really learned the stuff—negotiable instruments, municipal corporations, attachment and garnishment, the whole shot. Civil and criminal. I got straight A's in criminal procedure, interpretation of statutes, and constitutional law. I even got an A minus in legal ethics.

I probably could've done it even quicker except they kept throwing me in the hole. I mean, they were busting me for stuff like walking with my hands in my pockets or wearing a sweat shirt to lunch. I even got busted for possession of shaving lotion once. And when you're in the hole, buddy, they don't let you have no books.

Many times they would come in my cell and trash it. Once about halfway through the course they came in during a lockdown and ripped up all my books and papers. I sued them in court in Buffalo—sued the fuckin' prison officials and I won it on the Fourteenth Amendment. They were stupid that time; they handed me an issue. After that they went back to buckwheats again, the petty shit. I even got busted once for hanging up a picture my daughter painted in fourth grade, hung it up on the wall of my cell. "You gotta have a hobby permit to hang up that picture," the hack tells me. Bingo. Another fifteen days in the hole.

The other big problem, of course, was strictly mental. Personal frustrations in the cell. Sometimes you're thinking about home—sometimes you're thinking about a New Year's Eve or even your birthday. You get fucked up in the mind—you can't deal with it, you gotta put everything down. Sometimes it'd get so bad that even when I'd pass an exam, I'd feel good for maybe ten minutes. Then right back into that pit, y'know?

Only way to deal with it is to develop your mental powers to where you can overcome. I learned how to get myself to the point up there that I didn't even see bars anymore. I could look at a fuckin' steel door like it was nothing. Everything is mental. The physical beatings ain't nothing because it can only hurt so much and then it's over with. It's your mental area that's a lot of pressure.

I got my degree in December of '67. There was a big exam, a proctor from the state department of education came in. I honestly didn't know if I passed it or not. Six weeks later, my friends threw a big party for me in the feed-up room—a total fuckin' surprise. As a matter of fact, I was getting worried 'cause a lot of time had gone by and I still hadn't heard. "Come by the feed-up room," Fungi says. So I come by, and they're all sitting around eating lasagna. "How d'you think you done on that exam, Jerry?" Fungi asks me. "Well, I didn't get no letter yet that I failed," I told him. All of a sudden he pulls out a cake all decorated with graffiti and bad language, and he hands me a mailing tube with my law degree rolled up inside. Buddy of ours had pinched it out of the mail room before the censor got his hands on it. It was a beautiful party, though. It was like we all felt this little jolt of excitement, like now maybe things could really begin to change.

There'd been jailhouse lawyers for years, of course. Some damn good ones, like Caryl Chessman in California. And at Attica there was a black guy named Martin Sostre who'd won some really important cases in the area of prisoners' rights. He'd win another big one right before the riot. Plus there were maybe half a dozen guys in the joint who dabbled in simple writs. Writ-writers, they were called—they'd always leave their name off and let the other guy sign pro se. *It all had to be done on the sneak because of that fuckin' rule. But none of these guys had law degrees. And certainly none of 'em was in a position to say:* that makes me a lawyer.

Anyhow, my first big move after I got the degree was to file a writ of coram nobis *in my own case. That's a writ for newly discovered evidence. Had to be filed with the original trial judge, and that meant Leibowitz. Still on the bench at seventy-three. A treacherous bastard—but brilliant, and very shrewd. The toughest, smartest judge I've ever seen.*

He had this famous saying at the time: "When I send them away," meaning the Death House, "they never come back." So the first day of the hearing, he looks up at me from the bench and he says, "Not only did he come back, he came back a lawyer!"

The issue was the skin test, where they covered up the lab report that said I didn't have none of that tax-stamping ink on my hands. And right from the beginning Leibowitz was trying to knock me down—interfering like he always does, changing the facts, trying to lead the witnesses. I'd object every time, put it right on the record. At one point we had a big fight where the DA wanted to put me back on the stand, and I beat him on a procedural technicality. Leibowitz banged the table and went crazy. "You learned all the gimmicks, didn't you, Rosenberg?" he said. I said, "I learned them from Your Honor when you were my trial judge seven years ago. You were a great teacher." "This is my courtroom," he starts yelling, "and I'm going to hold you in contempt!" "No, it's not your courtroom," I told him, "it's the People's courtroom, and we're all here to determine the truth."

The main point at issue was the question of when the test was actually taken. Fact is that it was done in the courthouse in Brooklyn right after my arraignment. But the DA was claiming it was done at the precinct house the night before, in which case it wasn't part of what's called the pleading record, and they weren't legally obligated to disclose it at the trial. Leibowitz, of course, was backing the DA up. At one point I called Leibowitz a liar right to his face. "I'll have you gagged and chained," he screams. "You do what you want to do," I told him. "But don't try and bulldoze me and manipulate me the way you treat these regular lawyers and DAs—like that lackey of yours over there."

I lost the case, of course. A very short ruling. He said, quote, "After carefully reviewing all of the evidence, it is clear that the defendant Rosenberg was not prejudiced in his defense, that he received a fair trial, and that there was no denial of due process of law," unquote. But to me it was a moral victory, because I showed them up for what they really are. I brought it out in the open. I showed them what the truth was, especially Leibowitz. You can't hide truth. You can cover it, bend it, anything you want. But it's still there. That's the only kind of victory that means anything to me. And in the long run I honestly believe it's going to drive them nuts.

When he adjourned the hearing—it had been going on for like three or four days—Leibowitz called my parents into his chambers and he told them in Yiddish, "If your son had taken a different path in life, he might well have become one of the greatest attorneys that ever lived." You can imagine the impact a statement like that must have had on my mother. Anyhow, she translated it for me a couple weeks later. And she never lets me forget.

On February 24, 1969, the United States Supreme Court handed down a decision that would have nearly as profound an impact on Jerry's life as freedom itself. The case was called *Johnson* v. *Avery,* and it concerned a jailhouse lawyer in Tennessee who had been placed in solitary confinement for helping another inmate with a writ. While he was in the hole, Johnson had drawn up a motion on his own behalf asking for "law books and a typewriter." And it was this second writ, now heavily buttressed and amplified by outside lawyers, that had wound its way through the lower courts for several years and had finally been accepted by the Supreme Court for judicial review. Significantly, it was

Associate Justice Abe Fortas who would write the opinion—an opinion that grew logically out of *Gideon* v. *Wainright,* the landmark 1963 decision in which Fortas, then a partner in the prestigious Washington law firm of Arnold & Porter, had persuaded the Court for the first time that anyone accused of a felony had a basic constitutional right to be represented by a lawyer, starting from the moment of formal arrest.

In *Johnson* v. *Avery,* however, the justices were being asked to extend the logic of *Gideon* into an area where the Court had previously been very reluctant to tread: the internal operations of a maximum-security prison. *Questions of prison administration should be left to prison administrators,* the Court had ruled in a number of recent cases. And they had specifically given prison officials tremendous latitude in regulating the activities of jailhouse lawyers, as part of the state's overall responsibility for maintaining prison security and discipline. As recently as 1966 the Court had allowed a circuit-court decision to stand that said "prisons are not intended, nor should they be permitted, to serve the purpose of providing inmates with information about methods of securing release therefrom." Prison officials in many states were even in the habit of screening lawsuits to see which ones ought to be allowed to go to court. And at one prison in Texas the *World Almanac* was placed on the contraband list solely because it contained a copy of the United States Constitution.

The standard prison administration argument against jailhouse lawyering was loyally trotted out by Justice Byron R. White in a long and rather cranky dissent in the *Johnson* case. He wrote:

> According to prison officials, whose expertise in such matters should be given some consideration, the jailhouse lawyer often succeeds in establishing his own power structure, quite apart from the formal system of warden, guards, and trusties which the prison seeks to maintain. Those whom the

> jailhouse lawyer serves may come morally under his sway as the one hope of their release, and repay him not only with obedience but with whatever minor gifts and other favors are available to them. Many assert that the aim of the jailhouse lawyer is not the service of truth and justice, but rather self-aggrandizement, and power.

He neglected, of course, to estimate the percentage of free-world attorneys who were dedicated to any loftier or more selfless ideals.

In any case, *Johnson* v. *Avery* wiped the slate clean. Writing for a majority that included everyone except White and, curiously, Justice Hugo Black, Fortas based his argument rather narrowly on the federally protected right of habeas corpus. Fortas wrote:

> Since the basic purpose of the writ [of habeas corpus] is to enable those unlawfully incarcerated to obtain their freedom, it is fundamental that access of prisoners to the courts for the purpose of presenting their complaints may not be denied or obstructed.
>
> Jails and penitentiaries include among their inmates a high percentage of persons who are totally or functionally illiterate, whose educational attainments are slight, and whose intelligence is limited. For all practical purposes, if such prisoners cannot have the assistance of a jailhouse lawyer, their possibly valid constitutional claims will never be heard.
>
> Unless and until the state provides some reasonable alternative to assist inmates in the preparation of petitions for post-conviction relief, it may not validly enforce a regulation barring inmates from furnishing such assistance to other prisoners.

Justice William O. Douglas, in a strong concurring opinion, went even further: "The upheavals occurring in the American social structure are reflected within the prison environment," he wrote. "Prisoners, having real or imagined grievances, cannot demonstrate in protest against them. The right peaceably to assemble is denied to them. The only avenue open to prisoners is taking their case to court."

Johnson *v.* Avery *was the first important chink in the armor as far as jailhouse lawyering was concerned. And it was also one of the first court decisions that really reached down to the level of the hacks. One of the first ones to tell them: there's something you may not do.*

Of course they still had divide and rule—that was their other basic technique. Only with me it never worked. They tried it for a while—locking down the whole company every time I filed a writ—and a lot of guys in my position would've had to knuckle under. I mean realistically, you'd be a fool to take on the forty-three guys you lock with. But, fortunately, in my case I didn't have to. I had Red Hot and Fungi on my side, and the other guys pretty much just fell into line. Part of it was they didn't want to cross Red Hot, of course. But partly they really started to get behind the idea of banding together. We all knew they couldn't keep a whole company locked down for very long. It was a beautiful feeling. And in the long run it was that same feeling that finally destroyed the idea of do your own time.

The first important case I put my name to was the Bautzer case—right after Johnson v. Avery, *April and May of '69. Danny Bautzer, his name was. Just this kid in prison. A good kid—lawyers had been fucking him around for five years. This kid copped out to murder one and they gave him life. Supermarket holdup. Now what you gotta understand is nobody cops out to murder one unless they've been coerced. They told him he was going to the chair if he went to trial. They threatened him, and they scared him to death. His own lawyer was telling him: "People know all about this case, you'll never get a fair trial." Now the problem on the appeal was that all this coercion and intimidation wasn't on the record. There was only twelve pages of trial minutes because he pled guilty; they just stipulated certain facts. His family hired the biggest lawyers, but nobody could get him out. I got the case and knocked it out in six weeks. Got a new hearing for him and he repleaded guilty to manslaughter—ended up he did eight years instead of twenty-six.*

Then I won another big case up there, burglary case out of Buffalo. Very good case, got a reversal for a guy. All writ stuff, of course. Pretty soon I've got more cases than I know what to do with. Two big wins in a row and all of a sudden I'm swamped. I had to get a little bit selective.

One case I remember up there though, I took it right off the bat. This was a guy who cooked with Fungi in the officer's mess. He wasn't a hoodlum—just a pleasant guy, in for a stolen car. He used to throw me a couple of sandwiches every night—ham-and-egg sandwiches, BLTs. I was always up late studying. So now one day he calls me and says he's gotta see me, it's important. I was in a poker game in the yard. He comes over to the table, he says, "Jerry, I gotta speak to you, something terrible just happened." I was in the middle of a hand, y'know? So I said, "All right, wait a minute." So I finished the hand—I lost about sixty cartons of cigarettes. I was aggravated. I got up and I says, "What's the matter?" He says, "My wife was pinched, and now they're gonna take away my kids."

Turns out he had two kids—a little girl and a little boy—and one of them was a sick kid and the city was going to put them in a home. The mother got locked up for drugs, and they were claiming she wasn't fit. Now there were grandparents around—the guy's parents—but the city was claiming it was a common-law marriage, which it was, and that the grandparents had no legal relationship to the kids. "We gotta do something," the guy says. So I got all the information and I researched the hell out of it—I'd never handled a case in family court before—and I drew up a motion. I pointed out that the grandparents already had the kids living with them, that they were reliable people, working people, and that they were doing a good job. There was a de facto legal relationship there already, I said. Common-law guardianship, I think I called it. Plus the child was very sick and needed strict attention.

Fourteen days later the judge grants the motion and the family gets custody. He took the whole thing right out of my writ. Precedents and all the rest of it, to where the grandparents would be appointed interim guardians until the guy got cut loose and was in a position to resume custody himself.

The kid got better, by the way, the kid that was sick. He came in for a visit years later—one of the best visits of my entire life.

Meanwhile, I'm working on my own case all the time—the publicity issue, of course, and the torture of Richie Melville. But there was also a strong Sixth Amendment issue that was every bit as outrageous as the other two. The Sixth Amendment says you've got the right to confront the witnesses against you—in other words, they have to personally take the stand so your lawyer can cross-examine them and so forth. The whole idea was to exclude hearsay evidence so that a guy can't get up in court, for example, and say he heard a rumor that some other guy robbed a bank. But the amazing thing is that a lot of the most important testimony against me was of precisely that nature. Louis Ferrara, Linda Manzione, and Richie Melville—all three of them quoted other people as having placed me there at the scene. Melville quoted Portelli as telling him, "Jerry took the rest of it," meaning the loot. Ferrara claimed Delvecchio told him he was "going to pick up Jerry," and Linda said Delvecchio told her, "Jerry never learns." Vicious lies, all three statements, and totally inadmissible against me under the law. But the tricky point legally was that other parts of their testimony were admissible—against Delvecchio and Portelli—a distinction that Leibowitz pointed out to the jury, but only in the most confusing and half-assed way.

Now in early 1968 a Supreme Court decision called Bruton v. United States *gets decided where the Court rules that "cautionary instructions by the trial judge are not sufficient to correct the error inherent in such statements," a decision that was made retroactive in another case called* Roberts *v.* Russell.

Right away I drew up a writ of habeas corpus and sent it in to the United States District Court in Buffalo. It was a nice piece of work, and it eventually got shot all the way up to the United States Court of Appeals for the Second Circuit—a special three-judge panel—where the decision finally came down against me by a vote of 2 to 1.

"There is no doubt that the admission of those statements was error as to Rosenberg," the two judges in the majority said. "However, upon the record before us we find that the error in the admission of these three statements was harmless error." Harmless *error.*

But the third judge disagreed with them one hundred percent. "I must respectfully dissent," he wrote. "The case seems to me to be governed by the rule in Bruton v. United States *(88 S.Ct.1620), and I cannot agree that the evidence against Rosenberg was so overwhelming as to justify application of the harmless error doctrine. I would reverse the conviction and direct that the writ be granted unless the state chooses to retry the petitioner."*

One more vote and I would've walked out of there with forty dollars and a suit of clothes.

It took me another six months, but I finally got thrown out of that fuckin' metal shop. Me and Fungi both. He got assigned to the upholstery shop, which was a little better, and I ended up with a pretty good job as C-block porter. C-block includes the invalid company, about twenty-two guys.

And part of the job was me and a friend of mine named Al Victory would work the feed-up wagon.

First we'd bring it out onto the flats, then the hack would open the gate, and the invalids would come down—the ones that could walk. The ones that were really sick, we'd have to take a tray up for them onto the tiers. There were a couple of vegetables up there, guys who were mentally shot. One guy would just fuckin' lay there and we'd have to spoon-feed him in his cell—an old-timer, real skinny, with black hair pasted down on his scalp and a pair of glazed-over eyes that looked like Italian olives. Never said a word. If he didn't like his breakfast, he'd throw the stuff on the floor. Oatmeal or whatever. He was a complete fuckin' waste, that guy. A zombie.

Anyhow, me and Al Victory were very close. We grew up together on Coney Island, and believe it or not, we got sent away for the same thing. His was a traffic stop. His buddy grabbed the cop's gun and rang him out right there on the sidewalk. So you can imagine me and Al faced a lot of the same problems in the joint. I got him interested in the law. He'd read up on different cases in my law books sometimes, and we'd strategize together. I even represented him once in a narcotics case that he got pinched from in jail before Judge Frankel in the Southern District. We got him acquitted, proved the stuff was planted on him during a frisk.

He was a tough kid, Al Victory. Very bright. But when I knew him in the middle sixties, he didn't believe in bucking the system. That was before his big changeover. See, I'm a capitalist. Hundred fuckin' percent capitalist. I'll die a capitalist, you understand? I'm no revolutionary, even during the riot. The demands I held out for all had to do with changes in prison conditions and in the penal law: decent medical care, due process in prison disciplinary proceedings, decent food and wages so you wouldn't have to steal while you're doing time. Things that would've made a difference. I couldn't care less about transportation to a nonimperialist country—some guy actually slipped that one in there, discredited our other demands. Of course *there's gotta be prisons. And there's gotta be discipline in prisons. There's gotta be someplace you put some wacko that starts killing people. The point is you gotta stop the brutality in prisons, stop the dehumanizing process. Even Warren Burger said it, man. They're nineteenth-century institutions, and society is really starting to pay the price.*

But Al Victory didn't see things that way. He became a staunch fucking radical, this guy. To the teeth. All that revolutionary rhetoric. It shocked me. I'd tell him, "Boy, that's some changeover, my friend." I mean it was a drastic fuckin' change. Usually mob guys don't get involved in radicalism, but I guess that fuckin' hate in prison works on people in different ways.

Some of his ideas I know he picked up from Sam Melville, the guy who blew up the Whitehall Induction Center. He was very sincere and committed, Sam Melville. A real *revolutionary: he died proving he was real. He put out a newsletter in the joint called* The Iced Pig. *And he also made a lot of guys believe in their own courage—just the way he walked down the halls or talked to the hacks. I knew him a little. We'd have arguments sometimes. Just kidding around, but the differences were always there. "When you were out on the streets," I'd say, "you blew up a bank, right?" He'd say, "Yeah." "You blew up a fuckin' business building?" "Yeah." "Well then why the fuck didn't you blow up a prison?" I used to tell him. "We're in here dying!"*

To me a lot of that revolutionary stuff was fraudulent. I mean if you believe in something, don't talk about it, do it! *But I guess a lot of guys needed something to grasp, a myth, you know, something to pull themselves together. So maybe it served a useful purpose.*

I guess the most amazing thing about Al Victory was the way he escaped. From Greenhaven in 1978. Doesn't happen very often, believe me. See, for a long time he needed oral surgery on his teeth, and so they finally got him an appointment with an outside dentist. Him and another guy named Joe Tremarco were gonna go together. Three days before Al gets a wire that the hacks on the trip were gonna be two guys named McGibney and Panarello. These were hacks he knew pretty good—I mean the level of corruption in these joints is just incredible. So Al gets to them in advance and he works things out to where they agree to stop off at a motel room for half an hour on the way. He's got a girl friend and it means a lot, he tells them.

The rest of the story's so good I'm gonna quote it to you verbatim right out of a report by the New York State Commission of Investigation. Quote:

> Officers McGibney and Panarello stopped off with the two prisoners at the Ramada Inn in Newburgh. They waited in the bar with Mr. Tremarco while Mr. Victory left, ostensibly to go to a room where his girlfriend was waiting.
>
> When Mr. Victory had not returned after an interval estimated at up to an hour, Officer McGibney left the bar to look for him. Victory was not to be found. As nervousness turned into apparent panic, the two officers, with Tremarco in tow, began a frantic search of the Ramada Inn. McGibney unsuccessfully attempted to secure from the reservations clerk the number of the room registered to Victory's girlfriend. He then enlisted the aid of a barmaid, who found and gave him the room number, 126.
>
> Officers McGibney and Panarello, together with Tremarco, then ran to the first-floor room and pounded on the door, calling out, "Al, are you there?" There was no response. The three then ran outside and looked into the room through the window; they could see no signs of life.
>
> The officers then concocted an elaborate story about how they were ambushed on their way to the dentist's office by

masked gunmen. Mr. Tremarco was persuaded to go along with the fabrication on the promise of recommendations from the officers that he be given parole.

Immediately thereafter, Officer Panarello wrote a highly complimentary letter commending inmate Tremarco for his assistance during the Victory escape, stating that Tremarco's refusal to escape and the calming statements he made to the masked assailants had actually saved the officers' lives.

*The truth came out a couple of years later, just when Tremarco was about to get paroled out of Lewisburg. Poor bastard, they snatched it away from him at the last minute. What happened was the BCI went after McGibney on some other corruption charges, and the man totally fell apart. He confessed to everything and started working with the prosecutors. I never heard what happened to Panarello. But I can tell you one thing for sure: They're never gonna find Al.**

---

* Al Victory was recaptured on March 23, 1981, in San Diego. According to Jerry, there is "no clear story" about how and where Al Victory had spent the previous two and a half years.

14

Part of the buckwheats I had to deal with after Johnson v. Avery *was a lot of job transfers. Just to keep me off balance. Maybe they finally realized the best part of that C-block porter's job was it got me down to the feed-up room, no questions asked. I could study down there or work on my cases. Plus I was spending a lot of time drafting a federal habeas corpus on the hearsay issue—a helluva good piece of legal research that finally got thrown out of court because of delays caused by the Attica riot. Anyhow, the feed-up room was nice and quiet. We had a couple of soft chairs and an old three-burner stove for cooking. We fixed it up pretty good.*

But one morning when I came in there, must've been May or June of '69, they'd busted it all up. That same day they reassigned me to the electrical shop—a maintenance job, really. But at least there was some traveling involved. They gave me a big toolbox that weighed about fifty pounds, with some screwdrivers and pliers and a little light bulb with a light. I didn't know the first thing about it.

One of my first call-outs I get sent down to the mess-hall kitchen. They had these huge automatic toasters down there, the kind with belts, where you can toast a whole loaf of bread at once, and one of them is on the fritz. I walk in, and there's the kitchen hack waiting for me, a guy named Griffiths. He looked like Captain Munzy from that Burt Lancaster picture, Brute Force*—the guy with the glasses. What a mutt he was. He'd given me a ton of grief over the years. Anyhow, I walk in and he says, "Fix the toaster, Rosenberg, and get it fixed fast." So I go over there and I'm fooling around and I don't even know how to turn the fuckin' thing off. I'm sticking the screwdriver in there with the rubber handle so I don't electrocute myself, and nothing's happening. So he says, "You dummy! I'll do it. I know more than you and I'm not even in the electric shop." He says, "Gimme that tool!" So I turned around for a split second and picked up a regular screwdriver without the insulated handle and gave it to him. He stuck it in and his hair went up and he started to yell. He was shaking like a bastard and he couldn't get off. Nobody would even touch him till one of his buddies finally pulled the plug. I got thirty days for that one. I says, "What d'you want from me, he asked for the screwdriver." They says, "But you gave him the wrong one* on purpose.*" I says, "No I didn't, he took it!" A beautiful scene; it was worth the thirty days just to see his fuckin' hair go up.*

After that they put me on the grading company—an all-black gang, just about. A punishment gang. Chopping rocks and boulders and all that. They used it to fix cement.

The racial situation up there was truly horrendous. Over eight hundred blacks in that joint and not one single black guard. No black people in the whole town—this tiny little red-neck town where even the mayor worked as a hack. Any black guy who fucked up would automatically get it worse than the whites. The guards were much more severe. "He thinks just like a white man," that's the highest compliment they would ever pay a black. But the funny thing is if a white guy got caught playing sports with a black guy, they'd fuck with the white guy even worse. Nigger-lover, *they'd call him. Same thing with cards. Friends of mine started up an interracial football game one time and got the whole joint locked down.*

I never seen anything like it at Comstock, I'll tell you that. Take the Fourth of July. It's the biggest day of the year at Attica, parties out on the yards—the only day you could travel from block to block. My first year I couldn't believe it. Couple of hacks bring out this huge bucket full of ice and start yelling, "White ice, white ice." I thought they said white eyes *at first, until Red Hot took me aside and filled me in. I swear to God they had segregated* ice buckets *in that joint. It was embarrassing. It was a tradition, and it set a tone.*

By the spring of 1970—a full eighteen months before Attica finally exploded and all but destroyed itself in the riot of September 1971—the notion of an impending confrontation had already begun to take on a life of its own. "Where will you be when the crunch comes?" was the question on everyone's lips, and the rumor of a riot was inevitably the first rumor that every new prisoner heard during his first few days of Reception.

Behind this state of affairs was a massive sense of historical inevitability. And those who knew Attica best—guards and prisoners alike—had become grimly fatalistic about the possibility. Many guards had begun to leave their wallets and valuables at home. And many of the most able and experienced officers had begun to request assignment to the gun towers and to night-shift work when inmates were locked in their cells.

On July 29, 1970, the situation flared briefly into open rebellion for the first time when 450 prisoners—virtually the entire metal shop work force—sat down on the shop floor and turned off their machines. They were not only striking for higher wages, they said, they were also protesting the forced transfer of a small group of metal-shop workers who had approached Shop Supervisor Cunningham the week before and had formally requested an increase in wages. Cunningham had promptly keep-locked the group for seventy-two hours and had then prevailed upon Deputy Superintendent Karl Pfeil to have them transferred to other institutions.

But now, with 450 angry prisoners on his hands, Cunningham was clearly overmatched. He called in Superintendent Vincent Mancusi, who took one look and ordered the shop closed for the day. The prisoners went peaceably back to their cells, and Mancusi and Pfeil spoke to several of them individually. But the issue was left totally unresolved.

The next day the entire work force once again sat down on the job. And Mancusi—furious and baffled now, and totally out of his depth—called in Commissioner of Corrections Paul D. McGinnis. McGinnis summoned a group of elected representatives from the striking inmates, negotiated with them on the spot, and promptly agreed to increase wages from the previous 6 to 29 cents per day to 25 cents to 1 dollar per day. He also ordered a department-wide survey of all inmate pay scales and subsequently adopted a uniform, slightly improved pay schedule for all correctional facilities.

Given the generally harmonious result, the issue of reprisals was not even considered. A week later, however, a number of the organizers of the protest, including all those who had personally talked with the commissioner, were summarily transferred to other institutions. It was the first of many examples over the next fourteen months of prison officials apparently giving on the one hand and then taking away with the other—a senseless and ultimately tragic practice that produced a cresting wave of cynicism and rage in all segments of the inmate population.

From the administration point of view, however, the strike represented an alarming breach of prison security. Rather than seriously considering the grievances that were being expressed and at least accepting the fact that they were widely held, Mancusi and Pfeil continued to blame it all on a small group of *militants* and *troublemakers* whose rebellious attitudes, they said, were a dangerous influence on other inmates. In their Annual Report for 1970 they portrayed the situation as follows:

> Increased tension among inmates and between inmates and staff has constituted a difficult morale problem. The problem is directly attributable to the increased number of young militants in our population.

From their perspective, then, the problem literally seemed to be snowballing out of control with the arrival on February 12, 1971, of four additional *militants* from Auburn Prison who had been involved in an angry confrontation with officials there over permission to hold a Black Solidarity Day on the yard. And yet, despite an explicit promise of no reprisals from a deputy commissioner who had been on the scene during the demonstration, Mancusi promptly ordered the four transferees thrown in the hole as soon as they arrived at Attica.

It was another instance of an official promise being discarded like so much worthless fluff. But this time it would come back to plague them when U.S. District Judge John Curtin granted a writ of habeas corpus filed by one of the four and ruled that they could no longer be confined in the HBZ. Mancusi reluctantly released them into the general population, where they immediately assumed positions of substantial influence.

The reaction of the Attica guards to this latest piece of judicial intrusion bordered on outright panic. Already uneasy and frightened by the growing rebelliousness on all sides, they literally felt endangered by Judge Curtin's decision. Tragically, there seems to have been no awareness that the objective conditions at Attica might in any way be responsible for the growing climate of confrontation. And one anonymous corrections officer later analyzed the situation for the McKay Commission in the following unregenerate terms: "They should have left those guys in the HBZ a helluva lot longer," he said. "They can hear you awful good after a year or two up there, just like if you gassed them."

On January 1, 1971, Governor Nelson Rockefeller finally responded to the growing crisis by appointing a new commissioner—a fleshy, sixty-two-year-old, self-styled "reformer" named Russell G. Oswald. For the past twelve years Oswald had served as chairman of the New York State Parole Board, and he was acutely aware both of the dimensions of the crisis and of the warning issued by his predecessor, McGinnis, that there would be a "bloodbath" in the prisons unless more money were made available to alleviate the rapidly deteriorating conditions. And so, unlike any commissioner before him, Oswald chose to present himself both to the public and to the state's huge prison population as a reformer—a man with an alternative vision who would quickly leave his mark on the day-to-day experience of imprisonment in the state. And Rockefeller, in announcing the appointment, left no doubt that the Oswald approach represented his own personal answer to the crisis.

Within a week of taking the job, Oswald began making a series of highly ambitious policy statements that expressed his fundamental misgivings about the way the system was being run. But as the year wore on and no apparent changes were taking place, it began to seem to many inmates that Oswald's appointment was just one more example of a promise whose fulfillment had been snatched away. For the vision of reform that Oswald articulated over and over again remained just that: a vision. And despite repeated assurances to the effect that everything possible was being done and that he shared many of the prisoners' frustrations and concerns, the sum total of Russell Oswald's "reforms" in the nine months before the riot amounted to slightly liberalized visiting rules and the long-sought-after provision for uncensored "legal mail" between inmates, attorneys, and public officials.

* * * *

You can imagine there were a lot of petitions drawn up in the joint that year. I got one here from July, signed by a group that called themselves the Attica Liberation Front, where they asked for simple improvements in medical care, food, and sanitary conditions in the mess hall, personal hygiene, clothing, recreational facilities, and working conditions in the shops. Just the basic stuff. They sent it to Oswald, and they concluded the petition with this statement: "These demands are being presented *to you. There is no strike of any kind to protest these demands. We are committed to doing this in a democratic fashion. We feel there is no need to dramatize our demands." Unquote. Three days later the hacks started searching the cells for political literature and busting people right and left.*

And then came the murder of George Jackson in San Quentin. It hit a lot of guys real hard, including a good percentage of whites.

See, at a certain point I'd started following the radicals. I read George Jackson's book, Soledad Brother*—which had a tremendous impact on the whole joint—and it helped me relate to some of the Muslims and other radicals on the yard. I got to know a few of them, especially an older guy named Herbert X. Blyden. A great orator and strategist—and totally for real. He'd been through the Tombs riot, and he knew what the stakes were firsthand.*

Anyhow, a couple of weeks later I got the word there was gonna be a memorial for George Jackson, that we were all going to go silently into the mess hall one morning wearing black armbands, and nobody was going to eat or talk. I want to emphasize something here. Usually in jail when you try to organize something, it gets back. The stool pigeons get wind of it and the hacks bust it up. But in this case it was a complete fuckin' surprise. It just shows you the degree of solidarity we had. It just went through the grapevine, through all the cliques and crews and everything, and we had one hundred percent.

It was a breakfast one morning in the middle of summer. This day we all walked in and picked up a tray, but we didn't put nothing on it. It was a pinch if you didn't pick up a tray, so we picked up the tray, went right past the steam tables, and sat down empty. Usually the place is real noisy. With twelve hundred guys you can really hear it. But not today. Today it was like a church.

One guy didn't get the word. He took the oatmeal or whatever it was and then turned the corner and stopped short. He didn't know what to do with the fuckin' food. He wanted to bring it back. But two guys started to smile, so we winked at him: Don't worry, just don't eat. He caught the winks, y'know? There's a certain thing in jail, you know what a guy's saying just by facial or hands.

The hacks were just standing there with their clubs. Big, tough motherfuckers, right? All of a sudden they don't hear the noise. They see nobody's eating. What the fuck is going on? Now they're getting fidgety. They got their clubs behind them, they want to get out of the mess hall. They think it's going to jump.

And we just sat there, both mess halls waiting for the whistle to blow, waiting for that first company to get up and leave. You better believe they blew it early this time.

When you leave you've got three boxes. You've got to throw fork, spoon, and knife. Each guy. There's two lines, hacks on either side, watching. This time nobody took their fork, spoon, and knife. Just got up. Left everything on the fucking tables.

The hacks were petrified. They were really shaking. One guy actually told the papers it was the most frightening experience of his entire life. But the administration just glossed it over, tried to pretend like nothing happened.

A week later there was a sick-call strike, which was fine with me. I hate every fuckin' doctor in prison—for what I seen them do to other people and for what they did to me. They're worse than the hacks, some of them.

Anyhow, what happened was on August 30 somebody got a wire that Oswald was going to be in the joint that day, and five hundred inmates showed up for sick call. We knew outside officials always stopped off to check the infirmary. But as usual, Oswald didn't show.

Three days later he's there. Finally. He's going to meet with inmate leaders to discuss our grievances, they tell us. But forty minutes into the meeting, he's got to go. He's very upset, he says, he just got word that his wife is sick and they took her to the hospital in Albany. But he's going to leave behind a tape-recorded message, and they'll play it for us on the earphones after the four o'clock count.

Some guys actually thought he might have something on his mind. But when that tape was over all I could hear was earphones hitting the wall and people hollering.

Same old line of guff—he shares our concerns and so forth. But no concessions whatsoever.

15

The way the riot jumped off was truly spontaneous. The situation was so explosive, it didn't require any plans or leaders. All it needed was a tiny spark to set things off.

In fact, the whole thing grew out of an incident on the yard the day before, where some hack claimed an inmate pushed him. As usual, there was a lot of confusion, and the hack kept changing his story—it happened on one of the black spots, and the hacks were never very good at keeping track of who was who over there. But Mancusi and Pfeil figured they had to do something, so they locked up a bunch *of guys in the HBZ that night and keep-locked a couple more. Real overkill. It just shows you they were really scared.*

The next morning a friend of the guys on keep-lock hits the levers of the cell-locking mechanism and lets them all out for breakfast. Now that's totally unheard of. Never happened before. Ever. *But as usual, the hacks don't figure out what's going on till twenty minutes later. By this time the company's down in the mess hall already, and the administration's got a real problem on their hands. How the fuck are they gonna handle it? They decide to chase after the company and bring them back to the cell block. They finally catch up with them in D-Yard tunnel, some words were exchanged, and the fuckin' thing just blew apart.*

First I was aware of it was about twenty minutes later. I was still sleeping, as a matter of fact, and all of a sudden I woke up. I heard all this noise—shouting and crashing and tear-gas canisters going off. And then a friend of mine named Al Higby ran to my cell and said, "Jerry, the joint just went up. Come on downstairs fast. Get dressed." So right away I went downstairs to the feed-up room and we loaded up with knives and shanks. Was it a race riot? We didn't know what the hell it was. Nobody did. And then this other friend of ours came running down from A-Block with blood all over him. He says the joint just went down and we took over. "Is it a race riot?" Red Hot asks him. No, no, no, the guy says, everybody's *involved.*

So we rolled out into the corridor and headed down the tunnel toward Times Square. That's what they call it where the tunnels from the four cell blocks meet. And I can see that the security there is totally blown. The gates are smashed open, the control booth is wrecked, and guys are running around wearing football helmets and towels on their heads.

All of a sudden I turn around and here comes this fuckin' three-ton forklift truck from the metal shop, followed by four hundred and fifty guys with acetylene torches and tear-gas launchers and metal shivs. They'd just broken out of the metal shop and were smashing through the cell blocks, cutting guys loose. Unfortunately they never got to the real *arsenal or the whole thing might've been a different story.*

Just then a bunch of hacks wheel around the corner with a fire hose going full blast. But they take one look at this fuckin' army bearing down on top of them and they just turn around and run.

Finally I got out onto D-Yard, and everybody was just crowding around. There was a sense of panic at first, because nobody knew what was going to happen next. Would the hacks come storming back with shotguns? Would they drop a fuckin' bomb on us from a helicopter? I mean these were serious questions.

At first some of the guys just wanted to get out of there, and I really couldn't blame 'em. Maybe they had a parole date coming up or a couple of felonies on their jackets and were worried about kidnapping charges on the hacks. At that point we had close to fifty hostages out there rounded up and blindfolded and guarded by Muslims. And I think most people realized that every man who stayed on the yard was criminally liable.

The ones who stayed—close to thirteen hundred of us—were the ones who'd started to feel like we were part of something bigger than ourselves. It's hard to describe. But that night I saw a white guy come up to one of the really heavy Muslims on the yard and throw his arms around him. "Brother Richard," he said, "I've seen you before. I know you're a Muslim and I always called you nigger, and I'm white and I know Muslims hate whites. But I just want you to know that I'm with you one hundred percent." Scenes like this were going on all over. The tough facade was breaking down and guys were actually embracing. One guy started sobbing uncontrollably. It was the first time since he'd been in the joint that he'd ever really felt close to other people, he said.

At times it almost seemed like a religious feeling, all those barriers breaking down at once. We had a live band on the yard that night and we were sleeping out under the stars for the first time in ten, fifteen, twenty-five years. We actually built a city for ourselves—organized things, took responsibility, shared the work and the food. And these were guys who had been labeled asocial and incorrigible and worthless. And every fuckin' one of them was beautiful.

Soon as we got the sound system hooked up, we started to pull things together. Food and water, blankets, medical care for the guys who were hurt, tight security for the hostages. And then the leaders of all the different factions got together and there was an election on the yard. Two guys were elected from each cell block, and I was elected from C-block as the legal representative. I was pretty sure I had something to contribute, but it wasn't a job I sought out for myself. The leadership, we all knew, would be especially vulnerable to reprisals.

Anyhow, we all put our heads together right away—a lot of these guys were from different cell blocks and we'd never even seen *each other before. And we set our priorities. First of all we had to maintain discipline on the yard—no inmates get hurt, make sure the hostages don't get touched, get the medical people in there to treat the wounded on both sides.*

And set up our leadership table. Already we were thinking in terms of negotiations, and the first thing we decided was that everything would take place in public, in front of all twelve hundred guys. No secret deals, no vague promises. We'd been burned that way too many times in the past. Meanwhile the members of the committee were circulating through the yard, listening to grievances and ideas for demands. We're all *leaders on this yard, we told them. And we proved we meant it. All during those four days the microphone was open to any responsible person who wanted to speak.* Anyone. *We listened to our share of hot air, some of it from the members of the committee. But a lot of good ideas came out that way, and a lot of those speeches were pretty strong.*

I remember one in particular delivered by a twenty-one-year-old black kid from Rochester named L. D. Barkley. This was a kid who'd done four years at Elmira for cashing a sixty-five-dollar forged money order, who'd been paroled for good behavior, and who'd then gotten himself violated and sent back to Attica for driving his mother's car without a license.

"We are here today to put an end to the ruthless brutalization and disregard for the lives and well-being of prisoners here and throughout the United States," L. D. Barkley said. "What's happening here is but the sound before the fury of those who are oppressed. For we are men! *We are not beasts, and we will no longer allow ourselves to be beaten and driven as such."*

The yard was so fuckin' quiet you could hear the breathing. "We do not want to rule," this kid said. "We only want to live. But we have come to the conclusion, after close study . . . after much suffering . . . after much consideration . . . that if we cannot live as people, *then we will at least try to die like* men!"

That speech came later, of course—probably Saturday or Sunday, when the whole thing got dangerous and grim. But for the first couple of days, we were pretty optimistic. We had the hostages, we had TV cameras in the yard, and the conditions we were exposing were obviously horrendous. We really thought we had a chance.

By Thursday afternoon we had taken the best of the ideas—we'd boiled them down and kept them feasible—and we drew up a list of demands we called the Fifteen Practical Proposals, including political and religious freedom, decent medical care, the appointment of an inmate grievance committee, an end to censorship. Nothing outrageous whatsoever.

By this time Oswald was on the yard himself, along with a state assemblyman and a civil-liberties professor from Buffalo named Herman Schwartz. But all we could get from Oswald was the same fuckin' runaround—these things take time, he's gonna need the approval of the legislature, and so forth.

Now the only demand we left off that list was amnesty, the reason being we didn't trust him. We'd seen what happened after the metal-shop strike and the rebellions at Auburn and the Tombs in New York City, where the promises of no reprisals didn't mean shit. In fact, we had Herbie Blyden at the table, who'd been through the Tombs riot and who had been charged with one hundred and thirty-seven separate counts of kidnapping, assault, unlawful imprisonment, and destruction of state property.

So this was a big problem, and it was my idea that the only way to guarantee *that there would be no reprisals was to get a federal-court injunction or consent decree signed by the governor in advance. It would have worked, too, but as usual, the state started playing games. Plus we made a serious mistake on our part. Despite our best intentions, we overruled ourselves and agreed to let one of our guys leave the yard to work on the injunction with Oswald and Herman Schwartz in private. Now there are many ways to approach the drafting of a thing like this, but this individual, although he was popular with all segments and had a good reputation as a jailhouse lawyer, just couldn't stand up to them. He got run over, is what happened. But in the general optimism that surrounded the proceedings at this point, it was overlooked.*

By this time, even though it was eleven o'clock at night, there was still an incredible high running through the crowd. A lot of these guys hadn't been up this late in years. They were just strolling quietly, talking with their friends or straightening up the different areas. Believe it or not, the mood was carefree*—relaxed in a way that I'd never seen before except on the streets.*

No matter what happens later on, the feeling was, there's no way they can take this away from us tonight.

Nine A.M. *the next morning Schwartz is back with the injunction. He'd been traveling all night to get the judge's signature, but as soon as I took a look, I knew the thing was defective. Number one, there was no reference to criminal amnesty whatsoever. It spoke of "physical and administrative reprisals" only. Number two, it referred to "a disturbance at the Attica Correctional Facility on September 9, 1971." Well, it was now September 10 already, the "disturbance" wasn't over yet, and for what it was worth, the fucking thing no longer protected anyone. Number three, it wasn't stamped with the judge's official seal, and we'd all had writs thrown out of court for less than that. And number four, we had specifically demanded that Rockefeller himself sign on behalf of the state, whereas in fact the only other signature on that piece of paper was Oswald's.*

To me, the message they were sending us was clear as a bell, and one by one we denounced the thing as it went down the table. Oswald kept arguing back that we could trust him, that this time things would be different. But when we asked him about the promises that were broken at Auburn—about the beatings and the transfers and the long stretches in the hole—all he could say was that he'd heard about the problem, and that, quote, "the deputy commissioner who made those promises was very upset about the fact that they had not been kept," unquote.

When it came to me, I was so fuckin' angry I jumped up, tore the injunction in half, and threw it in his face. "This is garbage," I yelled at him, "and we're not even going to discuss it!" I was raving at him, but I was raving sense.

There was an enormous roar from the whole yard. And a couple of other guys at the table started screaming at Oswald that he was a pig and a liar and a stooge for Rockefeller, the whole bit. There was a total lack of trust on both sides, and I honestly don't think we could've gotten anywhere with the man after that. In any case, Oswald never came back onto the yard, and from that point on he basically turned the negotiations over to the group of outside observers we had requested, including Tom Wicker, Herman Badillo, William Kunstler, and close to thirty-five others, some of whom had simply showed up at the gate and appointed themselves.

Kunstler was very strong. I respect him enormously, and I learned a helluva lot from him over those three days. Of all the observers, he was the only one who really seemed to understand what we were up against. I still disagree with a lot of his politics, but on questions of tactics and strategy no one can touch him. We worked together on the drafting of the Twenty-eight Points, which was a more detailed and specific set of demands. And on Sunday, when things really started to look bad, I asked him if he'd take out a letter to my mother. "People have been pushed around long enough," I told her. "We may be prisoners and criminals," I said, "but if anything happens, I just want you to realize that the system we've been living under is even worse."

For me the point where the situation really became hopeless was late Saturday afternoon, when we found out a hack had died. His name was William Quinn—a young guy with two kids—and the fact is he wasn't a bad guy at all. He just happened to be in D-Yard tunnel when the whole thing flew apart, and the official report months later attributed the cause of death to a blow on the head. He'd been on the critical list at a hospital in Rochester ever since Thursday morning, and we'd hear reports about him from time to time. In fact, it was my most serious concern all along. But when they broke the news on the radio Saturday afternoon, they kept repeating that he died of injuries sustained when a bunch of inmates threw him out a third-floor window. Now that was preposterous on the face of it—every window at Attica has inch-thick steel bars on it. But it was just the first of dozens of official lies that the media picked up on and never questioned. This one they repeated endlessly, and it pushed the situation totally out of control. Number one, there were close to a thousand heavily armed state troopers on the other side of the wall by this time, and every one of them was convinced now that we were nothing but a bunch of bloodthirsty psychos. Number two, any possibility of criminal amnesty vanished out of sight. Number three, the officials were suddenly in a position to charge almost anyone they wanted to with first-degree murder—and we all knew there were only two death-penalty crimes left in the State of New York, one of which was the murder of a prison guard. And number four, it destroyed any possibility of a settlement based on trust.

It was the most extreme example yet of the betrayals and broken promises we'd been dealing with for years. And when the yard found out about it, it produced the biggest explosion so far. "How we gonna push a fuckin' hack through them *bars?" one guy yelled into the microphone, pointing up to the barred windows all around. "Fuckin'* heart attack *is what the mother must've had, he so fuckin' scared he seen the brothers runnin' loose!"*

The attack came thirty-six hours later, after a series of desperate but unsuccessful appeals by the Observers Committee asking Governor Rockefeller to come to the prison and lend his personal authority to the search for a solution. Rockefeller refused, explaining that "any duly elected official sworn to defend the Constitution and the laws of the state and the nation would be betraying his trust to the people if he were to sanction or condone criminal acts by negotiating under these circumstances." This despite the fact that he was well aware that the prison system had been long neglected and was in need of reform, that his commissioner of corrections had tentatively agreed to twenty-seven of the Twenty-eight Points (all except amnesty), and that Oswald himself had made an urgent midnight appeal on Sunday begging Rockefeller to reconsider.

It had been raining all night, and Monday dawned gray and wet. The twelve hundred residents of the jail-made city on D-Yard were now swamped and muddy and shivering—and increasingly hopeless. There was a last confusing exchange of demands with Oswald, who, fearing for his own safety, refused to come onto the yard—but no progress whatsoever on the question of amnesty.

A final voice-vote was taken shortly after eight thirty in which the inmates all but unanimously rejected any settlement that did not include immunity from criminal prosecution. And then, as if to emphasize their resolve and to forestall the attack that they now feared was about to come, the leadership ordered eight of the hostages bound and blindfolded and led up onto the catwalk near the intersection of the four tunnels.

This piece of news was quickly relayed to Oswald, who interpreted it as an "overt hostile act," ordered the power supply cut off to all four cell blocks, and reluctantly gave the long-delayed signal for the assault to begin.

Several minutes later a huge National Guard helicopter code-named *Jackpot One* took off from the main parking lot outside the prison, equipped with thirty-five pounds of powdered CS tear gas, a gas disperser, and instructions to create a huge immobilizing cloud directly over the middle of the yard.

Meanwhile several hundred state troopers and sheriff's deputies quickly took up positions on the roofs and catwalks atop the tunnels surrounding the yard. Many of them were equipped with shotguns and .270-caliber bolt-action hunting rifles, every one of which was loaded with "Silvertip" ammunition designed to flatten out like a dumdum bullet on contact.

From the moment the tear gas was released until the cease-fire order was given nine and a half minutes later, well over two thousand rounds of ammunition were fired directly into the yard, and the result was the biggest one-day massacre on American soil since the Civil War. In all, thirty-nine people were killed during those nine minutes—all of them by state-police weaponry—including almost half the remaining hostages, whose lives the assault had ostensibly been designed to save. Three other hostages, eighty-five inmates, and one state police lieutenant all suffered serious gunshot wounds of one kind or another, and hundreds of inmates suffered broken bones and other serious internal injuries from the indiscriminate beatings administered by troopers and corrections officers as they slowly regained control of the prison.

The immediate aftermath was in many ways more terrifying than the assault itself, as troopers and corrections officers stormed vengefully through the yard and the cell blocks, their rage fed by a series of official lies and deceptions that had once again been picked up unquestioningly by the press. And once again the subject of these lies was murder.

Approximately three hours after D-Yard fell, Deputy Executive Commissioner Walter Dunbar and the department's public information officer, Gerald Houlahan, gave newsmen waiting outside the prison the first official account of the assault—a briefing that was full of gross misstatements and hysterical fabrications, but that formed the basis of *The New York Times* lead story the following morning:

> In this worst of recent American prison riots, [the *Times* "reported"] several of the hostages—prison guards and civilian workers alike—died when convicts slashed their throats with knives. Others were stabbed and beaten with clubs and lengths of pipes.
>
> Deputy Commissioner Walter Dunbar said that two of the hostages had been killed "before today" and that one of them had been stabbed repeatedly and then emasculated. Of the remaining seven, five were killed instantaneously by the inmates, he said, and two died in the prison hospital.

The same set of fabrications inspired a *Times* editorial writer to majestic heights of lofty indignation the following day:

> The deaths of the hostages reflect a barbarism wholly alien to our civilized society [the editorial said]. Prisoners slashed the throats of utterly helpless, unarmed guards whom they had held captive through around-the-clock negotiations, in which the inmates held out for an increasingly revolutionary set of demands.

And a sidebar article in the *Daily News* on Tuesday headlined I SAW SEVEN THROATS CUT quoted one state policeman on the assault team as follows: "When the gas dropped, those cons didn't wait a second, they just slit throats." He went on to describe the resistance encountered by the assault forces: "We were hit by gasoline bombs, makeshift spears, rocks, iron bars, sticks, and other missiles," he complained. "It's a wonder more of us weren't hurt."

The rumors of atrocities, of course, had spread among the men of the assault team long before the newspapers hit the streets, and the mood among many of the troopers and the correctional officers who followed them into the prison was one of unbridled rage. A panel of outside doctors who examined the inmate population several weeks later found 634 examples of contusions, burns, abrasions, and lacerations on the D-Yard inmates, including 32 serious injuries to the head or groin, 38 fractured ribs, 2 broken elbows, a broken arm, numerous deep lacerations of the scalp and neck, and one example of first-degree burns on the buttocks.

Of the four hundred correctional officers on the scene, twenty-two of them were in fact dismissed for the day several hours after the assault began. The notations on their employment records purporting to explain why they had been sent home included "broke down," "emotionally unstable," "aggressive," "incapable," "irrational," "rambling," and eight instances of "incoherent."

It wasn't until Thursday morning that reporters finally obtained a copy of the official autopsy report, and the department's misstatements and outright fabrications were publicly exposed for the first time.

Every one of the ten dead hostages had been killed during the assault, the autopsy report stated unequivocally. And every single one of them had died of state police gunshot wounds rather than knifings at the hands of their inmate "executioners." Moreover, the report concluded, no hostages alive or dead had been castrated or sexually molested in any way.

The lies died hard, however, and as late as Friday afternoon departmental officials were still insisting that they had eyewitnesses to many of the atrocities and that a second "unbiased" autopsy report would confirm *their* version of events. A second series of autopsies was in fact performed by a team of expert medical examiners from New York City and Westchester County. But much to the embarrassment of Dunbar and Houlahan, this second report—when it was finally issued several weeks later—emphatically confirmed the first one in every single respect.

By that time, of course, the damage—in terms of rampant destruction, sheer terror, and permanent physical injuries sustained during the aftermath of the rebellion—had already taken place.

At first they were coming over the walls just like regular troops, firing indiscriminately, with one guy chanting through a bullhorn, "Drop your weapons—surrender and you won't be hurt," and the rest of them just firing at guys point-blank. They murdered L. D. Barkley in the first wave of the assault, and shot Sam Melville in cold blood five minutes later. The troopers had been watching the faces at the leadership table on TV all weekend, and in my opinion it was a regular hit list. The official McKay Commission report puts it this way:

> L. D. Barkley was struck in the back by a State Police .270 rifle bullet during the first minute of the assault. He was hit and died in the southeast quadrant of D-yard, about twenty yards from the hostage circle. Several inmates who knew him well told the Commission that they were with him in the yard and that they saw him hit as he was running toward his tent.

Samuel Melville was killed at least five minutes after the assault began by one rifled slug from a State Police shotgun fired by a BCI investigator standing atop Times Square. As he was standing there with the weapon, the investigator testified, he saw an inmate in D-yard bobbing up and down behind a crudely fashioned bunker made of fertilizer bags against the wall of D catwalk. The BCI agent said he lifted his gas mask and yelled to the inmate—whom he claimed he did not recognize—to stop his activity in the bunker. The inmate then reappeared, he said, with what appeared to be a Molotov cocktail in his right hand. Fearing he would throw the Molotov cocktail, the investigator said he fired one shot from the shotgun, striking the inmate in the chest. Another investigator stated that fifteen minutes later he went down into D-yard to examine Melville's body and could not find a Molotov cocktail anywhere near it, although there was a bucket of such devices in the bunker.

They probably would've shot me, too, except for a friend of mine named Rudy Moore. I'd got hit in the knee with a shotgun pellet almost immediately, and I was lying on the ground in front of a trench with my nose on the ground because of the pepper gas and a dead man right next to me. I really thought it was all over. It was raining and drizzling and there was all this mud. And like I'd said at the microphone the day before, I truly was ready to die. I think most of us had accepted that death was part of the equation going on. And the real surprise, even to me, was just how vicious and psychotic the troopers and the regular hacks finally turned out to be.

Anyhow, I was lying there in the mud with my kneecap shot off and all this rifle fire ricocheting off the walls, when all of a sudden some fuckin' trooper kicks me over and I could feel the muzzle of his gun pressing into my neck. He looked like a fuckin' Martian with an orange helmet and a fluorescent raincoat and these weird hoses hanging off his gas mask. "You're a dead man, you Jew cocksucker," he says, and then he kicked my glasses off and smashed them in the mud. He put the gun to my head and I closed my fuckin' eyes. I figured it was over with. And then all of a sudden something happened. It felt like a relief, like a weight lifted over me. I couldn't see nothing, and I couldn't hear nothing, but sure enough little Rudy had gotten up and grabbed the motherfucker and thrown him right over me into the ditch, like three or four feet down. So Rudy says, "Jerry, move fast!" So I started moving, and for a couple of minutes there, I actually got away.

Now the smoke's starting to rise and they're making sweeps through the yard and poking at the bodies—and I'm lined up against the wall, naked, with the rest of the leadership. We've all got these white Xs painted on our backs and we've got our hands folded on top of our heads. And all of a sudden this same fuckin' trooper comes over with his shotgun. He takes one look, spits at me right in the face, then hauls back and cracks me across the ribs with the barrel of his gun. I took my hands down, I honestly didn't give a fuck anymore. I'm shot in the knee, a couple of my ribs are broken now, and all of a sudden I started charging the guy and shouting at the top of my lungs.

"Let me tell you something, motherfucker," I told him—I actually had the guy backing up in confusion. "You want to beat me?" I said, "Go ahead and beat me. I don't give a fuck what you do. You want to kill me, go ahead and kill me." The guy finally digs in and cocks his weapon, and I'm still coming at him. "But you don't spit on me like that," I told him. "You do that again, and one of us is gonna die!" All of a sudden the guy flips his gun around at the last minute and cracks me over the head with all his might.

The next thing I remember, some guy's dragging me through the tunnel to the HBZ. I spent the next seven and a half months in there, along with the rest of the leadership. But despite the fact that many of us were seriously injured, we didn't get any medical treatment for weeks. In fact, there was martial law. We had no rights whatsoever—no outsiders allowed into the prison, including lawyers, no exercise or showers or decent food.

I filed a good half-dozen lawsuits while I was in there, all of them from memory 'cause I didn't have no books. Smuggled them out on toilet paper just like the old days. One of them was a class-action suit for five million dollars' medical damages on behalf of everyone killed or injured during the attack. Later on we even made a move to attach Rockefeller's estate. Another one was for Rudy Moore, who was in the box with me—the kid who saved my life. He had these open, bleeding sores from the pepper gas all over his face and neck. They were infected and he wasn't getting any treatment, but I put in a writ before Judge Curtin in Buffalo and got the kid treated right from the box.

As far as amnesty was concerned, it turns out we were absolutely right. Over fourteen hundred separate counts of murder, kidnapping, assault, and unlawful imprisonment were filed against inmates on D-Yard. Over the years all but one of those indictments was eventually dropped—especially when a blue-ribbon investigation proved that the prosecutors had tortured people and beaten them to testify. But in 1975 one poor guy was actually convicted of the murder of Officer Quinn, despite the fact that it happened in the middle of a huge, surging crowd. His name is John Hill, and he did close to ten years for it. One guy out of twelve hundred.

As *for the assault force, regardless of the fact that they murdered thirty-nine people, only one of them was ever charged with anything:* reckless endangerment, *for firing indiscriminately into the crowd from the roof of D-Yard tunnel. That was four years later, however. And as you can imagine, he was promptly acquitted.*

I saw that fuckin' trooper that clubbed me one more time while I was in there. His name was Lavagetto, and with his gas mask off he had these ugly, giant-sized buck teeth: old piano face, I called him. He must've been about six foot two, a real yahoo type of guy, hat cocked to one side. "Well, well, well," he said to me that morning, "looks like I'm going to have to feed this animal in the first cell. How d'you like your milk, Rosenberg," he said, "hot or cold?" And then he laughed and put his hand in the milk and stirred it around a little with his fingers—it was in one of those plastic styrofoam bowls for cereal—and he handed it to me through the bars.

"Yeah, you're right," I told him. And then I grabbed the bowl and I sloshed the milk right back in his ugly face. He cracked the cell and I got another beating, of course. But it was actually worth it just to see the milk dripping down all over his teeth and his fuckin' medals and gold braid.

For the survivors that's pretty much what Attica came down to. Just a lot more antagonism and suffering. And believe it or not, a candy bar once a week. The Attica candy bar, *they call it.*

But the Twenty-seven Points that Oswald had agreed to were promptly and completely ignored.

PART THREE

It's always been a fight. Only these days, instead of punches, I'm hitting 'em with strategy and words.

16

Seven and a half months later they adopted a policy of dispersing the Attica leadership and shipped me back downstate to Sing Sing. They just barged in on me one morning and said, "Come on, let's go, pack up your shit." I didn't know what the fuck was happening. They brought in a canvas bag for the little things—underwear, cigarettes, some legal stuff I'd accumulated. It was spozed to all be secret, but Fungi as usual found out anyhow. He and Red Hot were waiting for me in the tunnel. We couldn't talk much because of the hacks, but they fell in step alongside and walked me all the way to the gate.

We got to Sing Sing around eleven o'clock at night—after lock-in—and they made sure to clear the corridors. They were treating me like John Dillinger. I had these huge belts on with chains, and I still couldn't walk very good because of the beatings and the nerve damage. But they had to take me through Seven Building on the way to the hole, and all my friends in there gave me a big reception. A real boost, believe me. I just yelled to them, "Call my mother and tell her I'm here." She got all happy, came in to visit me right away. With a package, of course. They never let her visit once *while I was in the hole at Attica, the bastards.*

The next day a lot of hacks came up—guys I knew from the Death House—including Wiggins and the Genius and a guy named Fat Tony—and they were actually glad to see me. I expected a lot of animosity from the riot, but it wasn't so. "That's Jerry, all right," they said. "He always gave as good as he got." Plus there were a lot of black hacks now who sympathized to an extent. A lot of them actually respected me for being in the middle of that fuckin' riot. Take my word for it, Sing Sing is a different world.

Pretty soon all my friends started comin' up on the gallery. They're sneaking up. They're bringing me steak, whiskey, everything. And then that same afternoon Wiggins and one other guy walk me down the hill to the warden's office. They did it as a favor, instead of the truck. So I walk in, and there's Bill Gard, the captain, who's now a deputy commissioner in Albany. A good guy to the extent that he's very fair. He looks at me—I didnt know him then—and he says, "I'm Captain Gard." It was weird; I almost got mixed up—I thought he said "Captain of the Guard," like it was a new job or something since I'd been away. He says, "How d'you feel?" I said, "I feel all right, how do you feel?" So he looked at me. He says, "Oh, I feel all right." "Good," I told him, "that means we both feel all right. What am I here for?" He says, "Well, how would you like to get out on population?" I says, "I belong in population. I don't even know why I'm locked up." "Well, that's Warden Schubin's orders." I says, "Really? I don't believe I know the name." He says, "Well, you'll meet him. In fact, I got the authority to let you out from the warden. But you can't come out unless you agree to work in the law library."

They've got a law library? It's news to me.

"That's right," he says. "You take the job as head of the law library and you'll be free right now, you can go around the yard, meet your friends and everything. But if you refuse, you're gonna stay locked up!" A warped sense of humor, this guy—that's basically what I thought.

He wasn't kidding, though. Later on I found out that the Supreme Court had just handed down a decision called Younger v. Gilmore, *where they ruled that the Fourteenth Amendment required the states to establish "reasonably adequate" law libraries in the prisons. It was a beautiful decision, and it also had the effect of giving pro se defendants and jailhouse lawyers a kind of respectability and legitimacy in the eyes of the lower courts that we'd never had before.*

"All right," I told him. "When do I start?"

So he tells the two guards, "You don't have to take him back. He's out, he's free. Get your stuff and fix up your cell," he tells me. I said, "You got it"—and I walked out. Really felt good; it was like freedom for the first time in eight years. Over here you could walk around without a guard in sight. You walk up hills, you don't see nobody. Beautiful, like a big park, y'know?

Anyhow, I got a cell in Seven Building, right alongside of Johnnie-Boy Rizzo and a guy named Joe Perino, both of whom were gonna figure big in my legal work, though of course I didn't know it at the time. As far as fixing up the cell was concerned, I got all new stuff. I gave a list to my mother, scatter rugs and other things from the Sears catalog and Montgomery Ward's. Pretty much whatever I wanted. Plus some beautiful jail-made furniture from a dear friend of mine in the carpentry shop. I really enjoyed that prison. Unfortunately I was only there for twenty-one months.

Anyhow, the law library was gonna be in a room off the hospital they used for storage. Old mattresses and shit. We cleaned it all out, washed down the floors, robbed the typewriters from other departments. We really did a job on the place. My salary was sixty-five cents a day, and for the first four months all we had was my own personal books. A hundred and forty of 'em. But then the state got a grant from the LEAA in Washington and pretty soon we started getting the regular sets—state and federal. Guys were free to come in pretty much anytime they wanted. I'd work with them sometimes, show them how to use the books. But I finally had to draw a line between the cases I was helping out on and the cases I actually took.

Joe Perino was one of the first guys through the door. He was a knockaround guy doing twenty to life, same as me. And he was sick and tired of getting stiffed and manipulated by his outside lawyers. He asked me to take a look at his trial minutes, and right away I found an issue they'd never touched. The third day of the trial—this was in February of '68—the judge sent the jury out of the room for a few minutes while he entertained a motion from Perino's lawyers to dismiss the case for lack of sufficient evidence. It was a very weak case, by the way, and the motion was entirely proper. But the judge denied it out of hand. Not only that, but when he calls the jury back into the box, instead of just going on with the case like he's supposed to do, he turns to them and tells them he's just denied Perino's motion because in his opinion there is sufficient evidence.

I couldn't believe it; I had to read it over three times. It was blatantly prejudicial, and of course there should have been a mistrial right then and there, but Perino's lawyers just sat on their fuckin' hands. Sure enough, a week later the jury comes back with a guilty verdict, and Perino all of a sudden finds himself doing life.

A nice issue—there's a ton of case law on the subject, including a Supreme Court decision called Griffin v. California*—and as soon as I explained it to him, Perino grasped the significance right away. Naturally he wants me to get right on it, so I draw up a writ of habeas corpus and I send it in to the Westchester Supreme Court in White Plains.*

Six weeks later Perino gets a notice that the case has been accepted for oral argument. Now that's very rare. Usually they just bang it out on the basis of the paperwork, but this time the judge says he wants to hear the arguments in person. This had never come up in any of my cases before, and it raised a lot of complicated issues. But Perino, stand-up guy that he is, never gave it a second thought. "We're going all the way with this, Jerry," he said. "You're my lawyer, you did all the work, and the two of us are going in there—just you and me."

Everybody else thought he was crazy. "You're nuts," they told him. "He can do a writ and put it in, but how're you gonna go into court with the guy? He's not in the bar!" Anyhow, this went on and on. They're telling Perino it can't happen, you better get a lawyer. And he's saying forget about it, Jerry's my man. See, there's that idea of loyalty again. In prison, believe me, there's no way you can live without it.

Anyhow, I drew up another brief citing my legal education and experience and sent it in to Judge McCullough, the administrative judge for the whole Westchester County Courts. Now you gotta realize we're asking for something that's never happened before—an inmate representing another inmate in open court—and for six weeks more we didn't hear a fuckin' thing. Then one morning Perino runs up to me in the mess hall and shows me a notice he got saying he's going to court that day, that he's gotta appear. Unfortunately, since I didn't get one, we figure I'm out. But then an hour later all of a sudden they called me down to the DSO and they said, "Oh, Rosenberg, we just got a telegram that you're to appear for Joe Perino. So get ready." I ran back up the hill. I was very paranoid. I was sure the administration was gonna try and fuck it up. "I got it all right," I told Perino. "Now all you've got to do is get me through the fuckin' door."

Oddly enough, this hearing was gonna be held in a special courtroom they got right in the prison. It's strictly economics. The judge comes in every month or so for hearings and motions in various cases, and the department saves itself a lot of time and money on transportation. It's a regular courtroom setup, though, a permanent thing.

Anyhow, me and Joe walked over in our prison clothes and there's a hack sitting there at the desk. "What do you want?" he says to me. "I'm Mr. Perino's attorney," I told him. The guy looks at me like I'm out of my mind. "You heard him," Joe says. "His name's Rosenberg, and he happens to be an officer of the court." "Whatta you mean you're Perino's attorney?" the hack roars at me. "You're a fuckin' prisoner!" "Read it," I told him, and I showed him my ticket. He can't believe it. He runs into the courtroom and shows it to the judge. "That's right," the judge tells him—it's McCullough himself, the chief judge. "I want both of them in here right away," he says. Bang, we're through the door—and once I'm in there I know I'm not gonna lose it now. We walk up to the bench, and the judge turns to Perino and says, "You understand that you have a right to a regular licensed attorney and that whatever happens in here is binding on you," et cetera, et cetera. And Perino says, "No, I want my friend Jerry to represent me." "Well, this has never been done before," the judge says, "but the man does have law degrees . . ." He looks over at the DA, the DA consents, the judge bangs his gavel, and we're under way.

It made legal history, that hearing—was in all the papers and everything. And when the decision came down three weeks later, the judge ruled in my favor on every single point. He ordered Perino back to court for a new trial, and I was truly happy for the guy, almost the same as if it had been me.

Mostly what Jerry was doing in the brand-new Sing Sing law library, however, was working on his own case. For although the United States Supreme Court had denied *certiorari* (or judicial review) in 1966 and had thereby brought to a close the normal process of appeals, he was still free to file writs of collateral attack in areas that had not previously been raised before the courts. And so over the years, even though he could have papered his cell many times over with adverse decisions from state and federal courts at every level, he was still averaging at least one new appeal or writ of habeas corpus every year.

In one of his earliest complaints, filed in 1967, he had charged that the commanding officer of the Butler Street Precinct House, Lieutenant Domenico Carranante, "had encountered the jury in a corridor outside the courtroom and had told them, 'Well, it won't be hard to find those bums guilty. They're as guilty as sin, and their police records prove it.' " Carranante's comment was "an unwarranted extrajudicial communication," Jerry soberly informed the appellate division, "and was not only prejudicial in the highest degree, but also deprived petitioner of his Sixth Amendment right to confront his accuser (see *Parker* v. *Gladden*, 385 U.S. 363)."

In another writ that same year, Jerry charged that during the testimony of Anna Gandolfo, who was cataloging a long list of police threats that had been made to Richie Melville's wife, Fernanda, Judge Leibowitz had "repeatedly made a face of disbelief by puckering his lips and giving a sly smile." Jerry wrote:

> Later on when Justice Leibowitz cross-examined Mrs. Gandolfo himself, he made repeated facial gestures to the effect that she was a liar. It got so out of hand—the gestures and actions of the judge—that the witness herself even made the remark to the judge that he was "fresh." The judge then jumped up in a rage and started arguing with Attorney Wild [Portelli's lawyer], after which he turned to the jury and made some adverse remarks about all four defense lawyers—and then further stated to Attorney Wild that when this trial was over he was "going to cool him off in the cooler." (See Trial Record, pp. 3359–3375.)

Jerry got nowhere with either of these early efforts. But in his next series of writs, he began to concentrate much more effectively on the issue of prejudicial pretrial publicity. For not only was this an area where the deck had been stacked against him in the most flagrant way, it was also, in the late sixties and early seventies, a body of law that was evolving especially fast.

Still the results were the same. As always, the courts were more than willing to acknowledge massive levels of official misconduct. But somehow in their estimation the levels were never quite massive enough to overturn the decision. A ruling by U.S. District Court Judge John R. Bartels in 1969 is typical of the *yes-but* reasoning that the courts had consistently adopted in the case:

> It is hardly necessary to observe that the conduct of the police in their participation in the adverse publicity was shocking and reprehensible. Nor is the press to be exonerated in their irresponsible conduct in abusing their freedom. Nevertheless, this court has concluded from the record that there is no necessity for a further hearing and that petitioner Rosenberg received a fair and impartial trial free from any bias or prejudice.

But Jerry never gave up, and in another complaint a year later he cataloged a long list of false and inflammatory pretrial statements made by then Chief of Detectives Raymond V. Martin—a list that included such blatantly prejudicial assertions as:

> This man [Rosenberg] is a drifter and he is deceptive. When acquitted of a homicide charge, he told his girl friend simply, "I beat the rap." This man is more dangerous than he looks.
>
> As a result of pooling police information after the detectives' murder, five other holdups in Brooklyn have definitely been traced to these three hoodlums.
>
> Rosenberg is definitely one of the killers. We have ten witnesses who have identified him already.

In his writ, Jerry had gone on to specify Martin's role in obstructing and hampering his attorneys in their preparation of the defense, in orchestrating the reign of brutality and terror that had finally induced Richie Melville and Linda Manzione to perjure themselves against him, and in whipping up the climate of municipal hysteria that ultimately infected the conduct of the trial itself.

But it was all in vain. No matter how long the list of grievances, the courts invariably managed to satisfy themselves that the deliberations of the jury had not been affected and that the machinery of justice had functioned properly in the end.

Still he persisted. And in yet another writ, this one submitted in April of 1971, Jerry had skillfully attacked the "eyewitness" identification by Boro Park Tobacco Company co-owner David Goldberg—the testimony that underlay the state's entire case. Not only are eyewitness identifications notoriously unreliable, Jerry argued, but Goldberg had literally been "programmed" by the police to make the identification he did—and had been suitably rewarded afterward when Martin arranged to staff the Tobacco Company premises with a full-time plainclothes cop:

> At the trial, the witness Goldberg testified that "There was one time that I got a good look at him [Rosenberg] with the hat, with the glasses, with the gun, but with the handkerchief off the face." And yet this same Goldberg had told the District Attorney in a pretrial statement that he had "never" seen "this thin man, the first man, face-to-face at any time." When the District Attorney repeated the same question, saying "At no time?" Goldberg had again replied, "At no time." Goldberg also admitted that his identification of Rosenberg in a police lineup had occurred after he had been shown a photograph of Rosenberg by the police—although he insisted that the police were showing him numerous photographs and that they had not said anything to him about the person whose

> face appeared on the Rosenberg photograph. Goldberg further revealed that immediately after the crime he had seen newspapers containing pictures of the defendant Rosenberg, and that it was after seeing the newspaper pictures and the police photograph that he had gone to the lineup and picked out the defendant Rosenberg.

This time the court's answer amounted to little more than a single infuriating sentence: "The accuracy and truthfulness of David Goldberg's testimony," they said, "was a question that only the original trial jury in its collective wisdom was empowered to decide."

I had another solid issue on the question of jury selection where the record shows that every single one of them admitted they'd heard about the case. Of course they'd heard about it! The fact is there was continuous publicity right through the trial, and one guy on the jury even admitted that he'd read about my criminal record and that he knew I was a parole violator at the time of the shootings. The case law on this kind of prejudice is overwhelming. "One cannot assume that the average juror is so endowed with a sense of detachment that he can exclude his own preconceptions as to probable guilt, especially if those preconceptions have been built up by pervasive pre-trial publicity." That was the applicable standard at the time of the trial. But as usual, in my case the court of appeals found a way out. There happened to have been a newspaper strike right before the trial, they said, which allowed for "sufficient separation to take place in order to negate the prejudice against the defendant." Sufficient separation. *What are the standards they're applying here? What in God's name would be* insufficient? *Rulings like this aren't based on law or justice, in my opinion. They're arbitrary and capricious, and they're based purely on human whim.*

* * * *

Meanwhile Martin and his chief investigating officer in the case, Albert A. Seedman, were both being promoted briskly up the departmental ladder, Seedman to chief of detectives in Manhattan and Martin to a powerful citywide post known as deputy chief inspector. There's no question that the Rosenberg/Portelli case was a major stepping stone in both their careers, and Martin even went so far as to include a chapter about the case in a self-congratulatory book entitled *Revolt in the Mafia* that he wrote shortly after retiring from the department in 1963. Choosing his words carefully, Martin also brainstormed a brand-new explanation to account for the presence of the two detectives at the tobacco company:

> Detectives Fallon and Finegan had been working on a series of wholesale tobacco-company hold-ups. These robberies were committed on Friday afternoons after cash which could not be banked until Monday had come into the office. Following the second holdup, Captain Al Seedman C.D. of the Bath Beach area and I established a pattern chart—the location of each robbery, the time and method, how many minutes it took, the mannerisms of the two young gunmen who allowed their white handkerchief masks to slip down casually from their faces at times, etc. Since the next three robberies fitted the pattern chart exactly, it would be only a matter of time before our detectives caught up with their men. Checking the Boro Park Tobacco Company office this particular Friday afternoon, Fallon found himself in the midst of a holdup. One of the white-masked gunmen threw down his weapon and surrendered, only to shoot Fallon through the heart with a concealed gun a few seconds later. When Finnegan rushed in at the sound of the second shot, he was dropped in a fusillade of bullets.

Predictably, all the new twists that Martin had added to the previous official version—the concealed gun, the implication that the perpetrators routinely allowed their masks to fall away, and especially the bizarre claim that Finnegan and Fallon were literally on their tail—had the effect of buttressing the convictions and rendering the crime that much more reprehensible and vicious.

As for the charges of police brutality, which had been extensively documented and which even Judge Leibowitz had said would do credit to a "Gestapo wretch," Martin intransigently defended his command. "All three prisoners were treated with great restraint," he wrote, "and facts brought out later at their first-degree-murder trial substantiated this." Protests about police brutality came only from civil rights groups, he said, "and from individuals who didn't know all the facts." Characteristically, he was unwilling to back down even on the question of the official admonishment to Seedman by Police Commissioner Michael Murphy for roughing up Delvecchio in front of a phalanx of news photographers. "It was the first such rebuke in the history of the New York City Police Department," Martin wrote, "and it was not provided for in our rules and procedures. The admonishment was unwarranted, and I said so promptly."

To Jerry, reading the book in his cell at Attica one night in 1968, this latest batch of lies and distortions and denials merely hardened his resolve. And now, in February of 1972, with a "reasonably adequate" law library available to him for the first time, he began to devise an unprecedented course of legal action by which he hoped to hold Martin *personally responsible* for both the beatings and the pretrial publicity under an obscure hundred-year-old federal statute—Section 1983, Title 42 of the United States Code.

> Any state or local official [the statute reads] who, acting in his official capacity deprives a citizen of the United States of any

> rights, privileges, or immunities secured to him by the Constitution and Federal law, shall be liable to the injured party in an action at law, suit in equity, or other proper proceeding for redress.

Originally known as the Federal Civil Rights Act of 1871, the statute had been enacted shortly after the Civil War in an attempt to assist the newly freed slaves in asserting their constitutional rights. The *intent* of the law had been quickly undermined by racist federal judges in the South, however, and the statute had lain dormant until the late 1960s, when the Supreme Court, under the leadership of Associate Justice William O. Douglas, vastly simplified the procedures governing its use.

Most significant of all from Jerry's point of view, however, was a 1964 decision known as *Cooper* v. *Pate,* in which the Court ruled that state prisoners were entitled to use the statute to seek injunctive relief, and in some cases money damages, from state prison officials who had violated their federal rights.

Of course Jerry's grievances concerned a police officer rather than a prison official, but he could see no reason why the precedent in *Cooper* v. *Pate* could not be stretched to cover his own situation as well. And so by early spring he had thrown himself into a manic burst of research and writing that resulted in a forty-seven-page complaint in which he alleged that Martin had personally used his official position with the New York City Police Department to deprive him of certain "intrinsic rights, privileges, and immunities guaranteed under the Fifth, Sixth, Eighth, and Fourteenth Amendments."

Jerry knew that he had stepped out into a vast, uncharted legal wilderness here and that it was almost certainly the first time a prisoner had ever brought suit against his arresting officer under the terms of Section 1983. But it wasn't the possibility of money damages or even a primitive lust for revenge that had inspired him to devise this novel course of action. It was, on the contrary, the tenuous and still largely unspoken hope that somewhere down the line he might be able to use a Section 1983 judgment against Martin as the leading edge to reopen his entire case.

But for that to happen, he knew, his draft would first have to find its way to a judge who would not only be sensitive to the issues of police misconduct and pretrial rights that he was raising, but who would also have the courage to endorse the basic conceptual soundness of his approach.

A couple of months later my daughter came in to see me for the first time. A teenager already, I couldn't believe it. She'd been in Brooklyn a lot with my parents over the years, but for all those times Rose-Ann would never let her come up on a visit. She was worried about the stigma; it's understandable. But after the Attica riot I sent off a batch of clippings. I tried to send her the nice articles, for Ronnie's benefit, and I guess Rose-Ann finally decided she was old enough to handle it.

When she came in, she looked at me and tears rolled down her eyes. I had spoken with her on the telephone a few times so there was a little familiarity, but at first it was almost like she was scared to come over.

She's got a lot of problems, this kid. Got mixed up with the wrong people. Drugs and cops and so forth—the whole fucked-up Texas scene. The kid went to drugs and nobody knew it. She just went haywire, totally off on the wrong track. And I honestly believe it has something to do with me.

On that first visit all she wanted to talk about was what she could do to help me get out. It was like a total obsession. In fact, she was the first person to actually believe that I might have a chance at parole.

Anyhow, the first time she hugged me it was a hug that was frigid. But then we sat down and we started to talk, and pretty soon she could see that I wasn't a stuffed shirt. That I wasn't the regular kind of father who would automatically say this is wrong and that is wrong. She saw that I could relate to her, and she started to open up. After a while she just put her head down on my arm and lay there for a while, and I got all watered up. There's a lot of me *in that kid, and it hurts like crazy every time I see it.*

"It's rough when you find out what life is like," she told me at the end of the visit. "I mean it's pretty cold out there," she said, "isn't it?"

I truly wish she could've stayed in Brooklyn for the Martin trial. It would've given her a different image of me, hopefully. Something good *she could've identified with, instead of the street life that was eating her alive.*

17

"If it please Your Honor, counsel for the defendant, and members of the jury . . ." Jerry could hear his voice rising a notch, and he slowed himself down by glancing over at the defense table, drawing strength, as he knew he would, from Martin's silent intransigence. Martin, he reminded himself, was the one who had to worry.

"As the judge clearly stated this morning, this is a civil rights case," he told the grumpy-looking all-male jury. "And the first thing you have to understand is that in January of 1963 I was convicted of the murder of two New York City police officers. I protested my innocence, but that is not the issue here. I was found guilty by a jury and I am in prison for life." He quickly studied the double row of startled faces in the jury box, sizing up their initial response.

"The issue here is not really that complex," he told them. "In fact, it is a simple issue. When a person is accused of a crime, he has the right, according to law, to be protected *by* the law. And law-enforcement officials have the duty to protect that citizen no matter what the circumstances are—whether he is accused of a crime where their personal feelings are involved or not. The police officer's job is to arrest the accused. But in that act of arrest, he must use proper care, fairness, and, according to the law, no brutality."

He glanced up at the judge—Federal District Judge John F. Dooling, Jr.—a gentle, sixty-four-year-old practicing Catholic who had been an honors graduate of St. Francis College in Brooklyn and who was the father of five grown children. Despite his years Dooling was invariably the first judge to arrive at the courthouse every morning, and he also had a statewide reputation for impeccable legal scholarship, personal rectitude and, in the words of one former U.S. attorney, "the moral backbone of God."

"I will prove by a preponderance of the evidence," Jerry continued, "that both before and after my surrender at the Daily News Building on May 23, 1962, the defendant Martin personally assaulted me. That he caused me to be harassed, cursed upon, and beaten by other police officers, and that he repeatedly issued false and malicious statements to the press that were designed to prejudice [the public against] me in all matters. All this despite the fact that I surrendered voluntarily to prove my innocence."

He paused and looked over at Martin's attorney, an affable, fiftyish New York City corporation counsel named George Weiler, who was known as a shrewd litigator and a clever man with a jury. At the moment Weiler was sucking unconcernedly on a yellow pencil and paging through a sheaf of legal papers; he leaned back, whispered something to his associate counsel, William Greenough, and smiled broadly—a smile that would disappear completely from his repertoire by the end of the third day.

"At the station house I was interrogated for six to eight hours," Jerry continued, resting his hands lightly on the edge of the jury-box rail.

"I was spat upon by the police officers.

"I was beaten and kicked. And the defendant personally himself—who was in charge of the case—Martin himself placed his hand over my ear and suction-cupped my ear and seriously impaired my hearing on that side. This is not the function of the police.

"As serious as the crime was—and it was a serious crime; two officers were killed—still, the police had no right to inflame the public against me and cause me these humiliations and injuries.

"You will hear testimony from various witnesses," he said, "including myself, and documentary evidence will also be produced. I ask you to evaluate that evidence. And also to bear in mind that these violations took place at a time when I was entitled to the presumption of innocence."

And then he stopped himself short. He wanted to go on and complete the picture—to tell the jury in so many words that Martin's lies and distortions had been directly responsible for his conviction and imprisonment. But to do that would have violated the ground rules Judge Dooling had laid down in his chambers that morning. "I will not allow you to retry the original case," Dooling had warned him. And while Jerry hoped to be able to nudge the jury toward that conclusion on its own, he also knew from his experience with Leibowitz that it was absolutely vital to keep Dooling off his back for as long as possible.

"I will prove to the court," Jerry said in conclusion, glancing from face to face in the jury box and attempting to establish eye contact with each one of them, "that the tortious conduct of this defendant, in which he used methods of brutality and deceit, were acts of lawlessness incompatible with the civilized system of justice we know today. I ask you gentlemen," he said, "to render a verdict that speaks of truth and justice."

He turned back to the plaintiff's table, disoriented by the silence that hung over the room and totally unsure of the effect he'd just created. He was, after all, functioning in the real world for the first time in over ten years, and his real-world instincts were still a little rusty. But then he caught sight of his mother and father squeezed together in the third row, and he could tell from the look on their faces that he must have done okay. "Well, I guess this is it," he had told her nervously in the visiting room at the old West Street jail the day before. And the sense of pride and vindication and relief Rose felt as she hugged him there in his brand-new herringbone sports coat and flannel slacks was little short of overwhelming. She truly *admired* this strange person—her son—this person her son had become. She respected his courage and erudition. And as she sat there listening to him in the courtroom, she more than anyone was aware of the enormous obstacles he'd had to overcome, especially those within himself.

On this first day of the trial, the seats all around her were empty, of course, except for a marshal or two and a handful of elderly courthouse regulars. But in the days ahead, as word of the trial and her son's astonishing performance began to spread through Brooklyn's criminal-justice grapevine, the spectator section of Judge Dooling's courtroom would regularly be SRO.

Weiler, in his opening statement, revealed his basic strategy right off the bat—a defense that relied principally on undermining Jerry's credibility rather than dignifying the allegations and attempting to refute him on the facts. This whole thing is preposterous, Weiler seemed to be saying—a travesty, an affront to Martin, a waste of time.

"You have certain duties," he told the jury. "You are the finders of the facts. You will determine where to look for truthfulness—it is called credibility. You will determine which of these two gentlemen—and I expect there will be substantial areas of disagreement—is to be believed. Mr. Rosenberg, undoubtedly, will be a witness on his own behalf. And it will be your job to take his testimony and weigh what he says against Chief Inspector Martin's testimony—if the case should go that far—applying the test of your own common sense and life experience."

And then he rambled through a chronology of the manhunt and Jerry's surrender, emphasizing the *public-safety* aspects of the statements Martin made to the press. "It will come to your attention," Weiler told the jury, "that Mr. Rosenberg had previously been an inmate in a correctional institution—I believe his term was some five years or so—and whether a violator of parole or not, you will have the opportunity to learn during the course of this trial. This information and pedigree was immediately available to Inspector Martin, of course, and it was his professional judgment that the public as well as police officers throughout the region should be notified that Rosenberg was armed and at large and that he might be dangerous."

Weiler closed by brushing off the claim of assault, stating that Martin knew the *Daily News* had taken photographs of Jerry at the outset, and that assaulting him while he was in police custody "would have been a foolhardy thing, at best, to have done."

"I would ask you to decide this case," he told the jury in conclusion, "by searching for the truth of whether or not many of these things ever happened at all."

The trial itself got off to a sizzling start two minutes into Jerry's narrative testimony, when he began to describe the phone call he made from the basement of the Tremont Avenue Bar & Grill. "I was really debating whether to surrender or not," he told the jury, "at which time I spoke to my father. He told me the best thing to do, if you are innocent, is to surrender—"

"Objection!" Weiler shouted, jumping to his feet.

"Well, members of the jury," Dooling said, exhibiting the qualities of patience, thoroughness, and gentle irony for which he was justly famous, "this objection Mr. Weiler makes is to the fact that the witness has quoted what someone else said to him as a fact—to wit, his innocence. Now as Mr. Rosenberg has told you, innocence or guilt is not the issue. Mr. Rosenberg, senior, was not a witness to the crime. I assume he did not know whereof he spoke. He was speaking in the conditional to his son. So what you hear when Mr. Rosenberg repeats such a statement may be taken into account only for whatever action Mr. Rosenberg, junior, took on it. In any case, the gist of the statement was that his father advised him to surrender."

But Weiler wasn't satisfied. "Also an objection on hearsay, Your Honor."

This time, however, Dooling slapped him down. "No, he can testify to that. He is testifying on advice he received. Proceed."

"At which time my father made the arrangements," Jerry said, quickly picking up the threads, "and I surrendered at the New York *Daily News* in their offices. Prior to me surrendering, for three days straight every newspaper and television and radio station in the city gave accounts of the crime and of me as one of the killers—"

"Objection, Your Honor!" Weiler shouted. "On the grounds that he's failed to establish any connection between Inspector Martin and what the newspaper and radio stations may or may not have said."

"Sustained."

And so it went. At one point during that first afternoon, Jerry produced a thick stack of newspaper articles with statements attributed to Martin like "Rosenberg and Portelli tricked my men into relaxing their guard and then shot them down in cold blood," and "We've got him [Rosenberg], here's the cop-killing bastard, he's going to burn." But Weiler objected every time, insisting that mere publication, even when the quotes were directly attributed, was not legally adequate to link the statements to Martin. Dooling finally agreed. And in the end he ruled that Jerry would have to produce the original newspaper reporters to testify that the statements were authentic and complete and that Martin had not been misquoted in any significant respect—a task that would turn out to be every bit as difficult, ten years after the fact, as George Weiler had hoped.

Meanwhile Jerry went ahead with the rest of his case. And the first witness he called was his old friend and codefendant Anthony Portelli, who had just been brought down from Greenhaven Prison for the occasion and whom Jerry hadn't seen for almost ten years. They had had a boisterous reunion through the bars of the decrepit West Street federal jail in Manhattan the night before, both of them having kept close track of each other through mutual friends and determined now to squeeze ten years' worth of news and gossip into a couple of days. And then at six A.M. the next morning they had gawked out the window of the paddy wagon together as it bounced and shimmied over the Brooklyn Bridge to the Eastern District Courthouse near Grand Army Plaza, the landscape of their childhood flashing past them in a dizzy blur.

But now, sworn in and seated in the witness box—and dressed for the occasion in a snazzy dark blue blazer and rep tie that Jerry's father had provided at the last minute—Portelli made a surprisingly solid first impression.

"Mr. Portelli," Jerry asked him. "Do you know me?"

"Yes, sir," Portelli said.

"Mr. Portelli, in the month of May, year of 1962, how did you first hear that you were wanted for the murder of two New York City police detectives?"

"I read about it in the newspapers," Portelli said.

"Objection!" Weiler called out, flipping his pencil into the air in disgust.

"He may answer that," Dooling ruled.

"After you read about this in the newspapers," Jerry asked, "did you flee?"

"Yes."

"Where did you go?"

"Chicago."

"Why did you flee?"

"I was ascared," Portelli said. "I knew they would frame me."

"Objection!"

"Sustained."

"And then the next day you were brought back to New York City by Detectives Frigand and Shea?" Jerry asked him.

"Yes."

"Did anyone meet you at the airport?"

"Assistant Chief Inspector Ray Martin."

"Then what happened?" Jerry asked.

"He pushed me in a car."

"Were you handcuffed?"

Portelli thought about it for a moment. "Behind my back," he finally said.

"Once in the car, where were you seated?"

"In the center of two detectives. In the back."

"Who was seated in the front of the car?"

"Ray Martin, on the passenger's side," Portelli said.

"During this whole trip, did you have any words with Ray Martin?"

"Once we was out on the Parkway he turned to me and says, 'You sonofabitch,' and he hit me with a left hand right in the neck. Then he smacked me forward and back."

Weiler was on his feet in an instant. "Objection! Your Honor!" he roared. "The issue before us is what, if anything, Mr. Martin did to Mr. Rosenberg, not what, if anything, he did to Mr. Portelli. I move to strike that last statement as collateral and irrelevant."

"Your Honor," Jerry said quickly, the words pouring out of him in a deadly accurate rush, "I submit it is revelant as part of the *res gestae* of the whole issue. It shows a propensity under a parallel and connected occasion, and I offer Mr. Portelli's testimony to show that the inference of truthfulness in my account is a probable inference."

Dooling thought it over for just a moment. "The objection is overruled," he said firmly, "and the motion to strike is denied."

"Now, Mr. Portelli," Jerry continued, flashing his old friend a covert smile of triumph. "When you arrived at the precinct—before you entered the precinct—did you see anything unusual outside?"

"There was a large crowd," Portelli said. "Mostly kids. They were hollering 'Lynch 'em, kill 'em, hang 'em,' all sorts of things from all sides."

"Were there barriers up?"

"Yeah, regular police barriers."

"Television cameras?"

"Plenty. And a radio truck across the street."

"Could you describe to the jury in simple facts what occurred when you were brought into the precinct?"

"I was pulled into the police station. There was a large crowd, and I was pulled in and there were some newspaper people there and they stopped to ask Ray Martin: 'You sure this is the man?' And Martin said, 'This is the triggerman. This is the killer and Rosenberg is his accomplice.' "

"Objection!" Weiler yelled, stuttering out an incoherent jumble of legal blather that left Dooling thoroughly unimpressed. "I submit," Weiler shouted, "that on the basis of the alleged proponent and the alleged persons, there is no showing that it is either connected or that the person who said it had a duty to impart it or that it was a matter that was required to be given in the course of police duties—and general objection also."

"Please continue, Mr. Rosenberg," Dooling said evenly. "Objection overruled. The motion to strike is denied."

Jerry glanced over at the jury, aware that even the grumpiest of them now seemed at least vaguely receptive.

"Could you describe for the jury, Mr. Portelli," Jerry said, "the first time you saw me and the defendant together at the precinct?"

"We were sitting in the corner of the squad room," Portelli said, "and I was sitting in the chair and we were talking. And then all of a sudden the door smashed open and Martin whirled you around and he said, 'You face the wall, sucker, or I'll bust your other ear!' "

"No further questions, Your Honor," Jerry said. A quick sideways glance at the jury told him they were finally starting to come around.

On cross-examination Portelli was every bit as effective, even though Weiler immediately took him back to the car ride in from the airport and attempted a standard lawyer's job of mixing him up.

"Did you ever once during the entire ride see Inspector Martin turn around and place both of his knees and his body directed fully toward you?" Weiler asked.

"No," Portelli told him. "He was sitting at an angle, like this, with his arm on the window and one hand on the backseat. And then he turned and looked at me and that's when he made that statement [you sonofabitch]—and then he hit me right alongside my neck and he smacked me in the face, both forward and backward."

"Which of Inspector Martin's hands did you say was against the side column of the car," Weiler asked, "his right or his left?"

"His right."

"But you first told us he had his right hand on the back of the seat and he slapped you with his left hand. Now you describe that he brought his arm forward and struck you from the front seat with his right hand, is that correct, sir?"

"One of us is mixed up," Portelli told him, "and I know it ain't me. I actually showed the jury right before when I went like this with my arm."

But still Weiler wouldn't quit. "Your story is, then, that Inspector

Martin had his right hand on the column of the car, the upright column, and that he whirled around without putting his knees on the seat and struck you with that same hand, is that correct or not?"

Portelli flashed him a smile full of Brooklyn menace. "Could I demonstrate it for you?" he asked. "Come here. Let me show you." Weiler shook his head and backed away as gracefully as possible. "What way do you want me to put it?" Portelli yelled at him in exasperation. "He went wild. The man is a wild man. He's not human. If they only knew what he was like then!"

Jerry's first opportunity to cross-examine a cop came on the morning of the second day. The witness was a florid-faced, soft-spoken homicide detective named Donald Kunkel, who had been assigned to the Boro Park precinct at the time of the shootings.

"Detective Kunkel," Jerry asked him, "are you familiar with the Supreme Court decision called *Miranda* v. *Arizona?*"

"Of course," Kunkel snapped, "the Miranda warnings and so forth."

"Are you aware, Detective Kunkel, that the treatment of one of the witnesses against me, Richard Melville, was cited in that case as a flagrant example of police misconduct?"

"Objection, Your Honor."

"Sustained."

"Let me try it this way," Jerry said. "Do you know a Richard Melville?"

"Yes, I do."

"Did you ever speak to Richard Melville?"

"Did I speak with him? Yes."

"In other words you were in on the investigation of Richard Melville—questioning him about Portelli's allegedly hiding in his apartment, correct?"

"Objection."

"No. He may ask the question in that form, Mr. Weiler," Dooling said.

"Am I correct?" Jerry asked him again.

"I was part of the investigation, yes."

"And you spoke to Richard Melville in that investigation?"

"Yes, I just said yes."

"And earlier you told us that you got information that Portelli went to Chicago under the name Jim Davis?"

"Yes."

"And that information was in the alarm that resulted in Portelli's arrest?"

"Yes."

"Do you know where that source of information came from?"

"Yes."

"Who?"

"Richard Melville."

"Richard Melville. Did Richard Melville volunteer these statements to you and your brother officers?"

"Objection."

"Overruled."

"This information was given by Richard Melville."

"I said, did he volunteer this information to you?"

"Same objection."

"Overruled."

"Again, I don't recall whether or not he gave it to me personally or not. This was information that was given when he was in the station house."

"You seen him in the station house?"

"Yes."

"How was his condition?"

"Objection."

"Overruled."

"How was his condition?"

"He appeared to be all right to me."

"He appeared to be all right to you?"

"Yes."

"Did you notice any cigarette burns on Richie Melville's back?"

"Objection! And I now ask that this jury be instructioned to disregard any such statement."

"Overruled."

"Did you notice an open wound across his throat where he'd been sliced by a wire?"

"Same objection."

"Overruled."

"No, I did not."

"Detective Kunkel, were you ever brought before a Police Department Civilian Review Board in connection with this case?"

"Objection, Your Honor, this is new material."

"Mr. Rosenberg, I'm going to have to ask you to desist from this line of inquiry," Dooling ruled.

But of course the images Jerry had summoned up would be difficult for the jury to ignore. He then shifted to the issue of excessive publicity and asked Kunkel whether to his knowledge there was widespread media coverage of the crime and the ensuing investigation.

"I recall there was publicity, yes."

"Did you personally see any television publicity?"

"I was too involved in the investigation."

"You never seen any television coverage?"

"I may have seen a little television during breaks of investigation."

"Detective Kunkel, when you and I arrived at the Sixty-sixth Precinct, were we in different cars?"

"Yes."

"Do you recall me being brought out of the car?"

"I recall you were brought into the station house."

"Were there crowds outside the precinct when you arrived?"

"I don't recall any crowds. We got there about maybe one o'clock in the morning or so."

"I'm saying do you recall any crowds?"

"There were many people around all the time during the investigation. I don't recall any specific crowd that would be outstanding in my mind."

"Well, when you arrived at the precinct, were there crowds standing around with wooden horses blocking them off? Do you recall that now?"

"I don't recall wooden horses or things like that."

"Do you recall television cameras out there?"

"At that particular time?"

"At the time I arrived."

"There may have been. I don't remember."

"There may have?"

"I don't remember."

"In other words this wouldn't stand out in your mind, a scene like this, television cameras, crowds?"

"There were television cameras there all the time."

"There was television cameras there all the time?"

"Reporters, in other words. Reporters were there since the inception of this investigation."

"What I'm asking you, I'm going to reclarify this question. Simply, when you arrived and I arrived, were there crowds and television cameras outside the precinct? Simple question."

"Objection as to the form of the question, Your Honor."

"Sustained. The part about a simple question is stricken. Can you answer the question?"

"I don't recall."

"You don't recall very much, do you?"

"Objection, Your Honor, he is just arguing with the witness now."

"Sustained."

"No further questions."

"You may step down."

Jerry glanced over at the jury, pleased to see a flicker of awareness on several previously skeptical faces as Kunkel nodded to Martin on his way across the well of the court.

On July 25 William Federici, the *Daily News* lead reporter on the story, finally appeared—but minus the complete set of clippings and the videotapes from the *Daily News* television station, WPIX-TV, that had been requested in the subpoena. In fact, the *Daily News* lawyers, concerned about protecting the paper's First Amendment rights, had instructed Federici not to respond to the subpoena at all but merely to appear in the courtroom on a voluntary basis and to offer to authenticate whatever material was already in evidence.

"If it is here in the newspaper, and I am associated with it, then I say to you these are facts," Federici told the jury. He also testified that Martin was "obviously an important source" in his coverage of the case, and that whatever material had been attributed to Martin was accurate and complete. "When we put something in a quotation, it is exact," he said. "It is never rewritten. We don't change what people say. We can be sued for that."

Weiler, on cross-examination, inadvertently shed a great deal of light on Martin's penchant for cultivating personal relationships with reporters—relationships that Martin had exploited to the hilt in this case and that had worked to Jerry's disadvantage in almost every conceivable respect. "Chief Martin and myself were very close at that time," Federici testified. "I found him to be a very truthful and wonderful man."

And then, exhibiting an astonishing level of pre-Watergate naiveté, Federici explained his lifelong reportorial philosophy in the following terms: "I can only say that whatever Mr. Martin gave us at the time was used because Mr. Martin was an assistant chief inspector in charge of detectives. And if a newspaperman cannot trust a man in that authority to give him an accurate accounting of something, he cannot trust anyone."

To which Jerry added an emphatic and deeply ironic, "That is correct."

And then it was Martin's turn. Weiler took him quickly through the chronology of his involvement in the case—Martin emphasizing his *executive* role and the "extreme caution" he saw fit to exercise. "I knew the feelings were running quite high amongst detectives and policemen about two of their brother officers being killed, and I didn't want any repercussions or remarks or allegations that usually crop up in these cases," he said. Specifically, he denied that he had ever "spit upon, struck, or kicked the defendant. I as a commanding officer of that rank couldn't demean myself to do any act in front of my men or to have them see such a thing," he said. "That's the way I have always conducted myself in my job."

And then he went on to quote solemnly from a deposition he had given earlier in the case in which he had said, "In view of the serious nature of the crime, and realizing that pre-trial publicity would have a bad effect on the case, I was extremely cautious to protect the rights of the plaintiff in order to insure a valid conviction which would not be reversed on appeal."

As far as Federici was concerned, Martin paid tribute to him as "tops in the business" and "very enterprising" and admitted that he gave Federici and other reporters ready access to him during the investigation. But he insisted repeatedly that under Section 14.5 of the

Manual of Procedures of the New York City Police Department, he was "required to cooperate with the press."

Then Weiler took him through a well-rehearsed exegesis of his press statements, Martin denying some of them and modifying and amending others in certain key respects. As for the claim that he had "positive identification" of Jerry in ten other Brooklyn holdups, Martin now said he had no direct knowledge of those identifications but was merely relying on "reports from detectives in the field."

"But these were official police department data that were available?" Weiler prompted.

"Yes, sir."

"And these were positive identifications?"

"Well, at this point I can't say that they were," Martin told him, "because I have no record of it, and I have no recollection."

Jerry got his first crack at the man on the afternoon of the twenty-sixth, and after eliciting a *pro forma* denial of the assault charge—and of Portelli's assertion that he had been slapped around in the car—he plunged directly into the question of the extent of the pretrial publicity.

"Inspector Martin," he said, "I show you Exhibit Nine, portions of a book, *Revolt in the Mafia,* and I ask you whether that is your name underneath as the author."

"Yes, it is."

"Would you take a look at pages two hundred forty-three, two hundred forty-four, two hundred forty-five, and two hundred forty-six and tell us whether or not this is your work?"

Martin reached for the book and flipped quickly through the pages. "Yes, I already told you it was," he said, snapping the book shut.

"It *was?*"

"It is."

"Thank you. Would you kindly read for the jury the paragraph marked off in red on page two hundred forty-five?"

Martin opened the book again, fumbled for his glasses, and started reading in a gravel-voiced monotone. " 'A television news story showed Portelli arriving at the airport under heavy police guard, being greeted by a thousand hooting, cursing citizens,' " he said, his voice level dropping appreciably as he neared the end of the sentence. " 'I held him up by the arm and head to prevent him from falling in the path of the excited throng, and he thanked me while we were riding back to Brooklyn for protecting him from the angry crowd.' "

"He thanked you?"

Martin nodded.

"Was that before or after you hit him?" Jerry asked in a perfect Peter Lorre deadpan.

"Objection!"

"Sustained."

"I withdraw the question, Your Honor." Jerry glanced over at the jury, buoyed by a couple of appreciative smiles in the second row. He felt sure of his ground now, confident that he had his adversary on the run. The key, he had suddenly understood, was to force the man into a pattern of automatic denials.

"Inspector Martin," he asked softly, "were you emotional when this case happened?"

Martin looked at him for a moment, searching for a circumlocution. "My five hundred murder investigations and seven cop killings—I think we attack it with determination," he finally said. "Being emotional wouldn't help."

"Did you have any animosity toward me?" Jerry asked.

"I will take that word in its context and say no."

"Were you angry?"

"Of course not."

"You never got mad?"

"No."

A preposterous statement—and a quick sideways glance at the jury told Jerry that at least some of them thought so, too. "Inspector Martin," he said, "when you and I arrived at the precinct house the following day, do you recall a crowd of reporters and photographers outside at that time as well?"

"There were a lot of things around," Martin said, his anger boiling out into the open for the first time. "The fact is I wasn't looking at the crowds or what was there. I was busy with you, Mr. Rosenberg."

"Yes, I know," Jerry shot back. He riffled quickly through the papers at the counsel's table. "I'm going to show you an article from the New York *Daily News*," he said, "attributed to you and written by William Federici, and I'm going to ask you to read us the portion marked off in red."

Martin fumbled again for his reading glasses, his movements thick and clumsy with rage. "'In a revised account of last Friday's shooting,'" he read, "'Inspector Martin told reporters that Rosenberg, at the rear of the store, charged out holding a towel to his face. He stepped on Fallon, jumped over Finnegan, and bolted through the door,'" Martin related. "'Portelli followed, and they parted so fast that Portelli had no chance to get a split of the loot which Rosenberg carried.'"

"Did you make that statement, Mr. Martin?" Jerry asked him.

There was an immediate and unsuccessful objection by Weiler, and then a long pause during which Martin just stared fixedly at his fingertips.

"I would say I don't know those facts now," he finally said, "and I don't know that I knew those facts then, so I don't see how I could have given that statement."

"And yet the newspaper article clearly stated, 'Martin related this.'"

Again there was a long pause, Weiler silently rooting for his client to slide away from this in any way he could. The last thing he wanted was to pit his man's credibility against a pro-cop newspaper like the *Daily News.* But Martin, experienced courtroom hand that he was, had been forced by Jerry's interrogatory into a situation where he had no choice but to paint the issue in black and white.

"I deny making that statement," Martin finally snapped.

The trial finally drew to a close on the twenty-seventh, Weiler summing up in a brisk twenty minutes and once again hammering hard on the question of credibility. "In many respects there is a very great difference between what Mr. Rosenberg says and what Mr. Martin says," he reminded the jury, "and you all know who we have here and who the witnesses are."

He paid a wordy and only intermittently coherent tribute to Martin as a man of responsibility, "the commander of five hundred detectives, with twelve or fifteen precincts and a million and a half or more people under his day-to-day handling for their protection. He is a man who rose by responsibility, by civil-service examinations up to captain, and who is entitled to some consideration to determine his truthfulness by all of the excellent occupational and family circumstances of his career. On the other hand," Weiler said, "we have Mr. Rosenberg—and I'll say no more than that you all know Mr. Rosenberg's record, and I'll leave it to your own common sense how much of what he says can be believed."

As for the publicity, Weiler insisted it did not exceed the limits of proper police procedure. "The best test of that came on the twenty-fourth," he said, "when Mr. Rosenberg, in response to that very publicity, voluntarily surrendered himself. Clearly, then, the publicity served a reasonable purpose at the time and produced the salutary result of Mr. Rosenberg reaching custody in a way that he was not harmed. And while we're on the subject," he said, "let's not overlook the fact that there were many other ways to surrender. This man sought out the *Daily News.* He actively solicited publicity. Now, he's claiming too much publicity when he himself was the source of an exclusive to the largest daily circulation newspaper in the country."

Toward the end of his summation, Weiler dealt very gingerly and quickly with the question of money damages. "I submit to you that this isn't even a twenty-five-cent case," he said. "And the mere fact that I'm discussing this claim from the point of view of dollars—I don't want you to assume in any way, no matter how slight, that I believe there is anything to it. What would his damage be? Not one extra day of incarceration—he's serving life, and not a bit of that is compensable. Defamation of his personality? This is a man who admitted himself that 'I'm no innocent babe,' and who had already done four years in a state penitentiary. How much of his reputation was there left to defame?

"In conclusion," he told the jury, "I ask you one simple question. Did you ever hear Mr. Rosenberg ask to have a question repeated—this man who says he suffered an ear impairment, this man who has nothing better to do up there in his prison cell but dream up preposterous lawsuits like this one?"

Weiler glanced quickly from face to face. "We rely upon you as responsible citizens," he said, "to make a distinction between what is self-interested and what might be an ego trip on the part of Mr. Rosenberg—and what is truth. And we look to you to do equal, exact justice."

He returned thoughtfully to the defense table and sat down next to Martin, both of them clearly pleased with the jury's apparent reaction.

"All right, Mr. Rosenberg," Dooling said.

Jerry got slowly to his feet and anxiously scanned the double row of sober, skeptical faces. "Gentlemen of the jury," he said. "I'll sum up and get right to the facts, but before I do I would like to make a statement. Mr. Weiler brought out that never once during this trial did I ask to have a question repeated. Actually, I did ask a few times, but the truth is I can hear very well in this other ear. If I was here to deceive you I would have asked again and again. I'm here to get to the facts, not to impress the jury. The left ear is bad. The other one I hear from very well."

He stepped around in front of the plaintiff's table; unlike Weiler, he carried no notes with him as he spoke. "I'm not going to call Mr. Weiler a liar when he summed up on the evidence," Jerry continued, "but I will say that he was in error and that he was very careless with the truth. I'll give you the facts as they were. Of course it's up to your recollection, and of course you, the jury, will have to decide.

"Mr. Weiler says the publicity was necessary and proper. Does he really believe that? I was never arrested for ten other holdups. I was never even *questioned* about ten holdups. Other statements by Martin—'Rosenberg fired a shot,' or 'Rosenberg was at the rear of the store and charged out holding a gun,' or 'He, Rosenberg, stepped on Fallon, stepped over Finnegan'—these weren't just bulletins that I was being sought. Not at all. Bulletins are there to say that a man is wanted as a suspect, not to inflame the public before he can be brought to trial. Not to put in the people's mind, *your* minds, that a man is guilty because of official police statements given to the press.

"You heard the defendant read from his own book. There were thousands of people at the airport when Portelli arrived. There was extensive coverage. Mr. Federici testified he wrote fifteen or more articles. He also testified that he never saw the subpoena asking for television films and a complete set of news articles to be brought in with him."

"Objection!"

"Sustained. There is no evidence before the jury about the subpoena at all."

But Jerry didn't even break stride. "Now we go to the testimony of Detective Donald Kunkel," he said. "On direct examination Kunkel was clear and smooth, for what it was worth. But when I cross-examined him, he could not and did not recall a thing. He stated that his memory was hazy because it was an old case, but it was already an old case ten minutes earlier when he recalled everything Mr. Weiler wanted to hear. Was his testimony credible?

"He testified that he didn't recall one way or the other whether there were television crews or any news media outside the Sixty-sixth Precinct. And yet a small issue like the exact time of day we arrived he remembered perfectly. Kunkel did make one very revealing statement, however. He told Mr. Weiler that after we arrived at the station house he was placed in a room to *protect* me. Protect me from what? We have heard so far from the defense that nobody wanted to hurt me. Why would they want to protect me?"

Jerry moved a couple of steps closer to the jury. He knew he was making sense, but even from ten feet away he still couldn't read their faces. "Mr. Weiler also stated that I surrendered for publicity," he told them, an edge of authentic indignation in his voice. "This I did not do. A good friend of my father's was a newspaperman at the building; he assured my father that the safest way to surrender would be to the *Daily News*. I didn't go there to give them an exclusive. I went there to protect myself from physical harm.

"Mr. Weiler also brought up that I'm a convicted criminal. This is true. But I am also a human being. Mr. Weiler brought up I'm in prison for ten years. In fact, I could be there a lot longer, but still that is not the issue here. The issue, as the judge will instruct you, has to do with official brutality and deceit—and with the constitutional right we all have to equal protection under the law.

"Gentlemen of the jury," he said softly. "I'll close like this. The conduct of Inspector Martin was unlawful, reprehensible, and improper. And whatever balance must be struck between the rights of the accused and the right of society to protect itself against crime, physical torture and malicious pretrial publicity are both clearly intolerable.

"You have a priceless opportunity in this case—an opportunity to reassert that police lawlessness of this kind must never be excused in the name of maintaining a civilized society. I ask you to consider all the evidence carefully and think of all the testimony," he said. "And I thank you very much for your time."

The jury returned forty-eight hours later, and as the disheveled, sleepy-looking foreman lumbered to his feet and officially informed Dooling that they'd reached a verdict, Jerry's vital signs literally went on hold.

"Mr. Foreman," Dooling said, "how do you find as to the defendant, Raymond V. Martin?"

"We find for the plaintiff, Your Honor," the foreman said, his voice rasping with fatigue. "And we have awarded Mr. Rosenberg the sum of seventy-five hundred dollars in punitive damages."

"That's outrageous, Your Honor!" Weiler roared, as Martin slumped down in confusion and disbelief alongside. "And I demand that the jurors be polled one at a time."

"Juror number one, is that your verdict?" Dooling asked.

"Yes, Your Honor."

"Juror number two, is that your verdict?"

But Jerry wasn't listening. He was back in Brooklyn. And for the first time since the trial began, he allowed himself the fantasy of simply getting up and walking out the door. He heard Dooling pronounce the words "So ordered," then ducked away from the marshal who was approaching with a pair of handcuffs and reached out and hugged his mother tight from across the other side of the rail.

"It's sweet, isn't it, Ma?" Jerry said.

In his mind he had already drafted a brand-new writ of habeas corpus that incorporated the jury's ruling. And after more than ten years of struggle and pain and relentless determination, he allowed himself to believe that he had now finally acquired the means to reopen his entire case.

18

Three weeks after I got back from the Martin trial, I was out on the hill one day and I got a pain. In fact, I was heading down toward the Death House when all of a sudden I felt a numbness in my thighs and heat coming up my legs like a radiator. Then my whole body went stiff—like a contortion—and the next thing I knew I was in the hospital. I was numb. My blood pressure went down to forty. And the doctor, this sonofabitch named Michaud, didn't do nothing. I was getting worse and worse. My blood pressure dropped all the way. I couldn't get up. I had a fever of a hundred and four, a hundred and five.

Then, finally, a week later the nurse got scared and called the outside doctor, an internist from Peekskill named Dr. Froelich. He came rushing over and did a blood count, which turned out to be six times normal. "Holy Jesus!" he says. I was just lying there. I could hear him but I couldn't move.

Other inmates were helping me, like trying to talk to me. They said, "Jerry, everything will be all right." I couldn't answer. In fact, to be honest with you, it was blissful. I was right near death. A guy would put a rag on my head because I was burning up with fever. Inmates were coming up, how's he doing? Johnnie-Boy Rizzo, everybody. They'd bring me cake and ice cream and I couldn't eat, I couldn't even see or move. They fed me intravenously.

This guy Froelich saved my fuckin' life. Right away he gave me caffeine shots to get my blood pressure up. He said if it goes any lower, another three points, he's a dead man. And he got it up. Then he did a biopsy on the bone-marrow cells. He sprayed some anesthetic on my leg and took some stuff out of the bone marrow and had it rushed to the hospital. I didn't feel any pain. I heard a lot of crunching and stuff, but it really didn't matter, the way I felt. Turned out I had Guillain-Barré syndrome, some rare viral infection of the nervous system.

The first ten days were pretty rough. Thank God I had my good friends in there with me. Especially the Greek. He stood watch over me. Donald "the Greek" Frankos is his real name. Looks something like an Anthony Quinn type of character, only younger—dry sense of humor, the best in the world.

Years later I defended him in a murder case where we made new law in the Second Circuit. As usual, the guy who got whacked was a stool pigeon, a low-life bastard who'd been at it for years. They needed blood for the guy. They announced it on the prison speaker. And not one guy gave blood. That's the kind of solidarity we had over there at the time.

Anyhow, there was another guy in the infirmary with us, a client of mine named Gerald McCauley. He was always sick, McCauley, always complaining, even though he knew by then he'd be getting out in six months. In fact, this was the same guy whose case the special prosecutor's office—Nadjari's office—first hauled me in on a couple of months later.

What happened was in 1968 McCauley received a twelve-year sentence as a predicate felon—a three-time loser. The fact is, however, that one of those felonies was actually a misdemeanor that had been misclassified because of a change in the penal law. He had expensive lawyers on the case for years, and none of 'em spotted it. But as soon as he showed me *the minutes, I told him right away he had a shot. I drew up a motion for resentence and sent it off to the sentencing judge, Judge Dominic*

Rinaldi. And sure enough, a couple of months later Rinaldi ruled in our favor one hundred percent. Beautiful. McCauley's sentence gets cut in half and he'll be out on the street in six months.

Then all of a sudden I started reading in the papers that this special prosecutor, a real bulldozer named Maurice Nadjari, is planning to indict Judge Rinaldi for allegedly fixing a bunch of cases in Manhattan and Queens. But they never mentioned any of the specific cases. And I still didn't realize they were interested in the McCauley *case until a friend of ours in Inmate Records told me the special prosecutor's office had just subpoenaed my entire file.'*

By October of 1975, when Jerry had his first encounter with the special prosecutor's office, Maurice Nadjari was already on the ropes. He had been appointed by Governor Rockefeller in a blaze of righteous indignation in November of 1972—charged with cleaning up the city's criminal-justice system in the wake of a well-publicized series of hearings that had exposed multiple layers of corruption in courtrooms and precinct houses throughout the city. The *oomph* for the new office, Rocky said, would be supplied by an unprecedented $14 million operating budget and by a sweeping grant of inquisitorial powers that would render Nadjari totally independent of any existing governmental body.

But within a period of eighteen months, dozens of Maurice Nadjari's best-publicized cases had disintegrated before they even reached the courtroom, and many others had ended in prompt acquittals. Simultaneously, he had begun to come under attack from the city's liberal watchdog organizations. The American Civil Liberties Union's executive director, Ira Glasser, for example, publicly excoriated him as "a man who seems intent on carving a place for himself as a pathological example of prosecutorial misconduct."

As Nadjari's position slowly began to deteriorate, he became increasingly desperate for convictions and increasingly ruthless in the methods by which he sought to obtain them. Finally the abuses became so grotesque that he was dismissed from his position by Governor Hugh L. Carey. Three days later Nadjari held a press conference in which he charged that Carey had fired him because of the improper influences of "self-motivated persons." At which point longtime State Attorney General Louis Lefkowitz intervened and gave Nadjari a six-month extension in office in order to investigate the charges he had made against Carey and to prosecute those "self-motivated persons" whose cases otherwise would have been dropped.

One of those cases involved State Supreme Court Justice Dominic S. Rinaldi.

Six weeks after I got out of the hospital, I got word that the Court of Appeals had reversed the judgment of conviction in the Martin trial. It was a horrendous piece of legal scholarship, and they had to deliberately misinterpret the fine points of Dooling's entire constitutional argument to do it. But the closing paragraphs of the decision were nothing more than a rehash of the same old garbage the courts had been dishing out all along:

> It has been conclusively determined—not only by a state but by a federal court—that even though the prearrest publicity went considerably beyond what was necessary, and even though Martin's statements to the news media were thoroughly reprehensible—Rosenberg was not deprived of his constitutionally guaranteed right to a fair trial. In the light of these unequivocal rulings, we can find no valid basis for a verdict under Article 1983.*

---

* Jerry appealed, of course, all the way up to the United States Supreme Court, where the final vote was 8–1 against granting certiorari, or judicial review. Significantly, the affirmative vote was cast by Associate Justice William O. Douglas, who had resurrected the civil rights statutes in *Monroe v. Pape* thirteen years before.

I know it would've hit me a lot harder, but by this time I'd already started scheming something new. It had to do with a subject that everyone else forgot about over the years, including me: the fact that I was still legally on parole at the time I surrendered.

The only problem was that Leibowitz, when he sentenced me to the chair, never bothered to specify whether the two sentences were spozed to run concurrent or consecutive. I mean, why bother, right? If you're gonna burn, who cares? But by that same logic, once the sentence got commuted to life imprisonment, the whole issue suddenly became very important.

I finally had a hearing on it in April of '74 before Superior Court Judge Irving Lang, where I argued that the answer had to be concurrent. *Otherwise what were they gonna do, kill me first and then dig me up later to serve out the other sentence? "You got a good point there," the judge told me, and he reserved decision on it for a couple of months.*

Of course, once you start playing with these numbers it can get pretty ridiculous. I mean the minimum on a federal *life sentence is ten years. In California at the time it was only seven. And in Florida, believe it or not, it was just six months. In New York State in 1963, the year I was sentenced, it was twenty-six years and seven months. Then in 1972 it got reduced to a flat twenty—which, minus the forty-five months, would've meant that all of a sudden I was only four and a half years away.*

Meanwhile I was working on the Rizzo case practically fulltime—in a lot of ways the most important single case I'd ever been involved with. Everything was Rizzo, Rizzo, Rizzo. *But, unfortunately, I was so over-concentrated I totally lost track of Nadjari. In fact, the first I even* heard *that he was bringing Judge Rinaldi to trial on corruption charges was three and a half months later, when the sonofabitch hauled me in.*

Anyhow, it was the Rizzo case that really got me through the door as a lawyer. And in terms of prison medical standards, the decision we won is still working to the benefit of every prisoner in the state.

The facts involved were never in dispute. Rizzo hit a handball up on the roof of the Administration Building one day and, being a real clown, he decided to climb up a drainpipe to get it back.

All of a sudden something broke off or pulled away and he fell twenty feet, still holding onto the fuckin' pipe. It was horrible. He was in shock and tremendous pain and he was vomiting, and the Greek and Johnny D'Amato picked him up and carried him on a picnic table all the way to the infirmary.

Of course, it was that bastard Michaud on duty as usual, and as usual, he refused to treat him. All he did was give him some aspirin and a cell excuse for three days and told him not to masturbate!

It was incredible. The man was in excruciating pain. He couldn't walk for weeks, and even then he was still fucked up. One time his legs gave out on him completely and he tumbled down a flight of stairs. But Michaud just kept turning him away. Finally Dr. Froelich, the outside doctor, was in the joint one day and just happened to be there when Rizzo came up. He took one look and right away had him put in traction and other treatments and ordered him kept in the hospital for almost a month.

By that time I was so fuckin' angry I practically had the papers drawn up already and headed for the federal district court in New York City. We decided we were gonna nail this fuckin' Michaud personally. And as far as I know, it was the first time in history that a federal civil rights suit had ever been filed against a prison doctor.

What Jerry ultimately found himself asking for in the Rizzo case, however, went far beyond the threshold question of prison medical standards—and even further beyond the professional limits within which he had always operated in the past. For in this case, with Rizzo's wholehearted support, he was asking for nothing less than full accreditation as the attorney of record in a jury trial, including the right to cross-examine witnesses on Rizzo's behalf. It was an astounding request—a request that no prisoner had even *conceived* of in the past. And the situation became even more unprecedented six months later, when Rizzo was unconditionally released and Jerry suddenly found himself asking for the opportunity to represent not an inmate but a bona fide United States citizen.

The judge assigned to the case was a courtly, fifty-eight-year-old former Wall Street lawyer named Whitman Knapp, who had first come to public attention as the chairman of a blue-ribbon investigatory panel—the Knapp Commission—that had uncovered shocking levels of corruption in the city's criminal justice system.*

Jerry, of course, was well aware from his experience in the Perino case that judges—especially federal judges—have the discretion to do just about anything they want. But it was not until a lengthy pretrial hearing on December 9, 1974, that Knapp finally met the question of Jerry's participation in the case head-on.

In many respects it was Jerry's most impressive courtroom appearance to date. And Knapp's decision, even though he partially overruled himself several weeks later, would become the operative precedent for every one of Jerry's future court appearances and, in fact, for the mature phase of his entire legal career.

The central issue at the hearing had to do with the fact that Jerry, because of his criminal record, was categorically ineligible for membership in the New York State Bar. But after quickly thumbing through a thick folder full of diplomas and legal documents and clippings, Knapp pronounced himself satisfied that in terms of Jerry's education and experience "he *could* be admitted, there's no question of that."

---

* Ironically, it was the sordid revelations of the Knapp Commission hearings that had triggered Rockefeller's appointment of Maurice Nadjari as special prosecutor three years earlier.

"Your Honor, this man is a convicted felon!" Assistant Attorney General Ezra Coleman sputtered indignantly. "And if Your Honor is even *considering* the possibility of granting him the rights and privileges—"

"Assume it's a terrible precedent and I should get kicked off the bench for permitting it," Knapp told him. "How does it hurt your client?"

"A prisoner," Coleman said, groping for the words, "a man with a life sentence . . . there would be no way to discipline him, Your Honor, no way to insure that he conducts himself in a proper manner."

But Jerry rose to the provocation with consummate restraint. "Your Honor, I resent these gratuitous slurs," he told Knapp. "Moreover, I got a record here someplace where I represented a man at a hearing and the DA stated he had the highest respect for my competence and integrity. I will produce this for Your Honor's view."

Jerry produced a number of other documents that morning as well, including a tightly reasoned brief in which he argued that the legal premise established in *Johnson* v. *Avery* could logically be extended to cover his participation in *Rizzo* v. *Michaud*. "I personally don't see no difference between the verbal word and the written word," he told Knapp with a final rhetorical flourish.

He emerged from the hearing room fifteen minutes later with every one of the rights and privileges he had sought for himself, along with a bizarre admonition from Kanpp that if he revealed his identity as a prisoner or even hinted at any direct knowledge of the case, he would be immediately disqualified.

By a remarkable twist of legal circumstance, then, Jerry was literally being *required* to personify a free-world attorney. And for that day and a half in Judge Knapp's courtroom, he did an astonishingly successful and convincing job. His basic strategy throughout the trial was to place the jury in the shoes of a convicted felon—a strategy, although the jury didn't know it, that Jerry Rosenberg was uniquely qualified to carry out.

"When a man gets sent to prison and is locked up, that is one of the worst punishments there is," he told them in his opening statement. "But to treat him inhumanely, in any manner, only brings him out to society more bitter than he was before.

"What I'm trying to get across," he said, "is that any of us could catch an indictment someday. It happens all the time. God forbid any of you should get locked away. But let's say you did. And let's say you got hurt or you got sick up there—and of course you're not allowed to see your own doctor."

"Objection!" Coleman shouted, jumping to his feet. "Your Honor, these foolish ruminations—"

But Knapp cut him off in mid-sentence with a laconic "Overruled."

"The issue here is not just one crummy doctor and the suffering he inflicted on my client," Jerry continued. "The underlying issue is the horrendous conditions we have in these prisons, and a pattern of misconduct on the part of prison officials—"

"Objection!"

"Lay down, willya, Coleman?" Jerry shot back.

"I'm reminding you, Mr. Rosenberg, of the ground rules I laid down in my chambers," Knapp told him sharply.

But the outburst had loosened Jerry up a little, and he breezed into the facts of the case without a hitch.

His most effective witness that first morning was Dr. Dennis Froelich, the outside physician from Peekskill who had finally admitted Rizzo into the infirmary several months after the accident. In theory, Froelich was a witness for the other side, having originally been called by the defense as an *expert* witness and having testified earlier that in his opinion, Michaud's initial response was "clinically reasonable."

"Now, Dr. Froelich," Jerry said as soon as he got the man on cross-examination, "it says here that you also have a private practice in Peekskill, is that correct?"

"I am a board-certified neurologist and a fellow of the AANP," Froelich told him crisply.

"In other words you have a regular medical practice with a private office and so forth?"

"That is correct."

"Now, Dr. Froelich," Jerry said, "if one of your private patients, a regular patient of yours, let's say, was brought in on a stretcher, having fallen off the roof of a building—"

"Objection, Your Honor," Coleman roared. "The question is purely hypothetical."

"Of course it is," Jerry shot back. "I'm drawing on his medical *expertise,* Your Honor. Mr. Coleman qualified this witness himself."

Knapp thought about it for just a moment. "Proceed," he said, his voice inching up a bit above its usual low key.

Jerry looked over at Froelich, allowing the dust to settle. "If one of your regular patients came in like that," he said, "vomiting and shrieking with pain, would you send him home with a couple of aspirin and tell him not to masturbate?"

There was a long pause.

"I would not," Froelich finally told him as the courtroom sprang to life with a buzz of excitement.

"I have no further questions, Your Honor," Jerry said.

By far the toughest part of the case was proving that the medical treatment had been *deliberately* withheld—that the doctor had *known* that Rizzo needed medical attention and yet had refused to give it to him. It was a very strict standard, but Knapp kept hammering away at it over and over: "The question before you isn't whether Rizzo got good treatment or bad treatment," he repeatedly told the jury, "but whether or not it was maliciously and callously refused."

It was an area, Jerry felt sure, where the jury's *inferences* would make all the difference. And he approached the question only indirectly—but with enormous skill—midway through his closing statement. "The record in this case is detailed and very specific," he told them. "The record clearly indicates that the day Rizzo was brought into the hospital for the first time, Michaud gave him one pill and excused him to his cell. There is proof of that. It is in the record, and you will be able to observe the record if you wish. In fact, there is only one part of this case that *isn't* on the record," he said, "and that's the part where Michaud told him not to masturbate. The doctor told him, 'Here is a pill, stop masturbating for three days, and don't bother me.' That won't be on the record. Nobody in his *right mind* would put that on the record. If it was on the record, we would not be having this trial right now."

He paused for a moment and glanced from juror to juror. "Ladies and gentlemen," he said quietly, "even if John Rizzo didn't get one scratch on him from that fall, it wouldn't matter. The issue here is not the *injury* but the tortious conduct committed by the prison doctor working for the State of New York and the Department of Corrections. It is his actions that count. It is his intent with malice to commit an act like this against another human being that you should consider."

In conclusion, he told them, "We all have prejudices; that is human nature. But I will ask you one favor. If there are any prejudices in this case, try to put them aside and look instead for the right thing to do. And if you believe the evidence and the testimony you have heard—even though you may have no great liking for prisoners as a rule—then I ask you to return a verdict in favor of the plaintiff, John Rizzo."

* * * *

They came back with a verdict just two and a half hours later: guilty as charged with five thousand dollars in compensatory damages and three thousand dollars in punitive.

Of course the DA immediately started jumping up and down and screaming that the award was excessive and unreasonable, and he filed a motion thirty days later attacking the verdict on those same grounds. But by that time Knapp had changed his mind again and ruled me off the case—on the basis that since Rizzo was actually a non-prisoner, I didn't have the automatic right to represent him anymore. It's always possible Knapp was feeling some pressure, who knows? I mean it's just incredible how often these judges change their minds. In any case, that's why the papers attacking the verdict went to Rizzo directly, and that's also why—when Rizzo failed to respond within the specified time period—the verdict was eventually set aside.

But the very idea that a federal judge would allow a prisoner to bring a suit against a prison doctor was beautiful. "As an example to others," that's what Knapp told the jury punitive damages were all about. And I honestly believe that we've all been getting a little better class of treatment as a result.

As soon as the fucking gavel fell, they threw a pair of handcuffs on me and took me right across town to Nadjari's offices in the World Trade Center. It turns out there was an atmosphere of outright panic over there. They had this big trial underway where they were accusing Judge Rinaldi of taking backhanders, and as usual, they were making an absolute fool of themselves. They just didn't have the evidence.

Of course that's what got them interested in me. *With the proper testimony, they figured, the fact that my client McCauley was resentenced to a much shorter term could be made to look like Judge Rinaldi had been bought. And they also foolishly assumed that since I was doing life, I would automatically be desperate enough to take the stand against Rinaldi and testify to some kind of nonexistent payoff.*

See, if you're doing big time and they give you the opportunity, they always assume you'll pull a stool-pigeon move to get out. I mean, by their standards, who wouldn't? You take most of these criminal-justice guys and throw them *in the joint for a couple of months, and they'd turn on their own brother. They* know *they would. That's the way they've lived their whole lives and careers: by stepping on people and bribing them with deals.*

In my experience, that goes for almost all *prosecutors, state and federal. They introduce corruption into everything they touch. But even so, Nadjari was the worst. He was truly a special case. I can remember following one story in the papers where a bank vice-president testified that he'd been dragged out of his house by Nadjari agents in the middle of the night and driven around aimlessly for hours. They threatened to destroy him, he said, unless he falsely incriminated a Superior Court judge. "We will ruin you and we will destroy your family," he was told. "We will indict you for perjury, and even if you are finally acquitted, your career will have gone up in smoke."*

But even though I'd heard these stories, I still had no idea what to expect in person. They drove down into the basement on a spiral ramp and then took me up in a freight elevator to a conference room on the twenty-third floor of the World Trade Center. At first they treated me very nice. No handcuffs, plenty of cigarettes and coffee. "Look at you," they said. "This is most extraordinary. Here you just went out and made legal history on that Rizzo case. You don't belong in prison no more; we'd like to see you on the streets." Blah blah blah. Just strokin' me back and forth, y'know?

Twenty minutes later another guy comes in—very low-key type of guy, very businesslike. And he flat-out promises me parole if I'll take the stand against Rinaldi. "We have ways of arranging these things," he tells me, and he names some well-known cases of guys who got out. "We'll work with you on the details of your story later," he says. "All we want now is some indication of your willingness to take the stand."

I never even gave it a second thought. In fact, the whole idea made me nauseous and disgusted. I couldn't care if it was a fuckin' hack *they wanted me to rat on, I wouldn't do it. That's just the way I am. "You don't know who you're dealing with," I told them. "I'm no fuckin' stool pigeon and I never will be!"*

They couldn't believe it. They started repeating themselves, making sure I really believed they could get me out. "Yeah, I believe you all right," I told them. "But that's not the way we live in jail—the bright guys, the good guys."

When they finally realized I meant it, they went fuckin' nuts. Suddenly their whole case against Rinaldi had just disintegrated. And of course that's when they started in with their threats—every single one of which was ultimately carried out. The loss of parole, transfer to Dannemora up near the Canadian border, loss of my visiting privileges and my job in the law library, and a complete medical "blackout"—that was their term—unless, of course, I changed my mind and agreed to testify.

*"Go fuck yourselves," I told them. I was raving now, but as usual, I was raving sense. I knew exactly what I was doing. I walked out of that fucking office. "I'd rather die first," I told them. "I didn't become a lawyer just to rat on some fuckin' judge!"**

They drove me back across town through the rush hour. And as soon as we got back to West Street, they already had my bags packed and waiting for me and they hustled me onto the Dannemora bus.

"Better get yourself some warm clothes, Rosenberg," they told me. "Try suing a doctor up there and they'll kill you."

---

* Judge Rinaldi was acquitted of all charges on October 12, 1975.

* * * *

Several hours later Jerry was sitting alone near the back, handcuffed and smoking in abject silence as the bus jounced through the night in the direction of the Canadian border. Although in the years ahead he would go on to win scores of cases in federal and state courts at every level—including a near-miss in his precedent-shattering lawsuit against Nadjari himself—he was at this particular moment just about as discouraged and pessimistic as he'd ever been in his life. He flicked his cigarette in the direction of the brimming ashtray, then glanced over at a couple of black guys laughing and talking to each other in the pair of seats across the aisle. One of them eventually turned and studied him for a moment. "What happened, my man?" he finally said. "You blow your writ?"

"Something like that," Jerry replied.

"How much time you got in?" the second one asked.

"I'm doing life," Jerry answered quietly.

The first black guy whistled in astonishment. "You must've had the worst goddamn lawyer in the whole world!" he said.

"Yeah," Jerry told him. "The first guy I had was a real loser."

"Them lawyers is all the same," the second one swore. He leaned closer to Jerry across the aisle and lowered his voice to a confidential whisper. "Listen," he said. "We know a friend of ours who knows a guy—he's not exactly a regular lawyer, but he gets people out all the time."

"Oh, yeah?" Jerry asked. "Who's that?"

"His name's Jerry the Jew," the black guy whispered, settling back in his seat. "And let me tell you something, buddy," he chortled. "The sonofabitch is *really good!*"

Jerry smiled, took a long drag on the cigarette, and raised his eyes to the ceiling. It was, he likes to say, one of the finest compliments he has ever received.

EPILOGUE

He was always fast-minded, that's what makes this kid so great. But his stupid ideas from Brooklyn ain't there no more.

—ANTHONY DELVECCHIO, AUGUST 24, 1981

In the summer of 1981 Jerry Rosenberg is once again at Sing Sing, back on the crowded upper gallery of Seven Building where he and Rizzo and Tony the Greek locked together in the early seventies. It isn't the same, of course: None of the old crew is there with him anymore, and his health seems a little worse than it was even a year ago. But his legal career is flourishing. And his mind, if anything, seems a little sharper.

I am sitting in the third row of the prison courtroom at Sing Sing on a brutally hot midsummer afternoon, watching as Jerry and his client, Vincent Aloi, a tense, open-featured man in his middle forties, are brought in for a habeas corpus hearing. There is a momentary delay while the court reporter switches machines. And as I watch Jerry joking easily with the DA in the case, an experienced departmental workhorse named Eugene O'Brien, I find myself struggling harder than ever to come to terms with the questions and paradoxes that swirl around this man—questions, I have come to realize, that have at least as much to do with human nature—and the nature of justice—as they do with Jerry himself. Above all, I find myself wondering what it would mean for Jerry, for this born scrapper, to be cut off from the only milieu in which he's ever found something worth scrapping about. It was, I felt sure, a question that would begin to take on a special kind of relevance and urgency in the months immediately ahead. For today, after almost nineteen and a half years of imprisonment, Jerry Rosenberg is less than nine months away from his first legally mandated parole hearing.

"Your Honor," he says, with a nod to the court reporter, "in this petition for a writ of habeas corpus, we have a situation here which is very complex in one area and very simple in another. But the bottom line is that Mr. Aloi is entitled to the five and a half years he has done in the federal penitentiary to be credited toward his state sentence under Article 70.40 of the New York State Penal Law."

It is an area of law where Jerry is an acknowledged master—a fact attested to this afternoon by the eminence of his client, Vinnie Aloi, who was widely regarded as the heir apparent to the number-one spot in the Colombo crime family prior to his state conviction for perjury in 1973.

"Moreover, Your Honor," Jerry says, pivoting gracefully around the corner of the counsel's table, "Mr. O'Brien in his brief for the state is incorrect on his case law. In *People ex rel. Bridges* v. *Malcolm,* 44 N.Y. 2d 875, May 31,1978, which we have right here, it was held that a man that had spent time in another institution was entitled to that time under the doctrine of *constructive custody.* In other words, in our case, Mr. Aloi was constructively held by the detainer that was placed against him in the Feds."

Sitting there in the third row, I am once again struck by the uniqueness of Jerry's presentation—half Jewish lawyer, half Brooklyn hood—and by how confident he now seems that he has the full attention and respect of the court.

"Is the district attorney still confused on his case law, Mr. Rosenberg?" State Supreme Court Justice Albert M. Rosenblatt would ask him several minutes later in the hearing. "I understand you are a scholar," the judge would tell him with a twinkle in his eye. "Perhaps you might give Mr. O'Brien the benefit of your view."

It was a courtly hearing, and I found myself enjoying it for its formal qualities—and for Jerry's near-effortless display of legal virtuosity. Nevertheless, my mind frequently returned to the question of his parole. And to the larger question of what it would mean for *anyone* to try to reenter the real world after twenty years of confinement and brutalization and physical neglect. Twenty years in a set of institutions perhaps best described by one former inmate as "a human warehouse—a factory for producing a negative man."

The situation as far as my parole is concerned is very simple. They've got no valid reason to hold me no more, and under the law they're gonna have to prove they do. The whole idea of the parole law, of course, is that they're required to evaluate the person as he is now, *not as he was* then. *In fact, that's the main reason I've got no use for the word* rehabilitation—*which is their word, don't forget. See, if you look it up in the dictionary,* rehabilitation *actually means you went back to what you were originally. But* reconstructiveness, *which is* my *word, means you took those same raw materials and you started over from scratch.*

Anyhow, once the board has made their determination, they can do one of three things: cut you loose, hit you for less than two years—which is a pretty good indication they'll let you go the next time if you keep your jacket clean—or they can hit you with the full two.

Needless to say, I've been keeping pretty close track—and so far, with only one exception that I know of, everyone from the Death House has gotten out the first time. But let's say they hit me. These days, also by law, they've got to give their reason for a hit. And if they try using the nature of the crime, *I'll take them to court. That used to be their favorite reason, believe it or not—the nature of the crime—but it's an uncon-*

stitutional reason. It means the board is wrongfully assuming the right to redetermine the facts of the original case—and to second-guess the judge's sentence.

And if they try that stuff on me, they know I'm gonna sue.

Soon as I get out, of course, I'm gonna have to make a new life for myself. And one of the biggest problems as I remember from twenty years ago is the little things. You get very disoriented at times; you could spend your whole fuckin' day in a supermarket. And on top of that, of course, you've go to learn to resocialize yourself, to be the people's way.

I'd be lying if I said it didn't scare me a little, but fortunately I've got a wonderful woman in my life now named Dotty Tortorella, and she really cares for my feelings. For the first few weeks I'll just stick with her real close—in the stores and streets and so forth—and I'll try and learn by watching. I used to pick up on these things pretty fast.

She's an executive with a toy company in Manhattan, Dorothy, and a mutual friend of ours referred her to me on a legal problem. That's actually how we met. She's very stable and mature within herself, this woman, and it was almost like a shock at first to find out this type of person could even exist. Anyhow, we made our plans almost a year ago: As soon as I get out, we're going to be married in California near where her two daughters are living—two smart, beautiful girls named Dolores and Elena.

A little later, as soon as I get settled in and so forth, one of the first things I'm going to have to deal with is getting admitted to the bar. It won't happen overnight, of course, and in the meantime I can still do writs and appeals, which I plan to. But it's a situation that can definitely be dealt with. There's a major constitutional issue at stake. And just in the past couple of years, a number of people with previous felonies have been admitted to full membership—in California and *New York. In fact, that entire area of licensing and accreditation in law is beginning to open up now. And in my opinion, in another five or ten years we could start to see the whole Bar Association legal monopoly in this country beginning to shake loose.*

But I'm not gonna wait that long. I've been making precedent all my life, don't forget.

And like I always tell my mother—I can't see any good reason to stop now, just because one of these days I might happen to find myself on the streets.

POSTSCRIPT

Jerry Rosenberg was denied parole on March 9, 1982. He was denied every two years thereafter—until his death at age seventy-two on June 1, 2009, at Wende Correctional Facility, a maximum-security prison in Alden, New York.

Jerry had served forty-six consecutive years of imprisonment. He was the longest-serving prisoner in the state of New York.

* * * *

In recent years, at least eight former jailhouse lawyers—now released from prison—have been admitted to the bar and are practicing law as licensed attorneys on the outside.

Frankie Guzman, who served six years as a juvenile for armed robbery, graduated from UCLA Law School in 2012 and was admitted to the California bar in 2013. He is now Director of the California Youth Justice Initiative at the National Center for Youth Law.

Noah Kilroy served time in Florida on drug charges. After his release, he was admitted to the bar in Rhode Island and Massachusetts and became a prosecutor for the city of Providence.

Christopher Poulos did three years at the federal prison in Lewisburg, Pennsylvania for drug trafficking. He went on to graduate from Maine Law School, passed the bar in Maine, worked in the White

House, and is now Director of the Washington Statewide Re-entry Council.

Jarrett Adams was wrongfully convicted of sexual assault at age seventeen. He was exonerated after ten years behind bars and graduated from Loyola University Law School in 2015. He is now a licensed criminal defense lawyer in New York City.

Andres Idarraga served six years for drug-dealing offenses in Rhode Island. He graduated from Brown in 2008, and Yale Law School in 2011, where he worked on the campaign to end felony disenfranchisement. He is a member of the Florida bar and founder of a venture capital firm that invests in social impact projects.

Tara Simmons served three years on drug and gun charges, then graduated magna cum laude from Seattle University Law School. She won a prestigious Skadden Fellowship and passed the bar exam in 2018.

Shon Hopwood served a twelve-year sentence for bank robbery. He clerked in the law library at the federal prison in Pekin, Illinois, and had two of his cases accepted by the United States Supreme Court. He is now an associate professor at Georgetown Law School.

Reginald Dwayne Betts served eight years in Virginia for armed robbery—including a year in solitary confinement. A published poet, he graduated from Yale Law School in 2016 and passed the Connecticut bar exam. He is currently working on his PhD at Yale University.

* * * *

Jerry was part of an earlier era—before the courts required prison law libraries and better access to counsel. In those years Jerry was the only lawyer many prisoners had. And for many others he was an inspiration. In the pervasive atmosphere of violence and fear, he became a jailhouse legend—a role model who used his mind instead of his fists. And most inspirational of all in the world of prison, a man who insisted that he had a future.

About the Author

Steve Bello, a journalist and screenwriter, spent hundreds of hours with Jerry Rosenberg in prison visiting rooms across the state of New York. In 1978, because he had a case pending against a former NYC prosecutor, Jerry was held at the federal prison in lower Manhattan, where Bello taped weeks of interviews in the privacy of the attorneys' conference room.

Bello did the legal research for the book in Los Angeles, where he also worked on television projects including NBC's *St. Elsewhere.* His other writing credits include, *Hill Street Blues*, *Alfred Hitchcock Presents, Tour of Duty, The Untouchables,* and three NBC–TV films, including *Fatal Deception*, starring Helena Bonham-Carter. He also wrote the teleplay for the 1986 NBC–TV film *Doing Life*, starring Tony Danza. Bello was nominated for a 1985 Emmy Award for Outstanding Writing in a Drama Series for *St. Elsewhere.* He lives in New York City.